LEADER LOST

LEADER LOST,

A Biography of Hugh Gaitskell

BY GEOFFREY McDERMOTT

A VERTEX BOOK

Princeton   New York   Philadelphia   London

Published by AUERBACH Publishers Inc.
by arrangement with Leslie Frewin Publishers Limited

Library of Congress Catalog Card Number: 73-124628
International Standard Book Number: 0-87769-037-5
Printed in the United States of America

Contents

Acknowledgment

I AM MOST grateful to Ivan Yates and Anthony McDermott for their sage and constructive advice on numerous aspects of this biography. I, and the book, have greatly profited by it.

I am also much obliged to the staff of the Westminster City Central Reference Library for the courtesy with which they have produced so many reference volumes from the distant recesses of the building.

GEOFFREY MCDERMOTT

October 1969

LEADER LOST

Power

WHEN THE NEW Prime Minister announced his Cabinet after the elections of 1964, there were no great surprises. George Brown was given his heart's desire, the Foreign Office; Harold Wilson became Chancellor of the Exchequer. The Prime Minister's Winchester and Oxford friends and colleagues, Richard Crossman and Douglas Jay, received Social Services and the Board of Trade respectively.

The Prime Minister went into action with typical vigour. Having summoned a meeting of all his ministers, both in and out of the Cabinet, he described the strategy he intended to follow. The fact, he said, that our majority is slender calls for tougher and more radical thought and action on our part, rather than for caution. To this end he was appointing an inner Cabinet of seven people whose duty would be to keep things moving. As top priority matters he called for immediate and exhaustive studies of four aspects of policy: the possible devaluation of sterling; legislation designed to deal with the strikes which did so much to hamper our productive effort; a fresh look at the question of Britain entering the Common Market; and a plan, practical rather than theoretical, for détente in East-West European relations.

It never happened, of course. Hugh Gaitskell had been killed in January 1963 by a combination of overwork and a rare disease. As Leader of the Parliamentary Labour Party since the end of 1955 he had grown in stature year by year. Not only all his followers were convinced that he would be the next Prime Minister, and a good one; a large number of Conservatives were too. Statesmen all over the world, from

Kennedy to Khruschev, expressed their admiration of him and their sorrow at his passing.

Yet, to judge Gaitskell on the record, there is a mystery here. His one and only Budget, in 1951, split the Party wide open, and the rift with the Bevanites lasted many years. His election as Leader in succession to Attlee in 1955 gravely disturbed large numbers of grass-roots Socialists. Many asked whether it was good for the Labour Movement to have as its leader a man of his social background and, incidentally, relative affluence. Many came to resent his tough handling of a whole series of major issues: Clause 4, unilateralism, the Common Market. Furthermore, while confident of victory in the 1959 General Election, he in fact led the Party to a crushing defeat—the third one running.

Through all this Gaitskell sailed ahead in popularity, while his opponents either retired hurt or formed up behind him. How was it done? There is no simple answer; Gaitskell was a complex man. Aneurin Bevan's description of him as a desiccated calculating machine is remembered both because it is amusing and because it could be applied to one side of Gaitskell's character; but it is ridiculously inadequate as a description of the whole. Time and again we shall see evidence of this. Many of his friends, on the contrary, feared that he suffered from too much heart rather than too much head. He was a combination of gentleness and toughness, of sensibility and combativeness, of don and orator. He was in fact, as I shall try to show, a more considerable orator than most people realised, largely because he was for much of the time in opposition to the rich, whirling Welsh words of Bevan. He was a distinctly good television performer; yet, with his peaky nose and caricaturable face, he did not impress his personality on all members of his audiences. Then he could be harsh even with close friends who he considered were not thinking problems through to the bitter end; equally, he could give precious hours to apparently unimportant cases and victims of injustice. He was heavily criticised on many occasions by friends as well as foes for his uncompromising political tactics or strategy. He just kept moving, and kept his Party moving, towards what he had conscientiously elaborated as the right aims and objects.

And he is not remembered well enough. Amongst his family and personal friends the devotion is as warm as it could be for any man. Amongst those who worked less closely with him he is respected as having been a good leader of the Party. But in the country at large he is practically forgotten. That is life; and, even more, death.

In 1959 Gaitskell had authorised Gerald Sparrow, who in that year became Labour candidate at Exeter, to write his biography. Shortly afterwards, however, Sparrow revealed to the *Daily Express* his view that the Exeter Labour Party was little better than a bunch of Communists, and withdrew his candidacy. Gaitskell for his part withdrew his permission for the book, and also the photographs he had lent him. Obstinately, Sparrow worked on; and the book appeared in the 1962 autumn list of the Oldbourne Press, Lord Beaverbrook's private publishing house. But in fact it was never published.

A collection of tributes to Gaitskell by friends and collaborators appeared in 1964.* Roy Jenkins, whom he appointed with Anthony Crosland as his literary executor, was to have written a full biography, but got involved with other pressing matters. So it is high time that Gaitskell's memory was revived; and into the bargain it is tempting to speculate now on what his influence might have been if he had lived.

I knew Gaitskell, but not intimately; perhaps a satisfactory position for a biographer. I have been given enormous help by many who knew him better than I. I shall attempt to present an honest portrait not of a superman—Gaitskell himself would have laughed at that idea—but of a man with most of the human contradictions in his character; also, with the great special quality of zeal for improving the human

* *Hugh Gaitskell, 1906–1963*, edited by W. T. Rodgers, M.P.

condition wherever and whenever it cried out for improvement. A man, in fact, to be compared in many ways with his
friend President Kennedy: one who enjoyed life to the full in
all its variety; a relentless moderniser with a new style; one
who preferred to live his political life dangerously; one who
achieved much, and could have achieved so much more.

TWO

The First Forty Years

HUGH GAITSKELL WAS born in the same year as the Parliamentary Labour Party, 1906. This put him in the same category, give or take a few months, as such people as Kosygin, Hammarskjöld, Lyndon Johnson, and Quintin Hogg; also Auden, Ian Fleming, and Don Bradman. He came of an absolutely conventional upper-middle-class family, originally from Cumberland, with a house in a smart part of Kensington. His father was a member of the Indian Civil Service who served all his time in Burma. Hugh was given the extraordinary second name of "Todd-Naylor" in honour of his godfather. Soon after entering Parliament in 1945 he did the best he could by removing the hyphen. Better still, he was known in the family as Sam. His father died of a tropical disease when he was 45 and Hugh 9. His mother married again.

Hugh's education was *très snob:* the Dragon School in Oxford, then Winchester, then New College, Oxford. Curiously enough the Dragon School, which is to this day one of the most exclusive and expensive prep schools in the land, had at that time a headmaster—one of a series of Lynams—who was unconventional in many ways: he accepted girls and sons of tradesmen and, not least, he was a Socialist. Gaitskell remarked later on that it was here that he first imbibed the doctrine.

He was also much impressed by an older friend's remark to the effect that he should realise how lucky he was to be going to Winchester, as not one boy in 10,000 had the chance of an education like that. Winchester, then the third smartest school after Eton and Harrow and today the second, has for many years been *sui generis*. Its academic standards are the best. A good number of its pupils know so much by the time they leave that they tend to think further close connexions with the world at large are superfluous. They become bishops, dons, and ambassadors of a very superior but often ineffectual kind: they are remote. But Winchester also produces inde-pendent thinkers and politicians of high calibre. While all Tory Cabinets are crammed with Old Etonians, Winchester produces a number of people of the same class who are origi-nal enough to break away from the conservative tradition. In Gaitskell's time there, Crossman and Jay, apart from himself, came into this category, while Warden John Sparrow of All Souls and Warden Sir William Hayter of New College per-haps came into the other.

At Winchester, Gaitskell performed well but not outstand-ingly; he had not the brilliance of Crossman. He failed to get a scholarship to New College, where his elder brother Arthur had gone. His housemaster thought he should have been awarded one, and consoled him with: "Never mind. You'll be Prime Minister one day." However, he got a place there all right in 1924. The school of Modern Greats—Philosophy, Politics and Economics—had just been set up, and Gaitskell joined it. So did his life-long friend Frank Pakenham, at that time a pillar of the Carlton Club. Gaitskell was strongly in-fluenced by G. D. H. Cole, Reader in Economics and for a whole generation a leading theoretician of Socialism. He en-joyed his social life—he always liked the company of attrac-tive women and enough to drink—and he worked and played golf to near blue standard. He read his Proust and D. H. Lawrence with pleasure. His friends included Maurice Bowra, John Betjeman, Harold Acton, Cecil Day Lewis, Cyril Con-nolly, W. H. Auden, and, above all, Evan Durbin. He was, wrote Margaret Cole, "one of the gay intellectuals of the roaring twenties." Long political discussions were, as always in certain university circles, a normal feature of life, but he never spoke at the Union.

But in May 1926 Gaitskell took the business of being a Socialist a significant step further. When the General Strike broke out, the majority of hearty students saw it as a great lark, an opportunity for driving trains and so on, and, in the process, for putting the working class in its place. Gaitskell did not hesitate for a moment to come out in support of the workers. He joined the Labour Party. With typical intellectual honesty he admitted that the strike was perhaps unconstitutional in the strict sense; but in the human sense he regarded it as fully justified. He drove a car to help the strike effort, and under the guidance of the Coles he helped to organise those of his friends who were of a like mind to back the cause. And when it was all over he went on to get a first-class honours degree in Final Schools in 1927. His special subject was "Labour Movements."

So Gaitskell was now set on the straight Socialist path from which he never deviated. Even to this day there are many people who speak of such a man as "a traitor to his class," in the same way that Churchill was reproached when he joined the Liberals. The shires are full of them: Worcestershire, where I live and where two of our MPs are men of the stamp of Sir Gerald Nabarro and Sir Tatton Brinton, not least. The trouble with these people is that they are the class-conscious ones. Also, as a Socialist Cabinet Minister remarked to me sadly, practically all the inhabitants of Britain are conservative at heart; to which I would add, the women even more than the men. Gaitskell had no class-consciousness of any kind. He realised how lucky he had been materially in his upbringing and wanted more people to share such advantages. Moreover, while he was not unhappy at Winchester, and certainly happy at Oxford, he found the conventional upper-class atmosphere stuffy and oppressive. He never, of course, pretended to be anything he was not; he would have considered such an attitude as unbearable condescension. Furthermore, as a representative of a new generation of economists, he believed that the means of achieving fairer shares for all were to hand. He may have been over-optimistic in some respects. But the role of Socialists, after all, is to change things for the better by working with, and for, other people; that of Conservatives, to conserve or even attempt to return to "the good old days," by working each man for himself. Gaitskell knew as a fact that for very many people those good old days had never existed. With his keen analytical brain, and great energy, he could not bear the thought of sitting tight. He had to drive on.

There were plenty of parlour pinks about in those days, but Gaitskell was never one of them. At Cole's suggestion he went from Oxford to the unglamorous job of tutor for extramural adult classes, under the aegis of the Workers' Educational Association, at Nottingham University. His mother was disappointed that he had not gone into government service abroad, like his grandfather, father, and elder brother Arthur, who was making his name in the Sudan. His year at Nottingham was of great significance because it brought him into direct touch with working people, many of them unemployed, and showed that he got along with them easily. This was the equivalent for him of Attlee's early service in the army and then amongst the dockers of Stepney. Also, visiting a miner in his cottage near Worksop one day he met another visitor from his own social world who was to give him great encouragement and backing all through his career. This was the very up-and-coming Socialist politician Hugh Dalton, an old Etonian of large frame and booming voice. Dalton was struck by his fervent enthusiasm for social equality and justice and took him under his wing. For their part the miners, with all their great political influence over the next forty years, were always behind Gaitskell. He referred in moving terms to his experiences during this year when he made his first speech as a junior Minister—Parliamentary Secretary at the Ministry of Fuel and Power—in May 1946. In 1928 he moved to a teaching post in the newly formed Economics Department at University College, London, a rival to the London School of Economics. He rose to be head of it. He also stepped up his political activity.

Those were all too stirring days. The Wall Street crash of 1929 had repercussions all over the world, except in the Soviet Union, showing how much more dependent many countries were on the United States than they had realised. Gaitskell canvassed for Labour in 1929, but soon saw that the new Labour Government would be no better than the one that had fallen on its back in 1924. In the upshot it was much worse, and MacDonald did his best to ruin the Labour Party. Gaitskell, whose short history of Chartism appeared in 1929, became secretary of the New Fabian Research Bureau which, under the sponsorship of Hugh Dalton, Sidney and Beatrice Webb, and Arthur Henderson, flourished and took over the Fabian Society. Gaitskell did not go with a Fabian fact-finding team to the USSR. Like many others he was pro-Soviet at this stage, but he was not starry-eyed like some. He was also involved in a less flourishing organisation with the unprepossessing name of the Society for Socialist Inquiry and Propaganda. This used to meet, improbably, at the Countess of Warwick's seat, with Bevin in the chair. Known to some as the "loyal grousers," the jibe was made that their loyalty was more effective than their grousing.

In 1933–4 Gaitskell went to Vienna under a Rockefeller grant for economic study. In Germany Hitler's Nazis were by now well on their gruesome way, and Gaitskell recognised the monstrosity from the start. Red Vienna, with its fine workers' flats and other manifestations of practical Socialism, was a happy contrast. But not for long. Gaitskell was enjoying a party with some of his Vienna Socialist friends one day early in February 1934 when civil war broke out. He witnessed Dollfuss' Fascist Heimwehr in action, destroying those flats. He threw himself into organising funds, publicity, escapes, and showed great ability and effectiveness in doing so. But the Socialists were crushed. This was a decisive experience for Gaitskell, as it was for a slightly younger graduate from Cambridge who was also in the thick of it—Kim Philby. Gaitskell returned to England determined to strengthen the Labour Party's policies, and in particular their wishy-washy policy towards rearmament which, he hammered home, was playing into the hands of the dictators. He made no bones about it: we should have to fight them sooner or later. Philby's method to achieve similar ends was to write off his own country lock, stock and barrel, and clandestinely to enter the service of the USSR, to which he has remained faithful ever since. He hoodwinked Gaitskell, as he hoodwinked all his closest friends and colleagues. Gaitskell was horrified when Philby married a well-known Viennese Communist girl; he regarded him as an altruistic left-winger who would not go so far as Communism. Oddly enough, many people in Vienna were convinced that Philby was a Communist; in Britain no one seemed to know.

There were numerous things that the Government, stumbling along under MacDonald and Baldwin, and the Labour Opposition with their strong pacifist element, preferred not to know. One of Gaitskell's outstanding characteristics now displayed itself forcefully: he would always look facts in the face. An unpleasant fact might in certain circumstances deserve more attention than a pleasant one. Like the economist he was, or like a top-grade intelligence officer, he listed the facts, analysed them, weighed them against each other, and only then reached his conclusions on what could and should be done. In the 1930s his star was rising appreciably; but he had not the influence to move the old men of the Labour Party. He stood for Chatham in the General Election of 1935 but was soundly defeated. This disappointed him deeply, though it was a safe Conservative seat and the Tories ended up with an overall majority in the House of 249. In 1937 he was chosen, on Dalton's recommendation, as prospective candidate for the safe seat of South Leeds, in preference to a National Union of Railwaymen representative who had all the Union backing. He volunteered to contribute £100 per annum to Party funds from his earnings and private income. All the time Britain slid inexorably towards war. Gaitskell found that he could not conscientiously recommend the only alliance that might possibly have saved the day, one with the USSR. He was revolted by Stalin's purges and grew increasingly hostile to the Communist system as a whole. This hostility remained with him in later days and even led to rigidity of judgment in certain cases.

By the time war came in September 1939, Gaitskell, now 33, was established as one of the bright young stars in the Labour Movement although he had no influence on the Parliamentary Labour Party. The efficient economist was growing into an efficient politician. As early as 1933 his contribution to G. D. H. Cole's symposium, with the down-to-earth title of *What Everybody wants to know about Money,* had attracted attention. Gaitskell showed with great clarity that the existing economic system was not merely unjust, as anyone could see if he cared to look at the Great Depression of 1929–33, but also inefficient because it was wasteful and out of date. He returned to the theme in his own book *Money and Everyday* Life, published in 1939. Meanwhile, he proved a great success as a teacher; as an original thinker on economics he was near, but not in, the top flight.

His circle of friends widened to include the couple often named together like a music-hall turn, though different in so many ways, Balogh and Kaldor. In 1937 he married Anna Dora Creditor, of Polish-Jewish origin. She is tiny and attractive; throughout his career no one listened more constantly to his speeches, or admired them more. On important occasions, especially if they happened to be turbulent, she often appeared to be taking the strain for him, to be more under stress than he was himself. They had two daughters and much happiness together. They lived in a comfortable house in Hampstead and gradually built up the so-called Hampstead set, of whom we shall hear more at a later stage. His friendship with Hugh Dalton, who was highly respected in the Labour Movement and not least for his skill as a talent-spotter, led to fruitful collaboration. Dalton and he were alone, for instance, in their passionate denunciation of appeasement, on which some other leaders of the Labour Party had far less positive views. Gaitskell's stand on Munich was categorical; some people in the Party began to think of him as one of the potential leaders. When Cripps saw fit to state at this time that British imperialism was worse than Nazism and Fascism, in which he was supported by Zilliacus, Gaitskell reacted very strongly. But only after the Prague debacle of March 1939 did many of the Party follow his line. Even so, when he, Douglas Jay, and Evan Durbin put to Attlee, the Party leader, together with Dalton, Morrison, Alexander, and Shinwell, their proposed bargain—"conscription of wealth," or a wealth tax, in return for military conscription—the big five failed to persuade the traditionalists in the Party to agree. That same month, and in spite of all the portents, they voted against the Government's proposed conscription. Attlee later opined, in his measured way, that this was "probably a mistake."

In September 1939, Gaitskell was recruited on Dalton's insistence into the Ministry of Economic Warfare Intelligence Department, where his colleagues included such characters as Edwin Plowden and David Eccles. For Gaitskell this was the beginning of a short but intensive, and highly successful, career as a civil servant. For his first nine months he was Director of German Intelligence. He was all for action based on the available intelligence, as a remark of his made at this time shows: "What can we do about the neutrals? The Foreign Office won't let us bully them, and the Treasury won't let us bribe them."

In a heated debate after the war, some unnamed Tory interrupter, no doubt one of those red-faced majors or half-colonels who, curiously, like to flaunt through their rank the fact that they failed even in the not very demanding military career, shouted: "What did you do in the war?" To which Gaitskell icily replied, "My duty, as I trust you did?" Thank God we had the good sense to put men such as Gaitskell, Harold Wilson, Crossman, and a host of other highly intelligent people into key jobs at the centre for which they were well suited, while leaving the old-fashioned service officers to do the minor jobs on the periphery which were in line with their capabilities.

Gaitskell found time to write an introduction to his friend Evan Durbin's book *The Politics of Democratic Socialism,* which appeared in 1940; and it constitutes a profession of his faith. Referring to the circle of young Labour Party members and economists to which they belonged, he wrote: "The most fundamental ideal was social justice—but it was an ideal in no way inspired by class hatred. They were equally devoted to democracy and personal freedom. They believed in toler- ance and they understood the need for compromise. They were suspicious of large general ideas which on examination turned out to have no precise content. They wanted to get results. Above all, while accepting the ultimate emotional basis of moral evaluation, they had great faith in the power of reason. They were for the pursuit of truth to the bitter end."

In May 1940 Churchill brought in Dalton, whom he was gracelessly to vilify some years after the war as "the dirty doctor," as Minister of Economic Warfare, and Dalton at once made Gaitskell his private secretary. Two months later Dalton spread his wings to cover Special Operations Execu- tive, and Gaitskell interested himself deeply in it and par- ticularly in the side dealing with black propaganda. This lies behind his keen concern for intelligence and security matters which manifested itself on several occasions subsequently. In February 1942, Dalton became President of the Board of Trade and took Gaitskell with him as his political assistant— big Hugh and little Hugh, some called them—after persuad- ing him one evening with some difficulty, and whisky, not to accept a post in the United Nations Relief and Rehabili- tation Agency. In both these jobs Gaitskell could and did deploy his gifts in the way that suited him: devising active measures to help win the war—very different from the tra- ditional leisurely Civil Service grind—and also to see that people in general were fairly treated through such egalitarian measures as price control and coal rationing. He established close and friendly relations with the miners' leaders. He also found time to study the workings of the government machine, and some of its failings, and to get to know some of the top officials. The shape of certain things to come was seen at a party in 1943, when George Woodcock poured scorn on middle-class intellectual Socialists. Gaitskell was firm in his belief that the traditional identification of Labour with the industrial proletariat was not enough; but he admitted that the process of modernisation would be a tough and bitter one.

Gaitskell drove himself very hard and fully earned his CBE—one up on Harold Wilson and Crossman, who were rewarded with OBEs. But he paid the price. In the spring of 1945, when the first General Election for 10 years was in the offing, he had a slight heart attack—ominous at the age of 39. His doctors insisted that he could not undertake a full election campaign; the electors of South Leeds for their part insisted that he should remain as their candidate, and what is more they voted him in with a majority of some 10,000.

It was a famous victory. For the first time in history Labour was elected to power on that 5th July with a clear majority—very clear indeed: 393 seats to the Conservatives' 213 and other parties' 34. The final results were not announced until 26th July because the Services' votes took time to arrive. And such was the turmoil of those days that Attlee and the new Foreign Secretary Bevin had instantly to return to Potsdam, where the most important international business imaginable had been stalled while we had our election. (Attlee was offered Eden's assistance and declined with not too many thanks.) But the truth was that Labour now had the mandate, the men, and the programme. Men like Attlee, Morrison, Greenwood, Bevin, and Cripps had been at the very centre under Churchill in the war; they had performed valiantly and efficiently. Nye Bevan had shown his worth as a practically one-man Opposition, and was to prove it again as Minister of Health with a seat in the Cabinet. Others too numerous to mention had done their bit as Ministers not in the Cabinet. Some were older than they might have been, and a good many were tireder. But the landslide victory was a tonic. Here at last was the opportunity to put into practice the ideas formulated in the Party programme of 1918. The electoral manifesto set before the public had not, accordingly, been a modest one. On the contrary, it was revolutionary, constituting a revolution against the Tory sloth and mismanagement of the 1920s and 1930s. It called for the setting up of a National Health Service and the nationalisation of the Bank of England, coal, civil aviation, public transport, electricity, gas, iron, and steel, no less. All these objectives were attained by 1949.

And so Gaitskell was there with his comrades in the House on that triumphant 1st August 1945, when, with pardonable exuberance, the Labour Party sang "The Red Flag" and maddened the discomfited Tory Opposition with the reminder, in the words of Hartley Shawcross: "We are the masters now." Attlee did not know Gaitskell well at this time but was aware of all the favourable reports on him, and on such colleagues as Wilson and Durbin. He made Wilson Parliamentary Secretary at the Ministry of Works straight away but decided to wait and see how Gaitskell's health developed. He did not at this point give any major ministerial posts to the new generation.

On 16th August, Major John Freeman—today His Excellency the British Ambassador in Washington—looking incredibly handsome in uniform, was put up to move the address in reply to the King's speech. He spoke eloquently about the spirit of high adventure and the readiness to experiment that were in the air. "Today may rightly be regarded as D-day in the Battle of the New Britain." Gaitskell's maiden speech came in the debate on 21st August. In many ways it foreshadowed the style that he was to develop to such a high pitch over the years. It dealt largely, but not exclusively, with economic matters such as the nationalisation of coal, essential because of our technical inefficiency compared with other countries, and of the Bank of England. Exports and industrial efficiency must have the highest priority; too many industries thought only of their own profits. "There is generally in industry today a lack of enterprise." It was combative: he expressed surprise at the mildness of the Opposition's comments on a programme containing no less than twelve major measures, and commented that Churchill regarded coal nationalisation as a sort of gadget which he would watch in performance before deciding whether to buy it or not. On the recent White Paper on Full Employment he was donnish: he congratulated the Labour members of the Coalition Government on "the remarkable educational work they did" on their Tory colleagues. The aim must always be "full employment without inflation." He went on to praise the Civil Service, but also to say that it needed young "reinforcements." "We shall need to make changes here." He ended with an appeal to the House of Lords not to frustrate the workings of democracy "so that this country may live up to the famous words quoted [by Churchill]: 'Government of the people, by the people, for the people.' " He was warmly congratulated by his friends. For my money, the speech ranged rather too wide and in parts lacked the punch which he was later to develop; and the quotation of a quotation of a quotation was not the most effective possible ending.

A livelier speech came on 29th October on the Bank of England Bill. He commended the last Tory spokesman for putting up a fight. Previously, everyone had been smothering the Chancellor, Dalton, with congratulations. "They said it with flowers. Some of us on this side became almost overpowered by the scent of the flowers which were being thrown about." He questioned whether someone like Mr. Montagu Norman in the 1930s—"this mysterious figure who travelled about the world incognito" but always in a blaze of publicity —was "the ideal public servant." The Opposition would say: " 'The Bank of England will be a good boy and the joint stock banks will be good boys; please leave them alone.' But we have had bitter experience in the past of their not playing the game," and so the necessary steps were being taken. This was widely approved as a witty and—already—aggressive speech. One comment ran: "Hugh Gaitskell, a disciple of Mr. Dalton, with experience should equal his master as a political lepidopterist, excelling in the art of making the Opposition squirm on the pins of logic and irony."

Gaitskell's best speech ever as a back-bencher followed on 5th December. The Opposition had weighed in with a motion of censure on the new government. Oliver Lyttleton opened, and was followed by Clement Davies and then Gaitskell. He began with relish: "I have no doubt many hard things will be said in the next two days," and he contributed his quota. He compared the Opposition to mariners lured by the siren calls of the Lord President, Morrison: "We all know what happened to the mariners who listened to the sirens. Their bones were found a long time afterwards, white and bleached on the beaches." He offered special thanks to Churchill for his recent "delightful political fancies. He gave us the Gestapo, and the affection in which we hold our leader, the Prime Minister, was heightened by the beautiful notion of seeing him dressed up in jack-boots and a peaked cap." He suggested that the Opposition saw the Minister of Health, Nye Bevan, in the role of Rasputin. Towards the end he let them have it. They lacked any coherent philosophy. "We believe that the present capitalist system is inefficient, that it produces insecurity, and that it is unjust. Can anyone deny those things?" This produced the desired outburst from the Opposition. "If hon. members opposite want a shouting match they will be beaten in it easily." He foreshadowed one of his great themes of later years when he said that Labour were not proposing "wholesale revolutionary nationalisation," but only what was necessary for efficiency. "The Conservative Party is now left high and dry in an isolated position, bound by doctrinaire views of 'nationalisation under no circumstances.'" He described the motion as one of censure on the people of this country. "Just as the Opposition are going to be defeated in the division lobbies, so the country will defeat them in the next election." A curious prognostication in such early days, and as it turned out only just correct. But the speech as a whole shows Gaitskell at his combative best, and it was enthusiastically applauded.

As if to prove that his tired heart was tired no longer, Gaitskell deployed constant activity in the House of Commons and in his constituency. One question of his in April 1946 to the President of the Board of Trade elicited a reply from his deputy, Hilary Marquand, who was Secretary for Overseas Trade, that is redolent of the atmosphere of those days. "In view of the scarcity of accommodation, we are taking no steps to encourage tourists to visit this country before 1947. However, this morning, at Tilbury, I had the great pleasure of welcoming the first party of Swedish tourists since 1939. They have brought their own food and will be sleeping in the ship that brought them." This reminds us today of the fearful pounding which Britain had taken in the war and of the magnitude of the problems with which the Labour Government had to grapple.

On 10th April 1946, Gaitskell spoke on the Budget in his more academic style. Part of the object was, no doubt, to blind the Opposition with science. He exhibited his ability to reel off intricate economic agreements and relevant statistics. He welcomed the decision to make purchase tax permanent and called for a really hard blow at inheritance, by way of far heavier death duties, for the sake of social justice. He also used the daring new word "disincentive," in a suitably apologetic way. An awed Robert Boothby commented: "We have listened to an extremely able speech such as we always expect from the hon. member for South Leeds." In Gaitskell's last speech as a back-bencher, on 7th May, he took a few more swipes at the Opposition when speaking on the Borrowing (Control and Guarantees) Bill. "We on this side of the House take the view that we are going to maintain full employment. Hon. members opposite are so sunk in the past that they cannot envisage a state of affairs in which there is hope." He had a brush with Richard Stokes and Brendan Bracken on the odd subject of the London School of Eco-

nomics, which Stokes roundly accused of "corrupt practices."
It is true that Harold Laski was trying both to rule that in-
stitution with a Marxist rod of iron and to run the Labour
Movement into the bargain, though he was kept well in his
place by Attlee. However, Gaitskell refuted all allegations
that the LSE was influencing the Chancellor or the bill
under debate. He pointed out that he himself had never been
on its staff and that Dalton's connexion with it had ceased
ten years earlier.

By now Gaitskell was going great guns. On the record of
his ten months in the House there could be no possible
qualms about his health or stamina. Attlee considered appointing him his Parliamentary Private Secretary; but instead
on 10th May, just a month after his fortieth birthday, he
made him Parliamentary Secretary to the Ministry of Fuel
and Power, under the old stalwart Emanuel Shinwell. Not a
glamorous first ministerial post, but one, as we shall see, of
special importance in those days. In any case, Gaitskell was
never the type to fuss over superficial or incidental considerations; he liked to get ahead with the job. In this case he
certainly did. Fixing his feet firmly on this lowest rung of the
ministerial ladder, he proceeded to climb it at an unprecedented pace.

To understand how he did it we have to suspend the narrative for a while and consider in some detail the condition
of the Labour Movement within which Gaitskell was
operating.

THREE

Understanding the Labour Movement

COMPARATIVELY FEW PEOPLE even amongst those who vote Labour have a clear idea of just how the various constituent parts of the Movement interact and finally produce policy. Outside the Movement it would be fair to say that very few indeed attempt to understand, and the majority are baffled anyway. Gaitskell took great pains, in his thorough way, to analyse the various factors and bodies involved, and then to weigh their relative influence. Deductions followed, and after that he reached his conclusions and went bald-headed at the aims that flowed from them. With him this was a continuing process since he could not bear the static or the status quo. Indeed he was often ahead of the Movement, which after all is where a leader should be. This was one of the great causes of his success and strength; it also entailed sometimes riding roughshod over accepted ideas and the people who supported them.

Not the least confusing aspect of the Movement is the frequency with which its various parts have changed names and characteristics. In 1900 the Labour Representation Committee was formed out of the Labour Group in Parliament whose members came from the Trade Unions and some Socialist societies. After the General Election of 1906, the name was changed to Parliamentary Labour Party, or Labour Party for short. The Chairman, but only for two years, as parliamentary activity was not his forte, was the highly respected Socialist pioneer Keir Hardie. He was succeeded in 1908 by Arthur Henderson, who was followed in 1911 by Ramsay MacDonald. In 1914 Henderson returned; and after two changes MacDonald was back from 1922 to 1931. In 1922 the title was changed to "Chairman and Leader," which in view of some of the connotations of the latter term is perhaps regrettable; the Vice-Chairman became "Deputy Leader." Attlee was Leader from 1935 to 1955 without a break, and without anyone ever opposing him after the 1935 leadership election. Gaitskell then took over until his death, though he had to fight for his place.

Up to 1923 there was a Policy Committee of the PLP, which was then renamed the Executive Committee, only to become in 1951 the Parliamentary Committee as confusion threatened with the National Executive Committee, a far wider body as we shall see. The Parliamentary Committee consists of twelve Commons members elected each session by all their colleagues, plus three ex-officio members, the Leader, Deputy Leader, and Chief Whip. These sit on the front bench and are known as the Shadow Cabinet as a result of one of Attlee's last actions as Leader, when in 1955 he allocated specific subjects to individuals. Gaitskell was first elected a member of the Parliamentary Committee in November 1951, coming third after James Griffiths and Glenvil Hall. By 1954 he was equal first with Griffiths, who topped the poll every year from 1951 to 1955. Into the bargain there is a Liaison Committee when Labour is in power, with the duty of keeping the members of the Government fully informed of the back-bencher's views. From 1945 to 1951 it was chaired by Maurice Webb and in 1950 by Glenvil Hall; today the chairman is Douglas Houghton and, most confusingly, this committee is sometimes called the PLP. It all seems rather a plethora.

But the complicated parliamentary set-up is only one part of the Movement. This comes together as a whole in the Annual Conference of what is, perhaps misleadingly, called the Labour Party. These Conferences, held in rotation at different popular seaside resorts, are a combination of jamboree, letting the hair down, sentimental oratory, embattled discussion, and serious business. Votes are taken in mammoth blocks, presumably to emphasise the importance of the Unions. The method seems unwieldy, slightly absurd, and in the final analysis undemocratic, and Gaitskell gave it a hammering at the Annual Conference of 1960 when he considered that it had been abused. Moreover, he never blinked the fact that a good many Trade Union resolutions, decisions, and so on are undemocratically formulated anyway, because the great majority of members do not trouble to vote and the impetus consequently tends to come from the minority of activists who, as often as not, belong to the extreme left.

As a typical example of Conference's workings we may take Gaitskell's last one, held in the Sports Stadium at Brighton in October 1962. The annual elections for membership of the National Executive Committee duly produced a Mr. D. H. Davies of the British Iron, Steel and Kindred Trades' Association as chairman, because he had been vice-chairman the year before. Gaitskell was elected vice-chairman, which was unusual, for the Leader of the PLP had traditionally been content with the place on the Executive which he received ex officio. It put Gaitskell clearly in line for the chairmanship the following year. After the treasurer and Deputy Leader came, as usual, the twelve Trade Union members; next the one representative of the Socialist, Co-operative, and Professional Organisations; then the seven Constituency Parties' representatives; followed by five Woman Members, as such, though women were also elected from time to time as Trade Union representatives, and finally the General Secretary from Transport House. In round figures the Trade Union wielded six million votes and the Constituency Parties one million.

Thus the Chairman of the National Executive Committee can differ from one year to the next between some relatively obscure Trade Unionist and some influential MP, including the occasional Cabinet Minister—and once, very nearly, Gaitskell when Leader of the Party. What is certain is that the Trade Unions will always have a 50 per cent say in NEC matters, and usually more. This brings us, and brought Gaitskell, right up against the problem of the Trade Unions. The Labour Movement originated partly with them—and the TUC dates back to 1868—and partly with the thinkers who formulated its ideas, ideals, and objects. The Trade Unions were necessary because labour was exploited and disunited in the 19th and early 20th centuries. They could and did sponsor most Labour MPs until 1945. In 1918, for instance, they sponsored 49 out of a total of 57. In 1929 the balance was reversed with 114 out of 287, but this proved only temporary, and from 1931 to 1945 the old balance was restored. In 1945, however, the proportion was 120 out of 393, and it has stayed that way. The trouble with the Trade Unions was, of course, that they did not keep up with the times but still claimed their special rights under the law, which today appear to many people so extensive that they give the impression of going beyond the law. Even in the 1930s Low depicted the Trades Union Congress as a drayhorse—an amiable, heavy animal but hardly dynamic. The situation is no better today. Gaitskell reached two conclusions on the question at an early stage of his career, and they both stood him in good stead throughout. One was that the Unions were of the greatest importance to the Movement, and he got on famously with most of the important Unions for most of the time. The other was that he would on no account agree that the Unions, either on their own or working through the NEC, should dictate policy in anything but the broadest terms to the PLP, let alone the Labour Government when it was in being. The NEC met, and meets, monthly to draw up broad policy documents. These, together with resolutions from all kinds of other Labour bodies, were debated at the Annual Conference; but it was essentially for the PLP, whose members had been elected by the general public, to conduct practical, day-to-day political affairs and eventually to formulate national policy. This doctrine had in fact been established by Keir Hardie, but it had tended to be eroded over the years. Gaitskell indeed went further and was quite prepared not only to do battle with resolutions backed by the

NEC and the Trade Unions, but to overrule them when he thought it right and necessary. We shall see how some of his outstanding performances fitted into this pattern. It took courage, since even today after some rationalisation and merging, there are over 150 Trade Unions with a membership of nearly nine million. Admittedly, they are not all powerful: The London Jewish Bakers' Union, for instance, has a membership of 12; the Card Setting Machine Tenters' Society, 218; the Spring Trapmakers' Society, 90; and others are similarly insignificant. Gaitskell was well aware of the futility of this multiplicity, both from the point of view of the Unions themselves and, more important, of the British economy, and of its sad contrast with the efficient United States system. An offshoot of the NEC is the National Council of Labour, of which little is heard and which for some reason has an equal number of members from the TUC, "the Labour Party" (not the PLP), and the Co-operative Union.

And in addition, of all extraordinary things in our country, the Labour Party has a Written Constitution. This was put into shape in 1918 through the combined efforts of Arthur Henderson and the intellectual Sidney Webb. It was constantly tinkered with at Annual Conferences, but it annoyed Gaitskell that a rigid document which may have met the needs of 1918 could possibly be considered adequate in the 1950s and 1960s. He made a frontal attack on parts of it, and in particular on sub-clause 4 of Clause 4, which defines Party Objects. The sub-clause which especially offended him read: "to secure for the producers by hand or by brain the full fruits of their industry, and the most equitable distribution thereof that may be possible, upon the basis of the common ownership of the means of production and the best obtainable system of popular administration and control of each industry or service." This Clause 4 controversy, as it was a bit inaccurately called, aroused very high feelings, as we shall see. He declined, however, to alter Clause I, which reads simply: "NAME. The Labour Party." Perhaps he was right. The title "Socialist" has been sadly abused, not least in Germany in National-Socialist days and in both parts of that country today. Nevertheless, the Labour Party is a member of the Socialist International, and it professes Socialist faiths, and its existing name seems to me to have some out-of-date and rather lowering connotations. The Constitution runs to half a dozen pages of close print. The Standing Orders run to three more.

The Labour Movement, as Gaitskell profoundly understood, is and has always been a combination of voluntary collaboration and of rigid rules; of teamwork and of fissiparous tendencies. At all levels, from local parties to the parliamentary party, it operates for too much of the time through committees with their stifling minutes, standing orders, and the rest. Gaitskell had to force himself on occasions to be patient with this mumbo-jumbo. Nevertheless, the Party developed from nothing at all to being a government in 20-odd years. In the period from 1940 to 1970 (counting 1940–5 as a time when it was half in power), it has governed for 50 per cent of the time. It is a self-indulgent movement allowing for extremes of individualism, unlike the Conservative Party. The frightful schisms that rend it—the Trade Unions against the rest, the MacDonald debacle, the quarrels inside the PLP—are endemic. In one sense they are a sign of its strength and liveliness. In another they can prove to be self-inflicted wounds.

It is time to return to the narrative and observe how rapidly Gaitskell's political skill developed in 1946 and the next few years; and, almost as important for a politician, how the luck ran his way.

FOUR

Great Leap Forward

Do you remember the condition of Britain in 1946? Phlegmatic people though we are, we were beginning to think, a year and more after we had "won the war," that things should be looking better a little faster. The Labour Government knew, on a simple statistical review of our resources and capabilities, that a rapid improvement in food rationing, housing, and other basic essentials was out of the question, let alone in amenities such as petrol for motoring or allowances for foreign travel. The Government was faced with the gigantic task of clearing up the mess caused by the war, and not only at home but abroad. But, in addition, it had to clear up the mess, again both at home and abroad, caused by the feckless Coalition and Tory governments of the 1930s. Clearing up messes of all kinds has to be done every day by someone; but no one could pretend that it is an inspiring job. If you are tired, in particular, it is wearing; and most people in Britain were tired.

Two things, in the main, kept us going. We had won through the brutal contest, of which the final stages had been as rough as any with the V1s and V2s at home and the invasion of Europe for those in the forces. Secondly, the Government had a clear programme for the restructuring and reconstitution of our main industries through nationalisation and of our empire through decolonialisation. They were determined to put through these programmes, tough though the opposition would be, and they did so. But all this meant austerity rather than amenity, and as the years passed the Opposition's appeal to the ordinary feelings for a bit of a letup from stern purposes, a little more leisure and relaxation, could hardly fail to be attractive.

If I may mention my own experience, I had not had a hard war. I was in our legation in Sofia when it broke out and when I volunteered to fight was ordered to stay where I was. In due course, the legation was surrounded by Nazi tanks, and when we left in the diplomatic exodus train, we were, without being aware of it, presented with two large suitcase time-bombs, one of which severely injured my wife and killed our unborn child on our arrival in Istanbul. On our journey home through the Mediterranean in 1943, we were dive-bombed and the convoy lost one ship sunk. Then there were the V1s and V2s, including the V1 which artfully destroyed the Guards Chapel when it was full of worshippers on a Sunday morning, and incidentally shook us up pretty thoroughly in the Foreign Office a hundred yards away. And with it all the austerity and the drudgery. Not, as I say, a hard war for my family and myself; but when I was ordered to report for duty in early 1946 to Cairo, fleshpots and all, I was not sorry.

Meanwhile, the Government, which included many members who were tired as a result of their exertions in the war, had to slog on and carry through a peaceful revolution, the only alternative to which would have been a very un-British bloody one. Gaitskell's job as No. 2 in the Ministry of Fuel and Power was, at that moment, much more important than it sounded. First, under Minister Shinwell it was at the very centre of the earliest nationalisation processes which so inflamed the feelings of the Opposition. Secondly, this was the period at which Ernest Bevin said, with complete accuracy, that every extra hundred tons of coal we could produce for export strengthened his hand immeasurably in his activities as Foreign Secretary. He was the first holder of that post to realise how completely our influence in the world depended on our economic strength. Unfortunately, we could produce little coal for export then and had to import some. The combination of Shinwell and Gaitskell was in some ways an unlikely one. Shinwell, born in 1884 and a miner in his teens, was a class-conscious, grass-roots Socialist of the traditional stamp. He had first become an MP in 1922 and a junior Minister in 1924. At that time Gaitskell, 22 years younger, was at Winchester, and within a couple of years he would be working up his equally fervent Socialism from a totally different angle. It is not surprising that they were never close to each other; nor, perhaps, that Shinwell should feel and express his rancour at the young upper-middle-class intellectual's successes. Gaitskell for his part was always civil to, and about, Shinwell. And in the end it was the classless Gaitskell who was to render the greater services to the Movement.

Gaitskell made his first speech as Parliamentary Secretary on 13th May 1946, three days after his appointment. The subject, naturally enough, was the Coal Industry Nationalisation Bill. An Opposition speaker had described him as "a dove" on the subject. "I am not sure that that is entirely appropriate at all times. I am not sure that, as far as my home life is concerned, my family would take quite that view." He went on to warn the Opposition forcefully that the National Coal Board would not act like private monopolies in the past, with its eyes glued on profits; it would, rather, act in the public interest. A week later he moved the third reading and called for speed. He also reminisced a little. "In 1927 I was lecturing in a mining town. I do not know that I taught the miners much, but they taught me a great deal. They taught me what economic feudalism was, and what it was to be victimised. They taught me the reality of economic life. It is there, a legacy of hatred, bitterness and bloodshed." The majority for the Bill was 324–143.

Nationalisation did not produce a miracle, and the Opposition thought they could exploit this in a debate on 16th October. Gaitskell admitted that the coal supply situation was grave and that the winter would be difficult. The miners were still suspicious as a result of their treatment over the last 30 years. They wanted to overcome the existing "white collar snobbery," and he thought they should be valued more highly. He compared the situation to Dunkirk and used a rhetorical effect which was to stand him in good stead on two famous later occasions: "Just as then we had to improvise, and improvise, and improvise, so we have to improvise today." He called the miners the fighter pilots of 1946.

The 1946–7 winter was grave indeed. The cold was appalling; it was no hardship at all for me to pass the time in the perfect winter weather of Egypt. But, to put it a bit flippantly, the British weather was on Gaitskell's side. Shinwell, the ex-miner and already a senior member of the Labour hierarchy, was no great administrator; nor was he an able defender of a hard case. The nationalised industry had not got going yet. There was, simply, a breakdown in supply.

Meanwhile, the Government pressed on with the nationalisation of electricity, and Gaitskell on 4th February 1947 wound up the debate on the second reading of the Electricity Bill. He pointed out that action was long overdue, as even a good number of Tories had admitted. As early as 1926 the subject had been mooted in a Standing Committee: "I am told that the Conservative members of that Committee were divided into two groups—the undertakers and the mutes." Churchill had spoken vaguely in 1943 of the broadening field for state ownership; Labour would be very happy to take his advice on what more to nationalise as they were approaching the end of their immediate programme. A Conservative member suggested, facetiously, "Transport House." When Gaitskell claimed that the highly complicated coal industry had been nationalised "without any sign whatever of any dislocation," there was, of course, Tory laughter. "The dislocation argument is the last refuge of the reactionary. I have no doubt at all that when King John, faced with hordes of angry barons at Runnymede, was asked to sign Magna Carta, he said: 'Gentlemen, this will cause terrible dislocation.'" There was laughter on both sides at this. The second reading was approved by 340 votes to 165.

By this month of February 1947 the fuel situation was

clearly parlous. It was debated on 2nd April, and Gaitskell had to speak up for his Minister, whose grip of the situation was loosening. He declared himself disappointed with Eden for an unstatesmanlike speech, and with other Tories for being "slightly reminiscent of the barrack square. Really you cannot deal with the miners in this way." The miners all loved Shinwell, he said; and if they were asked in a reasonable way to increase output so as to help their fellow-workers, they would respond. Outside the House, Gaitskell was most active in doing just that with the miners, and he was on the best of terms with the first Chairman of the National Coal Board, Lord Hyndley, with whom he had worked during the war. We scraped through that winter, but in the following summer he was still warning the House that the fuel situation was unquestionably very grave. The debates on the Electricity Bill dragged on and gave rise to much acrimony. It was fairly clear that Shinwell's cutting edge was by now blunted, and Gaitskell was carrying him.

After more than two years of tough going, Attlee could see that some Ministers were wearing better than others and that it was time to sort out the men from the boys. On 29th September 1947 he moved Sir Stafford Cripps from the Board of Trade to the new post of Minister of Economic Affairs, with Dalton remaining Chancellor. This was a sensible innovation. Not only was Labour's domestic programme dependent as to 90 per cent on economic factors and the Government's judgments on them, but our foreign policy was fundamentally in a similar situation. A very young man called Harold Wilson—he was 31 at the time—achieved full Cabinet rank as President of the Board of Trade. Shinwell was eased out of the Cabinet on 7th October, which he much resented, and became Secretary of State for War, to the horror of all Colonel Blimps but not of the "other ranks." Gaitskell took his place as Minister of Fuel and Power and became a Privy Councillor, but without a seat in the Cabinet. This promotion *sur place* is rare in politics, as it is in the Civil Service. The fact that a trained junior knows the

work well normally counts for nothing, while the consideration that old Buggins from some other quarter is about due
for a ministry, or an embassy, though totally ignorant of the
matters at issue, is considered preponderant. But Attlee was
a sensible and decisive man. On the day of his appointment,
Gaitskell was down a Leicestershire pit; he made a habit of
seeing for himself on the spot. Another step in the process
that was to lead to Gaitskell's further promotion was taken
when Dalton out of sheer light-headedness revealed an
autumn budget "secret" to a journalist a few minutes ahead
of time, and so was replaced on 13th November by Cripps,
who also retained for the time being the office of Minister
for Economic Affairs. Anyway, at the age of 41, Gaitskell was
in charge of an important, but not top, department of state.
Good going, but not sensational. This job, he opined, was
going to be hell. But he got much useful advice and help
from Stafford Cripps, who had now settled down after his
earlier extremism and with whom, consequently, he was on
closer terms.

From now on, Gaitskell's speeches in the House and answers to parliamentary questions naturally increased greatly
in number. The style in these years was still largely donnish,
which is not to say that it was ineffectual. The sheer weight
of statistics and specialised knowledge, often mustered at
very short notice, was usually enough to stun the Opposition.
One of his Permanent Under-Secretaries remarked that he
was easily the most efficient Minister with whom he had ever
dealt. Not, of course, that this characteristic would necessarily
endear a Minister to his civil servants. The wit and the passion came through intermittently in Gaitskell's speeches of
this epoch, but the fully rounded style was yet to develop.

Gaitskell and his Parliamentary Under-Secretary, the able
37-year-old Alfred Robens, made a strong team; and the
weather in the winter of 1947–8 obliged by being less hostile
than a year before. In his second public speech as Minister
he called for reduced fuel consumption and recommended
people to take fewer baths. "Personally, I have never had a

great many baths. It does not make a great difference to
health. As to your personal appearance, most of that is un-
derneath and nobody sees it." He was duly twitted on this.
Perhaps he was thinking of the crude tubs used habitually
by both his miner friends and, to this day, by the more deli-
cately nurtured scholars of Winchester. His first speech in the
House as Minister, on 21st October, concerned the National
Coal Board, which he doughtily defended. "Do not let us be
continually sniping and snooping at matters of details. Do
not let us be continually examining the roots to see whether
the tree is really growing." A few days later in a debate on
a motion calling for the abolition of petrol rationing for
"pleasure motoring," he was accused of penalising the middle,
or motoring, classes. He was to speak up for them a few
years later when he became leader. (We have heard similarly
idle criticisms recently of Barbara Castle when Transport
Minister.) And by February 1948 Gaitskell was able to report
that the coal stock position was now so favourable that we
could push ahead more rapidly with our coal export programme. That same month he moved the second reading of
the Gas Bill in a speech of over an hour, which nevertheless
formed only a small part of an interminable debate. Brendan
Bracken, the pastmaster of the filibuster in all these nationalisation debates, and particularly in Standing Committee
upstairs, paid tribute to the "clarity and industry" of his
performance, and also the "dexterity which he derived from
long association with his former guileful master"—Hugh
Dalton.

A curious episode was Gaitskell's admission at this time,
in reply to a question by Anthony Greenwood, who has always been opposed to all blood sports, that a special petrol
allowance was made to the Master of the Quantock stag-
hounds and other masters of hounds "for purposes connected
with the hunt." On this he refused to budge. At the same
time he refused a special allowance for amateur cricket clubs.
He also indulged in some rather ponderous witticisms about
his own cricketing ineptitude and contrasted it with the first-

class skill of his brother-in-law, the Tory MP Hubert Ashton.

In an important speech on the Budget proposals on 13th April 1948 Gaitskell went for Harold Macmillan, whom he never much liked or trusted throughout both their careers. It was a sign of his personal standing, and of the importance of Fuel and Power at that time, that he was put up to make a major speech on the Budget. In Macmillan's speeches, he said, "There is always the rolling, rhetorical phrase, reminiscent perhaps slightly of Gibbon, and on occasion the most vitriolic and partisan approach to our affairs." He was able to report that the coal situation had recovered remarkably, thanks to the miners, to Shinwell, and to the National Coal Board—not to himself, he modestly added. Exports should now benefit our balance of payments by £40 m. Luck and judgment were working in Gaitskell's favour again. The Tory speaker who followed him called his speech "a lecture on economics." Throughout this period he had crisp exchanges with R. S. Hudson, the Tory spokesman on fuel and power, and the ebullient Brendan Bracken, who accused him of being petulant. The displaced Shinwell was unable to conceal his chagrin at the young man's success. Gaitskell took all this in his stride. He always enjoyed a scrap.

He attacked Bracken over the third reading of the Gas Bill on 16th June. Bracken had, he alleged, been deserted by his own side, and so had started a new group, which Gaitskell nicknamed the "Bracken Circus." "I feel the word 'circus' is peculiarly appropriate because, upstairs in Committee, we did have some excellent clowning, a lot of somersaulting, and indeed the whole atmosphere of the 'Crazy Gang,' led by the Rt. Hon. Gentleman from behind. As for his own patter, he does use certain weapons very well: invective, exaggeration, abuse and misrepresentation." Not content with that volley, Gaitskell hotted things up further. Bracken's speeches, he said, "are extremely reminiscent of that screeching, raucous voice we used to hear—the voice of Herr Hitler." There were furious cries of "cheap." When he mentioned Bracken's role as Minister of Information in the war several maddened

Tories took up the cry: "Where were you?" To which Gaitskell coolly replied: "I was also serving my country." As a
final sally he commented: "Never has anyone spoken so much
on subjects of which he knew so little." The debate was
stormy throughout. He gave Bracken another buffeting,
though less severely, in the debate on the King's Speech on
3rd November. He said condescendingly that Bracken had
been less "adjectival" than usual, less inaccurate, and indulging in less fantasy. He had no doubt that if he represented
the Opposition on the Steel Bill, he would repeat his performances on the Gas Bill. Bracken, of course, was quite
capable of looking after himself.

A favourite theme of Gaitskell's during this period was
praise of the miners, the National Coal Board, and the
Trade Unions. His stock reply to criticisms of production or
of price rises was that matters would have been infinitely
worse if coal had not been nationalised. In a debate on the
Coal Industry Bill on 28th March 1949, for instance, he
seemed to lose his temper with what he called "a disgraceful
attack on the leaders of the Trade Union Movement" and "a
most scandalous suggestion" by John Foster. The next Tory
speaker called him "offensive." On 6th July he made the outstanding speech to the annual meeting of the National Union
of Mineworkers, amongst whom he felt completely at home.
He appealed for intensive efforts aimed at winning the election "in a year or so." On 10th November he ended a long
speech on the National Coal Board's Annual Report, which
he pointed out was the first report of a nationalised industry
to be discussed in Parliament, by suggesting that the House
should join with the Board in expressing thanks to the men
in the industry. Similar thoughts so much moved him when
he was addressing a meeting of miners in Porthcawl that
tears overcame him. At last he was able to say: "I hope you
will forgive my emotion." Who would not? He even questioned whether, if he were to be called to more responsible
posts in the Party, he could keep this emotional side suitably
under control. This I find appealing; beneath the skilful

politician's exterior a true shyness remained. As he commented later, Churchill often became, to use his own word, "blubbery," when subject to strong emotion. So much for the "desiccated" image! One political commentator put it this way: "Gaitskell is very tough, tough enough for tears."

Meanwhile, on 24th May when addressing the Electrical Trade Union, he had developed what was to become a central idea of his: that the people who would decide the next election, and indeed any election in Britain at this time, were the floating voters. This may seem an obvious thought to many of us today, but it was an original one in large sections of the Labour Movement then. The less progressive elements tended to consider that if people were not loyal Labour supporters anyway, well, the hell with them; and a good many were suspicious of the sincerity and worth to the Movement of converts from other parties. Gaitskell drove home the message that Labour's principal aim was to keep, and later obtain, power. He was to run into much short-sighted opposition from such as Frank Cousins over this strategic question.

Nineteen-forty-nine was the year in which Gaitskell really made his name. It was not merely a question of his achievements as Minister of Fuel and Power: overcoming the fuel shortage, launching major expansion in coal, electricity and gas, creating a new oil refinery industry, collaborating fruitfully with Shell and BP. His successes went wider than that. Cripps had taken a grip on the whole economy since replacing Dalton in November 1947; production and exports were rising rapidly; the balance of payments was in surplus. Nevertheless, the US recession of the spring of 1949 and the resulting dollar crisis hit us hard: a familiar story. Also Cripps' health was deteriorating and in July 1949 he had to go abroad for two months. He and Gaitskell, while always on good terms, were never close. The strongly Christian side of Cripps' Socialism had no appeal for Gaitskell. The fact that they were both Wykehamists was neither here nor there. But the efficient and austere Cripps much admired Gaitskell's efficiency and readiness to use austerity as a means to that end. On his recommendation, Attlee took the extraordinary step of putting Gaitskell in charge of the Treasury. It fell to him to arrange for the devaluation of the pound, which, as on the next occasion in 1967, might with advantage have been done much earlier. Gaitskell carried it through with secrecy and efficiency. His circle of friends, and a good many people beyond it, were now convinced that he would be Chancellor in due course, if not Leader. Those less friendly to him in the Labour Movement regarded this possibility with apprehension. He was a disturbing phenomenon for them: a good Socialist, no doubt, but an upper-class intellectual who was showing signs of questioning the adequacy to the 1950s of a good many of Labour's established faiths and practices.

At the 1949 Labour Conference a new policy statement called Labour Believes in Britain was approved; Attlee thought the time had come to test whether Britain still believed in Labour. The Government's 1945 programme had been carried out; they had been going hard at it for over four years; not a single by-election had been lost in the last four and a half years; and at the same time several senior Ministers were showing signs of strain. Attlee decided off his own bat during the New Year holiday period to ask the King at Sandringham to approve the election being held on 23rd February. Many were surprised that he had not held his hand a little longer.

The results were deeply disappointing—much worse than any Labour leaders had thought possible. Labour's own Representation of the People Act, which altered all but eighty of the old constituencies, weighed heavily against them.

Labour actually raised their total number of votes by nearly 300,000, but the number of seats fell by 78 to 315. The Conservatives were up to 298, and the overall Labour majority in the House was a wretched five. This got Gaitskell's blood up, and he was determined to be more rather than less hard-hitting from now on. It was no surprise to anyone that on 28th February he was appointed Minister of State for Economic Affairs and official No. 2 to Cripps, while retaining the seniority of a head of department. He was still not in the Cabinet. On the same day Shinwell regained a place in the Cabinet as Minister of Defence. But he was not to outrank his former junior for long.

On 24th April, Gaitskell made his first important Commons speech in his new office. It was a long one and a good one, dealing in the main with the economic points in the Budget Proposals and Economic Survey, but also including a few pokes at Churchill. He said that everyone enjoyed his speeches, though they "are perhaps more lively than thoughtful, more witty than relevant, but always entertaining." Churchill had used the metaphor of the milch cow. "I keep no cows myself, but . . ." and here Churchill intervened to say: "It is only one of the Rt. Hon. Gentleman's examples of self-denial." Gaitskell pointed out that we were now in surplus on current account, and in balance on our dollar account. The major problems were to hold full employment without inflation and secondly to maintain the Welfare State, which involved redistributing incomes and retaining some rationing. "On these great issues the Opposition is split. Half the time they are back in their dream world. Some believe we ought to have more unemployment and cut the social services. Between the extremes is the great amorphous mass of Conservative opinion, led by one who has all the charm, but also the limitations, of Peter Pan, who never grew up." Oliver Stanley remarked: "He pulled you through the war," and the next speaker took Gaitskell to task for his irreverence.

Gaitskell's July 1950 programme shows him operating in top gear, as he was to do until the end of his life. Parliamentary questions then and in subsequent weeks covered such a broad spectrum as trade discussions with Canada, United Aid to China Fund, Colonial Empire dollar balances, timber supply for housing, purchase tax on fishermen's sou'-westers and on chemical closets, and greyhound racing bookmakers' licence fees. He made a big speech to the Economic and Social Council in Geneva, stressing the importance of full employment as a bulwark against Communism. He did much to get the Colombo Plan operating, and also the European Payments Union. On the third reading of the Finance Bill on 10th July, he spoke of past achievements and present difficulties. Since the end of the war, defence expenditure had declined and the national income risen. So expenditure on the social services had been raised from £600 m. in 1946–7 to over £1,200 m. in the current year. Indirect taxation had been much reduced, and a "very substantial surplus" achieved. But this year defence expenditure had risen from £741 m. to £781 m.—happy days, we may feel inclined to comment today—and "We must all have in mind the events in Korea." For on 25th June the Communists had decided to step up the Cold War by invading the southern part of that country. The disruptive effects of that war on the economies of the United States, Britain, and elsewhere were enormous. The United States Government put in hand a huge stockpiling policy; the prices of the UK's imports rose by 40 per cent in a year. And there was more to follow. The Moscow spymasters may well have been advised of these probable effects by Philby and Maclean.

By September 1950, Cripps was again away ill; and in Gaitskell's last speech from outside the Cabinet, he showed how well suited he was to enter it. It was a masterly survey of the Government's Defence Proposals, necessarily gloomy in tone and giving sombre warnings for the future. Having rebuked Macmillan for bringing party into the debate, Gaitskell explained that, as we were determined to do our duty in Korea and support our US allies, he foresaw an increase in defence expenditure of £1,260 m. over three years, or 50 per cent. It might even be heavier. This was bound to affect adversely our export trade and balance of payments. To avoid becoming once more, as at the end of the war, "a burden to our friends," we must bear Budget burdens ourselves. "It is not my business to discuss how the funds will be raised. That," he said, and the irony of the situation was almost tragic, "will be the job of my Rt. Hon. and Learned Friend the Chancellor when he introduces his Budget next spring." Defence would now have to take equal priority with exports. Up to then we had been paying our way; he meant, of course, thanks to tremendous help from Marshall Aid, which he was able to renounce in December, months ahead of time and of all other recipient countries. He paid a tribute to the co-operation between Trade Unions, management, and government since the war. On 3rd October he deputised for the Chancellor at the Lord Mayor's banquet for City bankers, the first time for 50 years that the Chancellor had been unable to attend. He painted a favourable picture of our economic achievements, but uttered warnings too. Our reserves had doubled, but were still far too low and much lower than before World War II. And, once more, the Korean war was bound to have a severe effect.

On 8th October, Hugh Gaitskell left for his first visit to the US and Canada, where rearmament problems were to the fore in his discussions. It was by now clear that Cripps' health had collapsed. For the second time Attlee accepted his recommendation to promote Gaitskell; and for the second time it was done *sur place,* on this occasion to one of the highest posts in the land. From his position halfway down the list of Ministers not in the Cabinet, Gaitskell leapt up to fourth inside it behind only Attlee, Morrison, and Bevin. Of his older colleagues, he thus overtook at a bound such as Dalton, Jowitt, Chuter Ede, Shinwell, and Bevan, who made no secret of the fact that he wanted the Chancellorship for himself; and of the younger Cabinet Ministers, Harold Wilson and Patrick Gordon Walker, who was at the Commonwealth Relations Office. It was only human that there should be a good many heads wagging, and some noses put distinctly out of joint. Bevan took it particularly hard. Not only did he regard himself as the archetypal Socialist, but he was nearly 10 years older than Gaitskell, had been an MP for 16 years longer, and a senior Minister for five years. Here the feud began.

Gaitskell actually received Attlee's offer while in Canada, by a cable sent to the High Commissioner, who jokily remarked: "I'm afraid what I am going to say may come as a shock to you." Gaitskell admitted to feeling alarmed and wondering whether he had dropped a brick of some kind. Of course, he accepted immediately. Exciting events made a habit of catching him on his numerous and far-flung travels, as we shall see again in January 1957 and August 1959. On his return he was duly installed on 19th October. At 44 he was the youngest Chancellor since Austen Chamberlain, at 39, in the Balfour Government in 1903. He had been in Parliament only five years. His temperament was such that he actively welcomed the looming challenges in the world situation, in the House where the Tories were now relentlessly harrying the government on every issue—the tiny majority came to be known as "the wheelchair majority" because intrepid invalids had often to be wheeled in to vote—and even inside the Labour Party.

Since Gaitskell had effectively been in charge of the Treasury for some little time he could go straight on with the operation of finding the money for rearmament. On 6th December he uttered the usual warnings to a meeting of the Foreign Press Association. He also said: "We must hold fast to the conception of the Atlantic Community . . . As a colleague of mine once said about 'third forces,' there is too much 'third' and too little 'force' in such ideas." Gaitskell stressed solidly throughout his life the importance of friendship with the United States; and this naturally aroused opposition amongst some of his more airy-fairy colleagues, not to mention many Tories with their traditional dislike of depending, as we do and must, on a younger nation that long ago made good.

On 10th January 1951, Gaitskell reviewed the 1950 record at a press conference. It had been one of great progress, in productivity, production, exports, surplus, and reserves, which rose in 1950 by £576 m. though they were still only one-third of our 1938 figure; yet the present and future problems were immense. Nineteen-fifty-one, he said, would be difficult. How right he was. In other speeches in January he put the blame for the world's ills squarely on Russia's aggressively imperialist policy. We on our side would have to give up what mattered least, luxuries, and to be content with a smaller surplus. In a far-ranging but sometimes edgy speech on 15th February he expressed disappointment that the Opposition should have put down a motion of censure on the Government's defence policy, and slated Churchill's speech as completely feeble and largely irrelevant. "My Rt. Hon. Friend the Minister of Labour [i.e. Nye Bevan], who is to wind up for the Government tonight, is a man with a vivid Celtic imagination who will no doubt be able to find bits and pieces on which to pick." Old Winston here began moving about in a way that seemed to annoy Gaitskell and intervened: "May I tell the Rt. Hon. Gentleman that I was only looking for a jujube." Gaitskell replied that he was sorry he could not help; he had left his outside. He then went back to serious business: defence might well cost £4,700 m. in the next three years. We might have to accept a deficit on our balance of payments, and the Budget would aim at keeping home expenditure down. Naturally, he did not yet specify what the measures would be. The next Tory speaker called for a General Election and Churchill back at the helm. The censure motion was defeated by a comparatively healthy majority of 21. In a broadcast on 6th March, Gaitskell said that but for Korea he would have been looking forward to quite a cheerful Budget.

Before that came he made his first major speech in the House on the conduct of foreign relations. The occasion was the comparatively limited debate on 20th March about the Sterling Balances Agreement with Egypt, which had just been negotiated though not yet signed. Egypt, he pointed out, had persistently refused our requests that all or part of the £350 m. balance in her favour should be cancelled on the grounds that it arose from our defence of the country. "It struck me that some hon. Members did not have much idea of what the feeling and public opinion was in Egypt. She did not invite us to assist her. She was not one of our allies. She was merely carrying out the 1936 Treaty. If we declined to pay when Egypt presented the cheque we were dishonouring it. This would have a very bad effect on our future relations." (This I can confirm personally from my service in our Cairo Embassy in 1947 and 1948.) Bob Boothby's arguments, he said, were simply based on the fact that he did not like Egyptians. Gaitskell went on to deplore Egypt's action in preventing the oil trade with Haifa through the Suez Canal and reminded the house that Sir Gladwyn Jebb had put our views very forcibly to the Security Council, who had referred them to the Mixed Armistice Commission. "We cannot really start introducing our fleet when the matter is under consideration by the United Nations. It is very rare to have an agreement in which one gets everything one's own way. We have made some concessions, and the Egyptian Government some very substantial ones." Here we see many of Gaitskell's best characteristics in his approach to foreign affairs. We must be fair in our negotiations and appreciate the other side's point of view; we must avoid force; we must respect and encourage the United Nations. Here was Suez casting its long shadow before. From now on, with Ernest Bevin dying, Attlee not too well, and Herbert Morrison since 9th March ineptly in charge of the Foreign Office, which Bevan had coveted, Gaitskell was officially No. 3 in the Government and took on more and more parliamentary work in wider spheres.

On 10th April 1951, Gaitskell presented his one and only Budget Proposals and Economic Survey, and in doing so split the Labour Party clean down the middle. His preparatory interview with the Prime Minister, who was unfortunately in hospital, had its farcical side. Gaitskell reported in his clean-breasted fashion that some of his proposals seemed likely to lead to important resignations in the Parliamentary Party, and he named the names. Attlee, who as is well known was a laconic man, muttered something to the effect: "Have to go then." Gaitskell was quite prepared for this to be his own

fate, though it would be a cruel blow. Attlee, in one of his
longer sentences, of ten words or so, then explained that it
was the dissidents who would have to go. His brief comment
on the affair afterwards was that Gaitskell handled it in a
business-like and resolute way.

By most people, however, both in and outside Parliament,
Gaitskell's speech of two and a half hours was greeted as a
masterly performance. For the first time in its short life every
seat in the new Chamber was filled. Ernest Bevin rose from
his bed to be present; he was to die only four days later.
Gaitskell analysed the world situation on the lines of his defence speech of 15th February. "The setting is the clash between the two great forces in the world today—Soviet
imperialism and the parliamentary democracies." After apol-
ogizing for bringing economics into the argument, he gave
an elaborately technical economic disquisition, which was
hardly interrupted at all—perhaps because it was above the
heads of most members? The out-turn for 1950-1 had been
good: instead of the forecast surplus of £443 m., in fact one
of £720 m. But—characteristically—the outlook now was a
different matter: and, sardonically, "I trust that I have thus
dispersed any optimism about the future." After all this the
Government's proposals did not appear too swinging: "a
modest charge in respect of some dental work and optical
services" [sic], profits and purchase taxes up in some spheres.
He claimed that the Budget was fair though he knew it
would not be popular. It was not one of his liveliest speeches,
but Churchill congratulated him on being lucid and comprehensive and avoiding malice or hatred. He had, in a very
practical and friendly way, helped the new Chancellor in his
task by urging him early on to speak more slowly. "I think
the Chancellor for a remarkable parliamentary performance."
But he also loosed off at the iniquities of "the whole period
of rule of the Socialist Party." Certainly life was not very
gay in the material ways which appealed to Churchill and
his colleagues. Only a trickle of new cars coming on to the
market; eightpence worth of meat and three ounces of cheese

per head per week; shortages of coal, gas, and electricity. As one Tory wag put it, "If all the wind and woolliness of the planners could be converted into electrical energy we should avoid power cuts altogether." In further debate on 16th April Gaitskell for his part warmly congratulated Sid Edward Boyle on his maiden speech: he always had a soft spot for him. Others he congratulated were Crosland, Jenkins, and Houghton, names which ring loud bells today.

Nye Bevan got very Welsh and proprietorial about the whole issue of the National Health Service, as if he had invented it single-handed and still ran it, which of course as Minister of Labour he did not. His personal statement on 23rd April about his resignation ranged very wide: he was clever enough not to concentrate on teeth and specs. He said that the Chancellor's arms-expenditure programme was impracticably large and that he knew it. The Budget was anti-Socialist and pleased the City. We depended too much on "the lurchings of the American economy"—some point in this—and we had allowed ourselves to be dragged too far behind the wheels of American diplomacy. "The only hope for mankind remains in this little island" was followed by other similar sentimentalities. Economic planning should be taken away from the Treasury, and the Chancellor confined to making an annual statement of accounts. There were too many economists around; worst of all, we now had one as Chancellor. "If the Chancellor finds it necessary to mutilate the Health Services for £13 m. out of £4,000 m., what will he do next year? It will be like Lavinia—all the limbs cut off and eventually her tongue cut out too." Splendid stuff, but not strong in logic. Gaitskell had actually increased expenditure on the National Health Service by £50 m. and Bevan had agreed in Cabinet that a ceiling must be set. His personal animosity on account of both Morrison's and Gaitskell's appointments showed clearly through. For what it is worth, my own view is that the specs and teeth charges could be criticised on two counts: the sum produced was indeed small, and there was something rather ridiculous, and hence vulnerable to the Opposition's shafts of wit, about the objects chosen. Harold Wilson in his statement the next day repeated some of Bevan's points, and said expressly that he was not resigning on the narrow issue of teeth and spectacles. "The Budget involves the first cutting into our social services, which I cannot believe to be necessary." John Freeman also resigned as Parliamentary Secretary at the Ministry of Supply. All this had a severe and prolonged effect on the whole Labour Movement. Gaitskell rode the storm in his usualy resilient way, described by some as obstinate and by others as arrogant. *Tribune* went so far as to compare him with Snowden in 1931 and accuse him of betraying the Labour Party. On balance the business turned out to his personal advantage. He and Bevan attacked each other lustily from time to time, but over Suez they became closer and by the time of Bevan's death they were collaborating warmly. Gaitskell and Wilson never really got together; Gaitskell felt more at ease with someone of a lively temperament such as George Brown. Freeman virtually left politics altogether.

"I did not join the Labour Party, I was born in it," said Bevan. In every major way but one, he and Gaitskell differed as chalk from cheese. Bevan was born poor in South Wales, followed his father into the mines at the age of 13, educated himself, was endowed with a golden tongue, was robust, extrovert, given to flights of exaggeration. On every one of these counts Gaitskell presented a contrast. His characteristics, and his success, infuriated Bevan for half a dozen years from 1950. Butskellism, with its subtle, friendly economic cut and thrust, appeared to him and his followers almost a betrayal of the Labour Movement. The question of "left" and "right" wing of course comes into the matter; but I agree with Attlee in thinking that these labels can and often are used with inaccurate rigidity. Of course, Bevan stood for most of his career on the left of the Party; but over unilateralism he was by no means as far to the left as Frank Cousins. "This," he said, "is a mere emotional spasm, there is no thought in it." After 1956 he moved towards the centre. Again, I should not place Gaitskell on the right, but about at the centre, though, like Bevan, with some variations. On the question of a détente in Central Europe, for instance, Gaitskell put himself on the far left by immediately supporting the Rapacki Plan and advocating the de facto recognition of the German Democratic Republic. But on the Common Market issue he was far to the right: though even here there was the complication that his "right-wing" trade unionist supporters favoured entry, in opposition to his views.

The one major characteristic the two men had in common was a passionate devotion to Socialism—yes, passionate in Gaitskell's case too—though they had come to it by such different paths. Their divergences were to cause the Movement untold harm. Their coming together in 1956 was something like the beginning of a new, hopeful era, all too soon curtailed by death. And in the end it was the cool Gaitskell who rendered the Movement the greater services, rather than the rambunctious Bevan. We shall see these themes working themselves out over the years.

For the time being, in 1951, Gaitskell played it cool and thus succeeded in further infuriating Bevan. For instance, he explained to the Scottish regional conference of the Party that the National Health Service was already costing much more than expected, and that a ceiling rise of £50 m. for the current year was essential. It was rubbish to say that this would disrupt the whole structure. On the second reading of the Finance Bill on 8th May he referred coolly, in passing, to "certain differences of opinion within our party," and not at all to specs and fangs. He obtained the endorsement of the National Executive for the Budget, which caused Bevan, Barbara Castle, Tom Driberg, and Ian Mikardo to write a letter saying that the National Executive, of which they were all members, had no right to do any such thing. He addressed the National Council of Labour on the Budget, a body curiously consisting of representatives of the TUC, Parliamentary Labour Party, the Co-operative Union, the Labour Peers and the *Daily Herald*. He found time later that month to slip over to the US, and in a National Broadcasting Corporation interview gave his audience of some 20 million Americans figures to prove that, taking the Far East as a whole, the British and French had more forces containing Communist aggression than did the US. Back to the Finance Bill, and on 6th June he expressed the view that salaried people generally would not be likely to work less because of increased taxation: they thought not only of their earnings but of other things such as family responsibilities, ambition, power. One Tory interjected: "Another lecture," and Gaitskell had some brushes with Churchill.

In July, Gaitskell called the TUC special economic committee to the Treasury and told them that Britain's financial position had much worsened since the Budget. There was a trade gap since then of £500 m., thanks to rises in world prices. Our gold and dollar reserves were diminishing. He asked that the TUC at their September meeting should postpone wage claims, but got the reply that the Government must first control prices, profits, and dividends. His speech at the Congress made a great impression by the force of its presentation, but the theme of wage restraint and general pessimism was rather coolly received.

Gaitskell's last weeks in office were a flurry of activity. Before the Blackpool Congress he had attended the Paris meeting of the Council of Ministers of the Organisation for European Economic Co-operation. After Blackpool he was off to Washington to attend the annual meetings of the Governors of the International Monetary Fund and of the International Bank for Reconstruction and Development. Then up to Ottawa for a week and a meeting of the North Atlantic Treaty Council; then back to New York where he addressed the Foreign Policy Association and told them of his belief that "the future happiness and peace and security of the world depend more upon Anglo-American understanding than anything else." On 23rd September he and his private secretary William Armstrong, now the very able head of the whole Civil Service, returned home. At the Lord Mayor's banquet on 3rd October, Gaitskell reported that in the third quarter the sterling area had run up a gold and dollar deficit of $638 m. Somehow a balance must be struck between the defence needs and the economic stability of the free world. Gaitskell played no great part at the Scarborough Annual Conference, which was held from 1st to 3rd October, and he was not on any committees. Although third in the Party hierarchy, he made no attempt to be elected to the NEC, for the good reason that he knew he would be defeated. The poll for the Constituency Parties' representatives was easily headed by Bevan, with his friends Barbara Castle and Driberg coming next. Attlee had suddenly decided that he and his government could no longer take the strain and had fixed the election date for 25th October. The election manifesto was discussed at length.

The rest of the month was devoted to campaigning for the General Election. I remember the atmosphere vividly, as I had just returned to England after two and a half gorgeous years in our Embassy in Chile. "Là, tout n'est qu'ordre et beauté, Luxe, calme et volupté"—or that was how it seemed in drab old England with its strict rationing and its gloomy economic outlook. It was true that the Labour governments had achieved much since the end of the war, both at home and abroad. They had provided the major industries with the new nationalised base that they needed. Harold Wilson at the Board of Trade had lit a "bonfire of controls." They had kept close to the US, through Marshall Aid which they had now renounced, through the Berlin airlift, through the founding of NATO, and through active collaboration in Korea. They had started work on our own nuclear weapon. They had given independence to India and Pakistan. But gratitude does not win elections. Many of the British people were sick of austerity and of the do-gooding style of some Labour politicians. Many were bored with nationalisation, past and prospective, and unconvinced of the need for it. They wanted more flamboyant leadership, and after all the great war-leader was to hand, even if he was nearer 80 than 70. The Tory cry of "Set the people free" may not seem, in perspective today, to have led to all that much achievement in practice; but it had great appeal at the time. And the Labour Movement was openly and bitterly divided. Nevertheless, the Labour vote rose by nearly 700,000 to just under 14 million: the largest total in history and 230,000 more than the Conservatives registered. Alas, the Conservatives got the seats: 321 to Labour's 295, and an overall majority in the House of 17. Gaitskell himself was safely re-elected.

So Gaitskell's brief Cabinet career was ended; as it turned out, forever. The Korean war had knocked our economy sideways and it was, disappointingly, in a worse condition than when he took over. But he had established himself in the hierarchy of the Labour Movement; he had shown that he was a fearless fighter; and he had proved himself a first-class House of Commons man. All these achievements would stand him in good stead in the next few years and would enable him to exercise increasing influence from the Opposition benches.

FIVE

Butskellism

THIS WITTY WORD was invented by the *Economist* during Rab Butler's long Chancellorship from 1951 to 1955. It implied two things. One was that Butler's policy of Keynesian control of the economy was little different in practice from Gaitskell's ideas. Indeed the scope for basic variations was limited by our economic performance and standing in the world, which obstinately deteriorated as time went on in comparison with that of more go-ahead nations. Secondly, the word referred to the fact that Butler and Gaitskell were throughout these years locked in unarmed combat. Butler looks back on it all with some pleasure. Being, as he says, on the left wing of the Conservative Party, while Gaitskell he considers was right of centre in his, there was in the last resort no great margin between their ideas. However, this did not inhibit the exchange of swinging verbal blows. Butler remembers Gaitskell with affection. Only one of his speeches in opposition to himself seemed to him unnecessarily vituperative, and this was at a later stage and on the different subject of immigration. At the end of this prolonged struggle, it was Gaitskell who won politically; but Butler lived actively on.

The tone was set as soon as 7th November 1951, when Butler opened the debate on the King's Speech and Gaitskell made an hour-long reply. He congratulated Butler on his frank statement, much of which was unexceptionable from the Labour point of view. "He was good enough to quote from some of my recent speeches" and he did not allege, as the Gracious Speech (drafted of course by the Tory Cabinet) had done "most dishonestly," that Gaitskell had withheld important information from the public. His speech was generally sympathetic to Butler as regards his heavy task. "What he is doing is precisely what I did myself last year. It is none the worse for that." Butler intervened: "I may be more successful." Gaitskell condoled with him over having to deal with the "Overlords," Lords Woolton, Leathers, and Cherwell. This was one of Gaitskell's more donnish speeches and not one of his most convincing. Bevan was on his back, getting at him; he missed no opportunity of suggesting that he was priggish, a dry-as-dust economist, and too kindly in his attitude to the Tories. And he was interrupted from time to time by ironical laughter. The next Tory speaker accused him of low tactics and called him "Satan rebuking sin." But it was a clear beginning to Butskellism. And the process continued when he spoke for well over an hour on Butler's first Budget Proposals on 12th March 1952. "On previous occasions I have had to comment on the contrast between the Chancellor's speeches and others made by his friends. I can see that it is annoying for them to see the Chancellor agreeing with me." Butler replied, mildly and all the more effectively, that the Rt. Hon. Gentleman must not be unfair. The going was hard for Gaitskell at this stage, especially as he was beginning to take over more responsibility from Attlee, now in his 70th year, and Morrison. But he often exhibited his skill in producing long and complicated expositions—sometimes a little too long—at short notice and with few or no notes.

As always, the debates on the Finance Bill were prolonged, and they extended through April, May, and June. Gaitskell bore much of the burden for the Opposition, and continued his divisive tactics, sometimes in a picturesque manner. "On the other side speaker after speaker has patted the Chancellor on the back in a perfunctory manner, and then proceeded, in the most treacherous way, to jab him firmly in the stomach about purchase tax and finish up with an uppercut to the jaw about the excess profits levy." He jokily congratulated Butler on securing all-party unity: "We are all agreed that this is a thoroughly bad Bill." He admitted, unblushingly, that the deficit in 1951 had been £500 m. as against the £100 m. he had anticipated. He attacked the Tories' "queer sort of inferiority in saying: 'We are only doing what you did before.' " The rearmament policy must be maintained, but Butler's increases in indirect taxation meant that 28 million of the poorer people would be definitely worse off. Butler again used the gentle retort: "He did himself far less than justice, but he is no less attractive in the role of Party agitator than that of an economist." On one matter of detail he admitted that he had had a private word with Gaitskell beforehand, who for his part expressed sympathy with Butler on having to deal with his "extremely reactionary" back benches, including Lord Hinchingbrooke who was "still in a dodo frame of mind." Gaitskell was capable of speaking at 4 a.m. on matters such as entertainment allowances. At the end, on 26th June, he commended the Chancellor for his even-tempered handling of the Bill; but equally he slammed the Government for muddle, incompetence, and vacillation.

Gaitskell had taken time out in May to address, somewhat improbably, the Executives' Club of Chicago, and what is more to tell them of the need for large-scale investment in the under-developed areas and for the lowering of import tariffs by the US Government. He did not find any great enthusiasm for these ideas in that particular audience. At home he addressed the annual congress of the National Union of General and Municipal Workers, of which he was a member. He attacked those who wanted large cuts in Britain's defence programme: we could not afford isolationism. But he said that the lowest-paid workers would be justified in making reasonable wage claims since Butler's reduction in the food subsidies had put up the cost of living. These were speeches in his coolest, most reasonable style. An hour-long speech in the House on 29th July, which aroused much laughter and applause from his colleagues, was different in tenor. He threatened that the Government would not get co-operation from the TUC and the workers unless they were seen to be behaving fairly. "They favour out-of-date economic doctrines consistent only with a high level of unemployment." The next day he was attacked by Bevan with considerable personal rancour, though of course Bevan denied that this came into it.

The Bevanites were in fact on the way towards over-reaching themselves. They made an almost clean sweep of the Constituency Parties' poll at the 1952 Annual Conference at Morecambe; Gaitskell stood for the NEC and was heavily defeated. But the Unions were beginning to get sick of the Bevanites' divisive tactics and what they often considered their bloody-mindedness. There was great indignation at their ousting of Morrison and Dalton from the National Executive, and Gaitskell seized on this in a speech—and a very strong one—the following week at Stalybridge. Morrison's defeat constituted both "gross ingratitude and blind stupidity." A most disturbing feature of the Conference had been the number of Communist-inspired resolutions and speeches. He had heard that one-sixth of the Constituency Party delegates were Communists or fellow-travellers: "Even if it were only one-twentieth, it is a most shocking state of affairs." The loud talk about withdrawing our forces from Korea and NATO was "silly nonsense." The Bevanites largely controlled the left-wing press and poured out misleading propaganda and malicious attacks on "Attlee, Morrison, and the rest of us." This would endanger a Labour victory at the next election. *"Tribune* is an invitation to disloyalty and disunity. It is time to end the attempt at mob-rule by a group of frustrated journalists." Such words were not the product of a "desiccated calculating machine." Gaitskell's blood was well and truly up; the gloves were off. The strictures on Communist influences may appear exaggerated to-day. But the line as a whole was well calculated to appeal to the more conservative sections of the Unions. This speech was also salutary because for the first time a representative of the responsible Labour centre had paid back the irresponsible left wing in their own coin. Attlee had never reacted as strongly, or effectively, to Bevanite and other provocations. Bevan realised with a shock, for the first but not the last time, that:

Cet animal est méchant.
Quand on l'attaque, il se défend.

In the debate on the Address on 11th November, Gaitskell spoke as his alter ego, the professional economist. The balance of payments had improved during 1952 and we might well have a surplus. This was due to luck rather than the Government's judgment, for import prices had fallen. Production had fallen too, and as a consequence about 500,000 were unemployed. If the supporters of a reduction in government expenditure had their way there would be another big cut in food subsidies and in the social services; in general the Government were returning to pre-war policies. This was not one of Gaitskell's most convincing speeches, and Butler was able to reply on the lines that, whatever truth there might be in parts of Gaitskell's analysis, the fact was that the economy was improving.

Active though Gaitskell still was in the House, he now had rather more time to travel around. In January 1953 he was in the Middle East, and he strongly criticised HMG's offer of jet aircraft to the Arab states and Israel. We should stand by the Tripartite Declaration, and offer economic aid instead. In May he went on a lecture tour in West Germany, and in August in the US, where he appeared on the television show named after the star chimpanzee J. Fred Muggs, but not in the ape's company.

In the House he gave a whole series of disquisitions on domestic and world economics, one of which led the bewildered Anthony Eden to comment: "The speech of the former Chancellor was very erudite and at times, for the ordinary amateur, almost incomprehensible." Though we were now in surplus thanks partly to a reduction in dollar imports,

said Gaitskell, our reserves were far too low for our situation
to be stable. He said any move towards the free convertibility,
or floating, of sterling, such as he had heard rumoured, would
be madness; Dalton had admitted it was a mistake in 1947,
but he had been obliged to do it on 15th July of that year
under the terms of the 1945 Loan Agreement with the US.
We must get together with the countries of the Commonwealth and of Western Europe before our next discussions
with the US Government. Butler assured Gaitskell that the
recent meeting of the Organisation for European Economic
Co-operation had been most successful and that no rash
moves towards convertibility would be made. A fortnight
later in debating the Budget, Gaitskell emphasised that for
the first time since the war industrial production had actually
fallen, by 3 per cent. "Did we work harder? Of course we did
not." In his heart of hearts Butler, he said, knew that the
economy was stagnant, in spite of the improvement in our
balance of payments. This Budget was opposed to social justice and the workers' interests and aimed to please the City.
(Bevan had said just the same about Gaitskell's own 1951
Budget.) As usual, the Tories were working to strengthen the
wealth, power, and privilege of the well-to-do. These rather
hard-worn criticisms made no very great impact. In a debate
on the Finance Bill in May he introduced a lighter note.
Butler had exempted cricket but not football from entertain-
ments tax, because, said Gaitskell, he said it was part of the
British tradition; and that word had a special appeal for the
Conservative Party. "My researches show that football is a
great deal older than cricket. It was played by the Greeks
and Romans. It was played in London in 1175. It was forbidden by Edward II in consequence of 'the great noise in
the City caused by hustling over large balls.'" In the debate
on the third reading of the Finance Bill on 12th July he
stuck to his criticisms of the Government for failing to stimu-
late investment and productivity. At the same time he praised
the contributions to the debate of Crosland, Albu, Jenkins,

Jay, and Houghton, the last of whom had gone so far as to call Butler "the cat's whiskers"; and he paid a handsome tribute to Butler himself.

The Annual Conference in 1953 was held in beautiful down-town Margate. Gaitskell was still not a member of any of the main committees, and he again failed to make the NEC. As usual, Bevan, Barbara Castle, and Wilson headed the Constituency Parties' poll for the National Executive Committee, though James Griffiths, who was to become a devoted Gaitskellite, came close behind. On the Executive Committee's long policy document "Challenge to Britain," Gaitskell spoke up loud and clear about a subject on which he always felt strongly, the public schools. The system was wrong because it was socially divisive, created snobbery, and was based on wealth, rather than brains. Half the places should be offered free. He never decried his own school, Winchester; on the contrary, the point he often made was that he was lucky to get such a good education because his parents were well-off and wished far more young people might enjoy it whose parents were not. One part of his argument, where he refers to brains as the right qualification, seems to me slightly misdirected. My own remaining parent was penniless, and I got my excellent public school and university education thanks to my brains, such as they were; and you could even in those days get an entirely free education at Eton or Winchester. But the rest of his charges have for many years been irrefutable, and remarkably little is done in the way of reform to this day.

On 15th October, Gaitskell made a party political broadcast, which he was frequently to be called on to do. While he was not a memorable television performer, he was almost always effective. His style was quiet, confidential, reasonable. He often spoke without notes. The image inspired confidence.

The Butskellite exchange continued. In the debate on the Address on 6th November, Gaitskell tried a lighter touch, with considerable success. He said he was always interested in Butler's metaphors, which normally came in three sets:

mountaineering, medical, and nautical. "We must get out of the slack water, lighten the ship and give her way." Now Tory colleague after colleague had walked the plank. The Overlords had sunk without trace. "Who is to be the next victim of [Churchill's] Stalinesque ardour?" But he criticised Butler's "doctrinaire Toryism." In a debate on 4th February 1954 he made play with reported discussions in the Tory Party about Churchill's successor. Neither Butler nor Eden seemed up to it, he thought. "I am not surprised that, between the two, the Prime Minister has decided that he will not retire after all."

Observing shortly after that the cost of living had gone up more steeply in this country in the last two years than anywhere else in Europe, except Greece and perhaps Norway, he concluded that we were pricing ourselves out of the competition with West Germany and Japan. He came out in favour of the proposed European Defence Community as offering the best means of keeping any West German rearmament under control. He said flatly that there was at present no prospect at all of a "free, united Germany," though at this time Eden and the Foreign Office were already deluding themselves with sweeping plans which had not the slightest chance of being accepted by the Russians. Gaitskell at this stage began to intensify his involvement in foreign affairs, which he tended to approach by way of his economic expertise. No approach could be sounder, and British diplomacy would have been in a better condition over the last 30 years if more of those concerned with it had acted similarly.

Nineteen-fifty-four saw further progress up the Labour Party ladder by Gaitskell, and a continuation of the struggle with the Bevanites. At one Shadow Cabinet meeting Bevan sneered at him: "You're too young in the Movement to know what you're talking about." A little hard, as Gaitskell had been in it since 1926. While Gaitskell saw no objection to the proposals for SEATO (Southeast Asia Treaty Organization), Bevan resigned from the Shadow Cabinet over them. June was a turning point. Arthur Greenwood, the Treasurer of the Party, died. Bevan summoned Sam Watson, the highly influential leader of the National Union of Mineworkers, to the House of Commons and told him that he wanted to become Treasurer and looked to this big Union to back him. Watson replied without hesitation that on the contrary they would vote for Gaitskell. Bevan exploded: "How can you support a public schoolboy from Winchester against a man born in the back streets of Tredegar?" The son of a miner, a miner himself at the age of 13, prominent in the councils of the South Wales miners' federation? Watson tried to explain that it was not Gaitskell's fault if he had been to Winchester and Oxford, and that it so happened that the miners liked him and trusted him, not least because he had given them a fair deal while he was at the Ministry of Fuel and Power. The fact that Bevan had been a miner himself was neither here nor there in this context. Anyway Bevan had represented the Constituency Organisations on the NEC since 1946 while Gaitskell, an ex-Chancellor, was still not a member. Bevan's intense dislike of Gaitskell at this stage had led him to be greedy and to over-reach himself. By 10th August the *Daily Mail* was already predicting that Gaitskell would succeed Attlee as Leader in 1955. Morrison had given up; Bevan—"God forbid," and it was clear that the Unions preferred Gaitskell. An interesting list of other possible candidates comprised Robens, Callaghan, and Hartley Shawcross; but for various reasons their chances were considered slim. The article went on to compare Attlee's and Gaitskell's careers. Attlee at 39 first worked alongside a Minister, Ramsay MacDonald; Gaitskell at 34, with Dalton. They became Parliamentary Secretaries at 41 and 40 respectively, senior Ministers at 47 and 41, Cabinet Ministers at 47 and 44. Attlee had become Leader at 52; Gaitskell was now 48. A kindly comment was that "Gaitskell resembles Attlee in nothing so much as the happiness of his family life." It was a compliment to him that he was denounced as "patronising" by the Bevanites. They had done the Movement much harm, and Gaitskell's job would be to exorcise them.

In the House the usual exchanges on the Finance Bill had been proceeding in June and July. Gaitskell now used the lighter touch more often. He twitted Butler for keeping them up till 6 a.m. on 17th June: "All sorts of queer things are said and this gives rise to hilarity." The Chancellor resembled Queen Elizabeth I: "He has a most charming manner and I do appeal to him to consider what we ask." But Queen Elizabeth I—Butler—stood firm. Gaitskell had fun at the expense of Frederick Erroll, who had presented a "tear-jerking account of the hardships of business executives having, under the pressure of taxation, to scrub the floor with aprons on or do the washing-up instead of thinking about developing their business. I always understood the tired businessman had other interests." Gaitskell defined a "large estate" rather surprisingly, as anything over £10,000. He was to leave many times that sum when he died.

The October Conference was a success for Gaitskell. He received over four million votes in the election of the Treasurer, which put him more than two million ahead of Bevan. He thus became a member of the National Executive Committee for the first time, and he remained one till the end. Bevan for once was turned off it. This was a tremendous kick in the teeth to Bevan and the Bevanites. For the present they refused to lie down, however, Gaitskell kept up the pressure. In a speech at Doncaster on 13th March 1955 he made a scathing attack. It was scandalous, he said, that although in the defence debate of 2nd March Labour had tabled a motion of censure, yet the Bevanites had personally criticised Attlee and in effect repudiated his leadership. This was an affront to the Party which had elected him Leader. "We have had to put up with a great deal of this kind of disruption in the last three years" (he might have said four). Meanwhile, in the House, Gaitskell kept up his criticism of the Government's actions in removing various controls and denationalising road haulage and steel. These rash measures led to social injustice; the investment class profited, but the workers suffered. This made matters difficult for the Trade Unions, he

said threateningly. When the Foreign Secretary, Eden, intervened in an economic debate, Gaitskell crushingly dismissed
him with the stricture that he did not understand what he
was talking about.

An epoch was ending. The next two years would see the
embattled Gaitskell rising to the very top of the Party and
triumphing over Butler, Bevan, and Eden in turn.

SIX

The Year of the New Leaders

AT LAST CHURCHILL made up his mind. He was 80 and had suffered strokes, bouts of pneumonia, and countless other ills that would long before have slain a lesser man. But the old warhorse had charged the Conservatives into victory in 1951, and it was clear that most of the people of Britain liked their policy and considered it successful. For the last year or two Churchill had led the Government in a fitful manner. A good deal was left to Eden and Butler, and there was considerable speculation about when Churchill would step down. He was capricious towards Eden, several times giving him half-promises of handing over shortly and then finding excuses for carrying on. One of his reasons was that he was none too confident of Eden's ability to cope.

But finally on 6th April 1955, Eden took over the reins. He was 58, in itself a reasonable age for the job. But he had in recent years suffered considerable ill-health, and the waiting had frayed his nerves. He was considered a well-nigh perfect Foreign Secretary by the Tories, who admired his style and assiduity in producing paper plans to deal with every international contingency. If these in practice seldom led to successful, or even useful, results, well, diplomacy was for most people a mysterious ploy best left to the experts. Eden was a self-confessed ignoramus where economic matters were concerned. Indeed, as his whole life had been devoted to diplomacy, he had made little impact on the home front at all, and he was none too confident about his own ability to lead on domestic matters. He and Gaitskell were very different in their style, their approach, and temperamentally, though to a foreigner they would appear to come of the same social and educational background. There was never much warmth in their relationship. Eden found it difficult to follow Gaitskell's economic exegesis and thought it a pity that, unlike himself, he had never had occasion to put on uniform. Gaitskell admired Eden's negotiating ability but did not consider him a very original thinker. Eden wisely kept Butler at the Treasury and put the dynamic Harold Macmillan into the Foreign Office.

On 20th April, Gaitskell made a wide-ranging speech of well over an hour on the Budget. His difficulty, which he did not altogether overcome, was that the Budget had proved popular in a good many quarters on account of its reductions in some taxes and controls, so that some of his criticisms appeared snide or doctrinaire. This, he said, was Butler's last Budget in the present Parliament and—optimistically—probably for a long time ahead. Production under the Tories had increased only half as fast as under Labour; he did not mention that in some spheres it had started from almost nil at the end of the war. Productivity had not increased at all; for instance, "The miners do not seem inspired with the same will to produce as under a Labour Government." The Chancellor had achieved only one-third of his hoped-for annual export surplus of £350 m., and while our exports under Butler had increased by 1 per cent per annum, the West German figure was 22 per cent. "Of course, home consumption has risen faster, because under Labour we had to pursue a policy of austerity—unpopular, but where would this country be today without it?" (Not much of a vote-winning argument.) Our gold and dollar reserves were still too small: true, they had increased by $330 m. since December 1951, but those of the rest of Europe had risen by $4 billion. Then on to the intimate, personal, Butskellite exchange: "The Chancellor, speaking at a Conservative Party Conference in October, said: 'Our future policy will emerge like a cat from the bag, in due course.' Last February the cat came out of the bag. But it was not a gentle pussy at all. It was a nasty, fierce, mangy, hungry cat called 'Bank Rate at 4½ per cent.' " (To-day we should welcome such a playful little kitten.) The Chancellor had decided to give £140 m. in tax reliefs, which would wholly benefit those already better off. The Stock Exchange boom would continue. Eden had just decided to go to the nation, and Gaitskell ended up: "We accept the challenge of the forthcoming election—eagerly, gladly."

Gaitskell was whistling to keep his Party's courage up. Eden had chosen his moment for a personal vote of confidence with skill. He was admired by his Party, and many had felt that it was really time that the old warrior departed. Moreover, Eden had not yet had time to show his own inadequacies, and Butler's policy of reducing taxes and controls naturally had appeal. On the Labour side, Attlee had been Leader for twenty years and, at 72, was getting on. His judgment was still crisp, but he had not gained control of the Bevanites. So once again a divided Labour Movement went ahead to defeat, this time disastrously. On 25th May 1955 the Conservatives notched 344 seats to Labour's 277, and the Tories had an overall majority of 58. Their total votes had decreased by over 400,000; but Labour's by an enormous 1½ million. The total poll was well down; people were too bored to turn out to vote for Labour.

Gaitskell frankly told the Amalgamated Society of Woodworkers on 2nd June what were the three reasons for the defeat. First was the immediate economic situation "as it strikes the ordinary voter." In other words, this was the run-up to Macmillan's euphoric "never had it so good"; and in spite of all Gaitskell's informed and realistic economic criticism, both at this stage and later, he could not get across to the floating voter the long-term dangers of our sluggish progress. Secondly, Gaitskell mentioned the obvious, and weighty, influence of dissensions within the Party; and thirdly, connected with that, the superiority of Conservative organisation for the poll. It is hard to picture what the morale of the Movement would have been if Labour supporters had known that the next election results would be considerably worse.

Bevan was not deterred from his disruptive tactics, but it was now being freely said that he was riding for a fall. In return for his announcement that he would again challenge Gaitskell for the Party treasurership, five of the big six Unions immediately came out in favour of Gaitskell. Up to July, Bevan had the meagre satisfaction of being nominated only by the National Union of Vehicle Builders, a laughable 40,000 strong. In September the National Union of Railwaymen, the sixth of the big Unions, announced that they were switching their 1954 vote for Bevan over to Gaitskell. Bevan's chief supporters now were the Electrical Trades Union, who were well known to be dominated by a Communist minority. The press began to forecast that Bevan would be lucky to get a block vote of 1 million, as compared with his ineffectual 2 million in 1954. Meanwhile, Gaitskell, having voted on the National Executive for Bevan's expulsion, made overtures to Bevan's friends Wilson and Crossman, for instance, by suggesting that Wilson should be put in charge of the committee to look into the Party's organisation. Privately he said that the only Bevanites he would have in a government were Crossman, Wilson, and Barbara Castle. And step by step they, or at any rate the first two, became less hostile to him.

Immediately after the defeat, Dalton had written both to Attlee and to the press letters strongly recommending the removal from the Shadow Cabinet of certain veterans, including himself but not Attlee. He pointed out that nine members were over 65. This was discussed acrimoniously, the veterans such as Chuter Ede objecting strongly. Morrison, at 67, resented the suggestion. Gaitskell paid a tribute to their services, especially Dalton's, and at the same time welcomed the initiative. Now for the first time Attlee said that he must depart before long. "We are now more than halfway through this century, and it's time the Labour Party had a leader who was born in this century and not the last." So much for Morrison and Bevan! Gaitskell was not yet considered by any means a certainty in leading Labour circles. But Attlee's hint was a pretty broad one; and Gaitskell came second to Griffiths in the election of the new Shadow Cabinet. It was not long before feelers were put out in his direction.

The other contest, between Gaitskell and Butler, worked steadily up through the summer to a climax in the autumn. In the debate on the Address on 16th June, Gaitskell included in his criticisms not only Butler but Eden and Macmillan. Monetary policy by itself, he said, would not put the economy right; we must increase exports and reserves. Industrial relations were at their worst since the war, and the inflation "endemic in Tory 'freedom'" was increasing. He suggested a capital gains tax. On 25th July he accused Butler of having cooked his Budget for electoral purposes and asked him straight whether he now planned an autumn Budget to put things right. Butler demurely answered: "I am not disposed towards such a step at present." The next day Gaitskell pressed him further, and rather more roughly than usual. While the dock strike had of course affected the economy, the real causes of the crisis, "if crisis is the right word," were the Government's incompetence and "blatant electioneering." He denied that he wished to paint too gloomy a picture, but gloomy it certainly was. This time Butler was nettled. He denied absolutely that there was any "crisis." "I shall not take great, violent or bitter exception to any of his remarks. He spoke with a little more of his undoubted ability as an economist" (a dirty word in Tory circles, of course) "peeping up over his rising ability as a politician. Therefore we were more interested than on other occasions . . . He was excitable in reference to the election speeches." The tone was collected and in part deliberately condescending, but Butler was beginning to feel the strain.

The 54th Annual Conference of the Labour Party, held at Margate from 10th to 14th October 1955, was an even greater success for Gaitskell than the 1954 one had been. Bevan received the rebuff which had been foretold in the election for the treasurership: Gaitskell 5,475,000 votes; Bevan 1,225,000. That was very much that. Although left-wingers as usual topped the Constituency Parties' poll, in the shape of Harold Wilson, Barbara Castle, and Anthony Greenwood, the Trade Unions had shown by their terrific vote for Gaitskell how sick they were of Bevanism and how confident that Gaitskell was the man to scotch it. At this time, though not for much longer, Attlee was still Leader and Morrison his Deputy. But even apart from this great success of Gaitskell's, he fairly got into his stride as a Conference speaker. He adapted his style with great skill to the requirements of the Conference atmosphere, and his annual speeches were from now on always an outstanding feature. They usually aroused wild enthusiasm amongst most of his audience, and sometimes bitter antagonism amongst the rest. He chose the Conferences deliberately to put forward the most provocative ideas which he had been pondering in the months before. He resembled Gladstone in that he positively preferred meeting opposition head on. He was as a result accused by a good many people of being a poor tactician; but the method was deliberate and the longer term, or strategic, results were usually what Gaitskell wanted. He also resembled Gladstone, though more in his House of Commons than his Conference speeches, in his ability to bewilder his opponents with an opening on the lines of: "It will be apparent to everyone that the subject under consideration is affected by thirty-four elementary factors," followed by a detailed list of them. At the 1955 Conference he most skilfully combined a report on the nationalised industries with some significant warnings of future trends. He was always proud of the setting-up and performance of the nationalised industries, and he said so again this time, with special reference to the atomic energy organisations and the airways corporations. Then came the warnings: nationalisation is a means and not an end in itself; if crudely presented to the public, it was a positive hindrance to Labour in an election. Clause 4 was all very well, but an enquiry was needed to bring things up to date. Finally, he gave the Conference an emotive, though deeply sincere, passage on "why I am a Socialist and have been one for some thirty years. I became a Socialist candidly not so much because I was a passionate advocate of public ownership but because at a very early age I came to hate and loathe social injustice, because I disliked the class structure of our society, because I could not tolerate the indefensible differences of status and income which disfigure our society. I hated the insecurity that affected such a large part of our community while others led lives of security and comfort. I became a Socialist because I hated poverty and squalor. I am a Socialist because I want to see a society of equal men and women. It may be that men are not equal in all respects but they are all equally men. I am a Socialist because I want to see fellowship, or fraternity, existing in our country more and more. And I want to see all this achieved by democracy. I want to see all this not only in our country but over the world as a whole. We say let the clear fresh wind of hard and fearless thinking blow through our minds and hearts." This was a masterly performance and he received loud and prolong applause. "Demagogy," muttered Bevan—high praise indeed from that quarter.

Gaitskell's next big speech in the House was also much applauded. Sure enough, as he had heavily hinted would be the case, Butler found it necessary to introduce an autumn Budget. On 27th October, Gaitskell tore into him. This was not merely a big speech, but a great one. It combined very serious, sometimes almost bitter, criticism of Butler with the lighter touch. He ridiculed his "orgy of metaphors" once more. "The most remarkable is gastronomic: we need to give up easy living on port and overripe pheasant. When we talk of the need to 'hold in the horse,' people do not think of themselves as the horse." Gaitskell was so biting about a series of Butler's statements since the beginning of 1955 that Butler burst out: "He has absolutely no business to make statements that I attempted to conceal the truth from the public at any point." Gaitskell waved him aside. The indiscriminate increases in Purchase Tax, particularly on household goods, were disgraceful; the decision to suspend the housing programme "not so much devastating as outrageous

—the most reactionary of the many reactionary things which this government has done since the election." The peroration was also the *coup de grâce*. "I bear him no personal animosity. He knows that. But as a politician and one-time statesman his record in this past year is, frankly, deplorable. He began in folly, he continued in deceit, and he has ended in reaction. Let him lay down the burden of his office, which he is so plainly unable to carry with credit any longer." Butler could only comment wanly on Morrison's and Gaitskell's speeches together that they were "trial gallops for the leadership of the Labour Party." He added with distaste, and less than perfect clarity: "The 'Third Man' [Bevan] in these stakes in which he is so bitterly engaged will no longer need to 'stoop to conquer.' "

It was the end of the Butskellite dialogue, and of a good many other things too. Incredibly, Eden was already feeling rocky on his throne, and the question whether Butler or Macmillan would succeed him was already being publicly discussed. Eden thought it advisable to do two things in December 1955. He issued a statement to the effect that he was doing nicely, thank you, and had no intention of stepping down. Secondly, he reshuffled his Cabinet. Four difficult years was a long time for anyone to be Chancellor, and Butler really was showing signs of sinking into a quicksand of metaphors and of incoherence, something like Ramsay MacDonald towards the end, though the process had not gone nearly as far. So, in line with Gaitskell's suggestion, he "laid down his burden" and became Lord Privy Seal. He was succeeded as Chancellor by Macmillan, a wilier politician, a high Tory, a man who, according to his own Chancellor Thorneycroft later on, positively enjoyed manipulating the economy up to the very brink of bankruptcy. There was never any love lost between him and Gaitskell.

Attlee now announced that the time had come for him to retire. At this stage Gaitskell was inclined to think that Morrison, who had served the Movement so well, should succeed.

Bevan offered a bargain: he would stand down if Gaitskell would too. Gaitskell declined this bit of barter, and the crudity of Bevan's manoeuvre worked in Gaitskell's favour. Attlee later declared that he did not influence the choice. But in fact he thought Morrison past it, Bevan a disaster, and Gaitskell the best option; and his timing and tactics favoured Gaitskell. The same applied to the Unions, to the influential group of "intellectuals" who were close to Gaitskell, and to many other Labour supporters besides. Gaitskell's recent performances at the Annual Conference and in the House strengthened these views. Attlee retired on 7th December 1955; Gaitskell had told Morrison and Bevan he proposed to stand. A few people with personal grudges went around blackguarding Gaitskell, like old Shinwell, who called him a phoney and a few other things besides. The faithful Dalton told him he would be in by a large margin. On 14th December 1955 the Parliamentary Labour Party met to hear the result, with Morrison in the chair. They had elected Gaitskell Leader with 157 votes, far ahead of the combined efforts of Bevan with 70 and poor Morrison with 40. This was the biggest majority ever for a newly elected Labour Leader, MacDonald having won by a mere five and Attlee only on a second ballot. The result was vociferously applauded. Morrison congratulated him and he took the chair. Morrison had just said that he was giving up the Deputy Leadership; Gaitskell appealed to him to stay on. "There is nothing between us but age." The embittered Shinwell shrieked: "Don't listen to him, Herbert." Morrison was not to be persuaded, and Gaitskell paid him a very warm tribute. He also appealed to Bevan to help end dissensions in the Party. His reply was ambiguous and contained a reference to his Celtic temperament, but in fact the worst was over. Dalton wrote to Gaitskell, wishing him good health and all success: "I, born nearly twenty years before you, count on you doing great things in my lifetime, and greater still 'far on in summers that I shall not see.'"

Who was this man? The press and the public widely asked the question. Bevan and Morrison were well known; Gaitskell was far more of a mystery. People tended to misspell his name. It was a fact that at 49 he was the youngest leader of any British Party for 60 years (though he was to be narrowly beaten on this by Harold Wilson, and equalled by Ted Heath, a few years later). Everyone knew of his upper-middle-class background; nobody, except Bevan and some of his cronies, took it amiss. It was in fact similar to Attlee's. The resemblances between his early career and Attlee's, and indeed Harold Wilson's, were striking. Attlee: son of a well-to-do solicitor, Haileybury, University College, Oxford, 2nd class Honours in Modern History, secretary of Toynbee Hall in the East End, lecturer at Ruskin College for working men, and later on tutor and Lecturer in Social Sciences at the London School of Economics. Gaitskell's story we have already traced. Harold Wilson: grammar school, Jesus College, Oxford, 1st class Honours in PPE like Gaitskell (but he was dubbed "the cleverest man at Oxford"), Lecturer in Economics at New College and a Fellow of University College; plus a similar Civil Service career during the war.

One of the first Labour personalities to have spotted Gaitskell as a future Leader of the Movement was the tough miners' leader Will Lawther, who did so after personal dealings with him in 1947 in his first, junior ministerial post at the Ministry of Fuel and Power. Hostile critics accused him of intellectual arrogance; most of these were Tories from the shires and backwoods who hardly understood the meaning of the word "intellect," and not at all its workings. His apparent arrogance was on some occasions due to shyness. He had taken only ten years to make the grade from new MP to Leader. If all went well he could expect to be Prime Minister before too long. He was not impressive to look at, with his peaky nose and crinkly hair. But the forthrightness, the intelligence, and the warmth combined soon made a favourable impression on anyone from a miner's wife to a socialite lady. He enjoyed social life thoroughly and believed that

Hearts just as brave and fair
May beat in Belgrave Square
As in the purer air
Of Seven Dials.

though his closest circle of friends were not denizens of Belgrave Square but the "Hampstead set" of the Croslands, Jays, and so on, known as the Gaitskellites. Attlee himself criticised him for having too closed a circle here. Where Paul Johnson of the *New Statesman* once took Ian Fleming's books to task for "sex, snobbery and sadism," Gaitskell with more humour wrote to him: "Thank you very much for sending me your latest. As you know I am a confirmed Fleming fan—or should it be addict? The combination of sex, violence, alcohol and—at intervals—good food and nice clothes is, to one who lives such a circumscribed life as I, irresistible." More seriously, it soon became clear to more and more people that he was a firm, combative, direct character, prepared to tackle anyone and anything in the interests of social and international justice. He had proved himself a good speaker, highly articulate, in the House, at the Conferences, and up and down the country. If he was not an impassioned "orator" like Bevan, the great majority preferred it that way. Two of his comments on Bevan were to the point. He once remarked, not smugly but reflectively, with reference to the Bevanite conflict: "No, I can't see that I made any mistakes." And of the man: "His weakness is that he can never use the words 'I don't know.'"

One man who did not applaud the selection was Eden, who would have preferred Morrison as his opposite number. It is easy to see why. Indeed there is reason to think he had advised Morrison to take the Foreign Office for the short but disastrous period in 1951, which led up to Labour's defeat. He would have been much easier for Eden to deal with than the active younger man. Eden's own words on the selection of Gaitskell are extraordinarily harsh: "I had no doubt that this was a national misfortune." He adds that he was unable to establish with him the political and personal relations which he had enjoyed with all his predecessors (this is an exaggeration). Mock-modestly he continues: "This was one of my failures, but curiously enough in all my years of political life I had not met anyone with his cast of mind and approach to problems. We never seemed able to get on terms." Gaitskell for his part was quite ready to do so, until the crunch came. And finally Eden was the loser.

The new Leader lost no time in turning his attention to foreign affairs. In a speech at Keighley on 18th December he criticised the government for denying to Cyprus the self-determination which must come sooner or later. In the Middle East the supply of arms by the Communists to Egypt was a dangerous new factor, and in a different way the fact that Eden appeared to favour the Arabs complicated matters. We should stick to the Tripartite Declaration and the guarantee of frontiers. Soviet political aggressiveness, as shown in Bulganin's and Khruschev's speeches in India and Burma, must be contained everywhere.

On 24th December a 15,000-word essay by Gaitskell on "The Ideological Development of Democratic Socialism in Great Britain" appeared in the bulletin of the Socialist International. This was symptomatic of the more active interest which Gaitskell always took in that body as compared with Attlee and his principal lieutenants.

The tone of the new leadership was established without delay and with crispness. On Labour Party matters Gaitskell attacked "stale slogans" in January 1956. The Labour Party, he said, needed to think afresh and shed illusions. In his first television appearance as Leader he reiterated that nationalisation must be a means and not an end in itself. The Party paid him the unique compliment of keeping him on as Treasurer as well for the time being, rather than letting in Bevan. (A warm supporter of Gaitskell, James Griffiths, defeated Bevan for the Deputy Leadership.) Nobody doubted that Gaitskell was going to show pugnacity and liveliness.

As regards foreign affairs, and in particular the Middle East which was coming to the boil, they could say that again. Gaitskell, presumably taking it that there was not much point in seeing the new Foreign Secretary, Selwyn Lloyd, asked to see Eden. He was quite right, of course. Just as Eden when first Foreign Secretary in the mid-thirties had never been allowed to carry out his duties without interference by the Prime Minister, Neville Chamberlain, so now Eden as Prime Minister proposed to dominate Lloyd, who seemed quite happy to be dominated. Eden saw Gaitskell on 2nd January 1956, and Gaitskell reported to the House in a debate on the Export of Surplus War Material on 24th January, his first major intervention on foreign affairs. He was very critical of the Government and of Eden himself. They had discussed the Middle East intensively. "Our complaint is that, contrary to government policy, surplus arms went to the Middle East at a time which was extremely dangerous. It shows the Government have been guilty of slipshod and lax administration and of extreme incompetence in public relations." He asked pointedly who was responsible, the Prime Minister or the Foreign Secretary? He criticised the Templer mission which, aimed at bringing Jordan into the Baghdad Pact, had on the contrary led to her joining the Egyptian group. He insisted again that we must base our policy on the 1950 Tripartite Declaration, to which the Labour Government had of course been a party and which guaranteed the present frontiers until a peaceful settlement was reached. Eden intervened that he did not consider it as specific as this; but "I have said many times that we will stand by it." We shall see! Gaitskell's rather unpractical suggestion was that the Soviet Government should now be formally asked to collaborate in a full peace settlement. "I am not pro-Arab or pro-Israel, but I am pro-peace." Generally speaking, he was in fact considered pro-Israel, and there have always been close relations between the Socialists of Britain and Israel. Eden, for his part, had much more of the traditional British love of the Arabs—always provided that they kept their proper place, of course. This debate was a lively and suggestive prelude to the massive conflicts of the summer and autumn to come.

On 21st February, Gaitskell spoke in the House, both gravely and wittily, on economic affairs. "We now have a crisis, and it is at least admitted that it is a crisis"—a last backhander for the departed Butler. The Chancellor, Macmillan, was walking in his sleep into unemployment. This caused loud laughter. "Well, he was rather somnambulatory during his speech." Macmillan decided it was funny too, and interjected the sporting comment: "Jolly good." Gaitskell said there were far too many people getting their money far too easily. Death duties, capital gains, and expense allowances all needed attention.

On 1st March there was a happening which really triggered off the Middle East crisis, though this was not clear to all concerned at the time. King Hussein of Jordan unceremoniously, and at a moment's notice, dismissed Glubb Pasha, the British general who over the years had built up the Arab Legion into the best Arab army. Glubb himself took the rebuff with admirable calm; Eden did not. Gaitskell made a speech in the House on 7th March which contained some shrewd analysis and some mixed thinking. What he did not appreciate was that Eden's judgment on such matters was becoming erratic and undependable. Gaitskell paid tribute to Glubb as a restraining influence in Arab-Israeli problems. But he added, correctly, that the Jordanians had got sick of his being virtually a dictator of their country, and that the Arabs were not going to tolerate a semi-colonial status any longer. Britain must give up the paternalistic policy of which the Baghdad Pact was the embodiment. His suggested remedies were as before: activating the Tripartite Declaration and bringing the USSR in on the act. Nothing whatever had come of Eden's recent talks with President Eisenhower: "It is not enough to have meetings and consultations unless decisions are taken." (This of course is easy for an Opposition leader to say; but at the same time he had put his finger on one of the main weaknesses of Eden's diplomatic method, according to which talks, plans, minutes, memoranda, and so on were regarded as achievements in themselves.) The Government's policy had contrived to be both weak and provocative at the same time. Now Gaitskell uttered a warning. Some would like to reimpose our will on the Middle East by force. "But we do not have adequate force, and the US will not join us in such a policy." Also we should be in conflict with international law and the United Nations. He rashly suggested that an alliance with Israel should be considered: he was lucky not to be taxed with this later in the year. Even as regards oil supplies, he said, force would not be justified; an Anglo-US understanding was required, and in any case the Arab states did not want to be Communist-controlled. Eden, in return, defended the Government's policy, including the Baghdad Pact, on which he suggested that Gaitskell might be "a milder echo of Moscow radio." This caused indignant protests on the Labour benches. Gaitskell had now given Eden fair warning, though not perhaps altogether in the clearest terms, to watch his step in the Middle East. He had also nettled him, at a time when Eden was getting the bit between his teeth.

In the same month a pretty compliment to Gaitskell was announced: he was to be a member of the faculty of Harvard University during 1956 and 1957 for the purpose of delivering the Godkin lectures on the subject of "the essentials of free government and the duties of the citizen." As we shall see, he made excellent use of this opportunity after the Suez turbulence was over. In a speech at York a few days later, he said that the Government decision to deport Archbishop Makarios from Cyprus was wrong, especially as the remaining differences in the negotiations were narrow. This action only made matters more difficult for our troops, and such repressive measures were not worthy of us as a democracy. In a speech to the Conference of the Party's Scottish Council, he said that he welcomed both Khruschev's recent denunciation of Stalin and his forthcoming visit to Britain with Bulganin, but we must not expect too much from either development.

He was dead right on this. On 22nd April, Gaitskell, Griffiths as Deputy Leader, and Robens as Shadow Foreign Secretary were invited to lunch at Chequers by the Prime Minister to meet Bulganin and Khruschev. Gromyko, Butler, Lloyd and various others were there. After lunch the three Labour representatives had half an hour alone with B & K. They raised the question of the Social Democratic leaders imprisoned in the Eastern European countries, but the discussion was interrupted because the Soviet leaders had to leave. The following day the notorious dinner took place at the House of Commons, the object being to introduce B & K to the Labour National Executive and Parliamentary Committee. In due course Bulganin responded amiably to the toast of the Russians' health. Khruschev also began his speech amiably enough but gradually became both more eloquent and more truculent. At one point George Brown interpolated a critical remark and Khruschev took this very much amiss. He worked himself up and spoke for over an hour. Gaitskell, dogged as ever, replied that there were many points in his speech with which the British side could not agree. He must mention two things: the plight of the Social Democratic colleagues in Eastern Europe and that of the Jews in the USSR. This was not only tactless; but, done in this public fashion, it was bound to be ineffectual, if not positively counterproductive. In return, he received the firm "nyet" he ought to have expected, and the comment which Khruschev was to utter more than once that the Conservatives were better people to deal with than Labour. Of course on such matters they were, because they had none of the broad humanitarian principles of Labour. The evening was not constructive. On 26th April, Gaitskell went along to Claridges with Griffiths and Edwin Gooch, chairman of the NEC that year, and mollified B & K as far as his conscience allowed. He said that they had come to wish them well on their departure and were sorry the dinner had ended as it did. Khruschev said that they had been disappointed, hurt, and provoked by interruptions. Gaitskell said that he would like to visit the Soviet Union, and Khruschev welcomed the idea. They all parted on reasonably cordial terms, and we shall see how in a matter of three years Gaitskell had established friendly relations with Khruschev. However, on Independent Television the next day Gaitskell said that when he had raised as tactfully as possible, the question of the imprisoned Social Democrats, "we got a rough answer." He did not think George Brown had wanted a row, but Khruschev was not used to being interrupted and "he flies off the handle too easily." He was struck by the visitors' "terrible ignorance about what our democracy is like." It was a pity that on their return home they had started up a violent campaign against the Labour Party. "We have no regrets and no apologies." He looked forward to frank talks from time to time.

There was a curious backlash to the visit in the shape of the Crabb case. Commander Crabb, it will be remembered, was the retired naval frogman who was found by the Russians swimming about in a suspicious manner near the cruiser *Ordzonikidze*, in which B & K had just arrived in Portsmouth harbour. As soon as they had returned to the Soviet Union, the Admiralty blandly announced that the frogman "did not return from a test dive in connexion with trials of certain under-water apparatus in Stokes Bay in the Portsmouth area, about a week ago." The press, naturally enough, played the mystery up, and on 9th May Eden made a statement. The Soviet Government had enquired in a Note what Crabb had been up to. Eden had replied that he had acted without permission and expressed his apologies. While HM Ministers generally accepted responsibility for departmental blunders, in this case he thought it essential to make it clear that no ministerial authorisation had been given; and he added that disciplinary steps were being taken. Gaitskell, however, pressed him very hard and even insisted on a debate on 14th May. His line was that there had been gross incompetence by the Secret Service, a breach of security, an insult to our guests, and ministerial irresponsibility. "The Prime Minister is responsible. Is he up to it?" Eden, quoting the national interest, said that there was ample precedent for governmental silence, particularly as international relations were also involved. "I deplore this debate and will say no more." The Government had an unusually high majority, indicating that some members thought that Gaitskell was making Party capital out of a delicate matter of national interest. It was so much on Gaitskell's mind that he even referred to it a few days later in a broadcast in the US, explaining that he felt in conscience bound to investigate this grave blunder. In fact, he always took security questions very seriously. What Gaitskell could not know, but as it happens I did thanks to my duties in the Foreign Office at the time, was that the fiasco occurred as a result of a colleague of mine, who for personal reasons was under stress at the time, giving the go-ahead to the project without sensing its important political implications. The project had originated with the Secret Intelligence Service, for whom Crabb did odd jobs from time to time. Khruschev for his part took the matter lightly, remarking that the cruiser was hopelessly out-of-date anyway. He later sold it to the Indonesian Government. Amongst the incident's widespread effects was a considerable embittering of relations between Eden and Gaitskell. Eden heatedly described him to a friend as a "paranoiac."

Gaitskell's American tour was a great success. As in Britain, he established good relations with the Trade Unions. He talked with George Meany, the president of the merged super-union called the American Federation of Labor—Congress of Industrial Organisations; he addressed the Amalgamated Clothing Workers; and he and his wife were the guests in New York of the International Ladies' Garment Workers' Union. Neither of them, as it happens, was very dressy. In Washington they stayed with our Ambassador, Sir Roger Makins, and Gaitskell had discussions, and got on well, with President Eisenhower and Secretary of State Foster Dulles. That is more than Eden ever achieved. His appearance on television, when he spoke of the West's need for unity in dealing with Soviet foreign policy, was very well received. On his return to England he reported that the state of Anglo-American relations was "pretty good." He had been asked a certain amount about the Middle East, "but I never like to emphasise Party differences when abroad." In this respect he was more scrupulous than many Tory politicians, both before and since. Altogether his trip, and his comments on it, constituted a fair warning to Eden on the Middle East and other matters, which Eden chose to ignore.

In June and early July, Gaitskell kept up the pressure on Eden about Cyprus. HMG should either bring back Makarios and reopen negotiations with him, or put the whole problem, except the question of the British base there which was not in dispute, to the United Nations. When Eden said that no new Constitution could be put into effect until terrorism had been overcome, Gaitskell asked whether he did not realise that the terrorism was the direct result of HMG's refusal to give assurances that the principle of self-determination would be implemented. Major Legge-Bourke saw fit to call this question "highly treasonable." He was ordered by the Speaker to withdraw his comment and did so. Gaitskell was to hear plenty more in this gutter style before 1956 was out.

On 24th July, just two days before President Nasser's coup, Gaitskell surveyed the whole field of foreign affairs in a debate in the Commons. He emphasised the continuing importance of the Anglo-American alliance and of NATO, in spite of doubt and confusion on both in many quarters. On the Middle East he took Julian Amery to task for speaking of "our oil resources." "They are not ours. This idea that the Middle East is a British preserve is totally out-of-date. How does he imagine that on our own we could defend that area for one moment?" We should work to bring the US and NATO in on Middle Eastern problems, including Cyprus. We also needed sympathy in the uncommitted countries, who tended to give it to the Communists. We should end all colour bars, give up bases in hostile territories, agree that those countries which wished to be neutral should be so, and give them much more economic aid.

Now the testing time, the Suez crunch, was at hand. Gentlemen, on my right the ailing Anthony Eden, keeping himself going on tranquillisers and other pills, and on nostalgia for the British Empire of the past. He is backed to the hilt by his parliamentary majority, and by much of the British nation. On my left, the younger, fitter, and cleverer Hugh Gaitskell, less versed in the methods of traditional diplomacy; and determined to bring into the situation a sense of fairness and of contemporaneity; and, ineluctably, incurring immense hostility in the process.

SEVEN

The Suez Aberration

THE SPARRING BETWEEN the two new leaders was now over. The serious in-fighting was about to begin. Who would win? Certainly not Eden. In an important sense, not Gaitskell either. The *tertius gaudens* was Macmillan. Internationally, Britain and France were humbled; Israel, and to a lesser degree the United Nations and Egypt, were the gainers.

A great deal has been written about the Suez affair. As early as 1957 the Brombergers' book, published in France, revealed numerous aspects which the British public were not supposed to know, particularly on the crucial issue of collusion between the Anglo-French allies and Israel. It was published in an English translation the same year; yet for years after this the British public still preferred, on the whole, not to know. Various essential sources are still not available. Eden himself and Selwyn Lloyd have resolutely refused to testify on the collusion question. The official papers are not yet open to examination; and when they are, there is good reason to suppose that many vital pieces of evidence will be found to be lacking, either because Eden forbade records to be made or because he ordered them to be destroyed. I myself had a good Foreign Office purview of the affair as I happened to be one of only three officials who, under Eden's direct instructions, were fully in on both the intelligence and planning sides. I was Patrick Dean's deputy, and he in turn was deputy to Sir Ivone Kirkpatrick, the Permanent Under-Secretary.

On 26th July 1956, Nasser seized the Suez Canal. Up to then Eden's attitude to him had not been unreasonable. He had come to an agreement with him, signed by Anthony

81

Nutting, in 1954 arranging for the withdrawal of British forces in 1956. He was collaborating with the US Government in a scheme for financing the Aswan Dam. The only time he met him personally, in early 1955, absolutely no rapport was established, which was hardly surprising. But even when Nasser turned to the Communists for arms in September 1955, the US and British governments continued to consider aid over the High Dam. It was Foster Dulles' action in suddenly telling the Egyptian Ambassador in Washington, in mid-July 1956, that aid would not be forthcoming which triggered Nasser's action. HMG were not consulted by Dulles but immediately followed suit. And now Eden's true feelings about Nasser, and indeed the wogs in general, surged up. He had already got inordinately excited over King Hussein's dismissal of Glubb Pasha in March and had considered sending British troops into Jordan. He now immediately gave orders to the Chiefs of Staff and the Foreign Office to make plans to topple Nasser, though the official written directive was more discreetly phrased, and if possible by August. These plans were my principal preoccupation throughout August, September, and October.

Eden's biggest single blunder, amongst a rich collection of them, was to equate the US's interests in the Middle East with our own, and hence to rely on the US's support and sympathy or, at the very least, neutrality. The facts were otherwise; and he also failed to allow for the personal hostility of Dulles, who had walked out of the 1954 Geneva Conference on the Far East because he could no longer stand the sight of Eden, and had found no reason to change his mind since then. Gaitskell's position was much closer to the US Government's. He appreciated that their interests in the Middle East were different from ours; for instance, they did not depend on the oil or the Canal to anything like the same extent. He also appreciated that they sincerely disliked what they considered our neocolonialist attitude in that part of the world. In earlier speeches he had reminded Eden that the Middle East did not belong to Britain; that any attempt to restore our former position by force must fail, because in the 1950s we no longer had the force to succeed against the resistance of the emerging countries and the United Nations; and that in any case we must base our policy on respect for their interests.

The factor that was to bedevil the months-long discussion of Suez both inside and outside the House was that Gaitskell appeared at first to be behind Eden. A close examination of his statements shows that he never was, in fact; but to the euphoric Eden, and to the blimps beside him and on the benches behind who were roaring for Nasser's blood, he unfortunately contrived to give this impression in the early stages. He had been at a formal dinner given by Eden for King Feisal and Nuri es-Said when the news came in on 26th July. When he asked a Parliamentary Question the next day, he also emphasised that "On this side of the House we deeply deplore this high-handed and totally unjustifiable action by the Egyptian Government."

But the crucial utterance by Gaitskell, the one that wrong-footed him, was the bulk of his speech in the debate on 2nd August. Eden had opened proceedings with a speech which found great favour with his supporters and did not seem too unreasonable to the Opposition. Then Gaitskell weighed in. "I think," he said, "that we are all grateful to him for the statement he has made about the attitude of Her Majesty's Government to Colonel Nasser's action." (Even Gaitskell could only bring himself to use President Nasser's proper title by fits and starts.) He recalled that for a long time the Opposition had been critical of the Government's policy in the Middle East. But he was not now going to develop those criticisms; and "I must make it abundantly plain that anything they have done or not done in no way excuses Colonel Nasser's action in seizing the Canal." He then analysed with care the reasons why we objected so strongly to this action, and also the Egyptian Government's reasons for taking it. First, he had to say that nationalisation as such was not wrong, even in the case of a foreign company, so long as proper compensation was paid, though he doubted whether the Egyptian Government could in fact afford this. He admitted he was not sure of the legal aspects; and he was prudent to do so, for the chief Foreign Office Legal Adviser, Sir Gerald Fitzmaurice, later expressed doubts whether Nasser's action was really illegal. "The real objections, it seems to me, are three." In the first place, as the Prime Minister had rightly emphasised, this was no ordinary company but one controlling an international waterway "of immense importance to the whole of the rest of the world." Here he exaggerated. To most countries in the world the Canal was not "of immense importance," and these included the United States. As for the Egyptian Government's assurances that they would abide by the 1888 Convention, which guaranteed freedom of passage through the Canal to ships of all nations, he had grave doubts because of their refusal to allow Israeli ships through in accordance with the 1951 Resolution of the United Nations. The second strong objection was the fact that Nasser had done the deed by force. Gaitskell speculated on whether the Egyptians could run the Canal efficiently, which in fact they soon proved they could, and on whether they would put the charges up. Thirdly, the action must have grave political repercussions throughout the Middle East.

At this point Gaitskell made, I think, a cardinal error. "The French Prime Minister, M. Mollet, the other day quoted a speech of Colonel Nasser's and rightly said that it could remind us only of one thing—of the speeches of Hitler before the war." And a little further on: "It is all very familiar. It is exactly the same that we encountered from Mussolini and Hitler before the war." These comparisons were unworthy of Gaitskell's intellect; and they played into the hands of Eden and his wog-bashers. Writing now, I must own that hindsight is a facile weapon; and the atmosphere at the time was heated. But Gaitskell was here borrowing the phraseology of the Tory fire-eaters, and a moment's reflexion might have shown him that, while all historical equations are unsound since history does not repeat itself exactly, the equating of Nasser and his Suez action with Hitler and Mussolini and their various enterprises was absurd. As it turned out, Eden was to play the Mussolini this time round. Gaitskell went on to say that Nasser's general policy endangered our relations with Iraq, Jordan, and Saudi Arabia; though he did not mention that they were not a trio of progressive, let alone Socialist, states under the régimes existing at that date. He reminded his audience that "we are pledged under the Tripartite Declaration to go to the assistance of whichever state is attacked—Israel or her Arab neighbours." Now that he was discussing the action to be taken, the tone of his speech altered. "This is not our affair alone. It would be ridiculous to treat ourselves as though we were the only Power involved." He welcomed the consultations going on with the French and US governments. A conference of all the nations principally concerned would be a good thing, and this should certainly include the USSR. Any control commission that might be set up as a result should be a UN agency. He approved the economic measures already taken by the Government against Egypt, and also the ban on arms shipments to her, which should be extended to cover other Arab states.

The peroration was for Gaitskell the nub of his speech. "Last of all, I come to a matter which cannot be ignored at this moment just before the recess. There has been much talk in the press about the use of force. We need to be very careful what we say on this subject. Obviously, there are circumstances in which we might be compelled to use force, in self-defence or as part of some collective defence measures. I do not myself object to the precautionary steps announced by the Prime Minister today; I think that any government would have to do that, as we had to do it during the Persian crisis." (Here I must comment that the logical sequence from "self-defence," etc., to calling up reserves over Nasser's seizure of the Canal is not clear.) "I must however remind the House that we are members of the United Nations, signatories to the UN Charter, and that for many years in British policy we have steadfastly avoided any international action which would be in breach of international law or, indeed, contrary to the public opinion of the world. We must not, therefore, allow ourselves to get into a position where we might be denounced in the Security Council as aggressors, or where the majority of the Assembly were against us. If there were anything which [Nasser] had done which would justify force at the moment it is the one thing on which we have never used force, namely, the stopping of Israeli ships. I believe that we were right to react sharply to this move. We should try to settle this matter peacefully on the lines of an international commission, as has been hinted: while force cannot be excluded, we must be sure that the circumstances justify it and that it is, if used, consistent with our belief in, and our pledges to, the Charter of the United Nations and not in conflict with them."

Gaitskell had the roaring lions of the right purring at his feet. The fella's heart's in the right place after all, said the half-colonels and the knights of the shires. Of course, he had to put in all that gup about the United Nations; Labour always does that. But you could tell from the way he approved our sharp reaction and spoke of the possibility of our using force that that was all a bit of lip-service. Captain Charles Waterhouse described it as "an extremely courageous speech, in which he aligned himself with the essentials of the British attitude" [sic]. Denis Healey spoke at some length and encouraged Eden to stand up to the "dinosaurs and teddy-boys" in the Conservative Party. Viscount Hinchingbrooke, rapid as ever to grasp the wrong end of any stick, spoke of the support given "in splendid words" by Gaitskell to Eden. William Warbey tried to raise the temperature by a little anti-imperialism and fell foul of the Speaker in doing so. A good many anti-American sentiments were expressed on both sides of the House. All Labour speakers wanted consultation with the UN, but most also insisted that that body must take effective action against Nasser. Eden later reflected wanly in his memoirs that the House did not seem to be

divided on Party lines, and that to the Socialist Lord Stans-
gate, who was listening, Gaitskell's comments seemed more
warlike than his own. Then, crisis or no, the House broke up,
as arranged long before, for the summer holidays.

Gaitskell's speech of 2nd August, and what flowed from
it, were central points in his career, in his relations with the
Tory Government, and even in the Labour Party's history.
The entire Conservative Party, practically the whole of the
press, and a vociferous majority of the nation had taken
Nasser's action as a direct personal insult, timed to follow
on the withdrawal only weeks before of the last British troops
from Egypt. Whether other nations were involved seemed, in
this mood, irrelevant. Gaitskell had, in fact, given perfectly
clear warning that we must not get into a position where
we were condemned in the Security Council or the General
Assembly, never mind whether we considered such condemnation justified or not. But the point made no impact because people were not in a mood to take it. The press gave it
no prominence. And in the Foreign Office, the Joint Planning Staff, and the Chiefs of Staff Committee, we proceeded
with our projects for removing Nasser by force.

From now on Eden's deception operation gathered mo-
mentum, and Gaitskell for his part tried to clarify his position. Thus on television on 14th August he condemned
Nasser's action as "wrongful," but also insisted that it did
not justify the use of force by us. Four days later he expressed the view that the threats of force were fading out.
When Dom Mintoff, visiting London, told him that a large
expedition was being mustered in Malta he declined to believe him, though Bevan did. On 30th August he said in a
press review that the London Conference of 18 interested
Powers had cooled the atmosphere and shown the British
and French governments that none of their allies would
support use of force. They should stop sabre-rattling. Gaitskell insisted on seeing Eden but got nothing definite out of
him one way or the other. His suspicions were more than
aroused. Yet as late as 30th September he could say that the

Government's "most dangerous wobble very nearly brought us into war over Suez," as if the danger were past. Eden had hoodwinked Gaitskell completely and Gaitskell never forgave him for it.

Nevertheless, in early September suspicious signs and portents were accumulating, and anti-war feeling in Britain showed signs of increasing. Gaitskell, therefore, forced a brief recall of Parliament on 12th and 13th September expressly to discuss the Suez Canal situation. The atmosphere had completely changed. All hell broke loose; there was pandemonium from now on until mid-November whenever Suez was discussed. Eden began quietly by referring to the remarkable measure of unanimity in the House and the country early in August. But interruptions and cries of "resign" soon supervened. Gaitskell made two speeches in which he pinpointed, with force, the great issues to be faced. Wide differences of opinion had emerged in the country in the last six weeks, and what the Prime Minister had just said could only divide the nation even more deeply. The fundamental points at issue were the Government's attitudes to the use of force and to the United Nations. The Prime Minister had spoken of the former, but he had not told the full story. (This was true enough.) He and his colleagues, Gaitskell reported, had seen Eden both before 2nd August and again on 14th August. So far from giving assurances as demanded, the Government had leaked to the press that they might well use force. India was shocked, the US worried. No power other than France favoured force. If the Government were really prepared to go it alone with France, they were heading for disaster. Also this would be an open invitation to other countries to follow suit in the future. (This was prescient.) There would be a risk of a general war. Even if a quick victory were achieved, what then? Here Gaitskell put his finger on a tender spot; for the fact is that with all our planning to topple Nasser, we had no clear idea in the Foreign Office of whom to put in his place. The best bet seemed to Eden to be the totally discredited Nahas Pasha, known as a lurking figure from the past even 10 years earlier when I was in our Cairo Embassy. Gaitskell then repeated that force would be justified only under a collective decision of the United Nations, or to help Israel, if attacked, under the terms of the Tripartite Declaration. President Eisenhower had made the US Government's disapproval amply clear. The Government had reached the position where it must either use force or execute the greatest diplomatic climb-down in history. What Gaitskell could not foresee was that matters would be even worse—an almost unimaginable and totally disastrous combination of both these courses. HMG, he went on, might even be themselves in breach of the 1888 Convention. This produced enraged cries from the Government benches. They should take more trouble, he said, to find out what people in other countries were thinking. "Of course many hon. Gentlemen opposite do not want a settlement at all. We have a good case. We must not lead back to international anarchy." The next day's debate was highly acrimonious. Gaitskell again pressed Selwyn Lloyd on the United Nations aspect; Lloyd passed the buck to Eden, who remained deliberately vague. Gaitskell expressed approval of the statement just made by Dulles that the US would never use force over the Canal, but would send her ships round the Cape instead. He then put the record straight: "In my view a strict comparison with our relations with Hitler before the war does not apply. I said that the words which Colonel Nasser used reminded us of Hitler. That is quite true. But it does not mean that the whole situation is by any means the same." This was regarded as a bit shifty by the Tories; but it was sensible and sincere, if a little late in the day. Again with acute prescience Gaitskell warned that if we were not careful we should give Nasser an even greater prestige victory than he had already won. Finally, a striking appeal to commonsense: "If the United Nations are slow, what is wrong with weeks and weeks elapsing without war?"

Eden wound up and released the usual smoke-screen. He was constantly and violently interrupted. But commonsense played no great part that day, and the Government had a majority of 321 to 251.

Gaitskell had hit the nail on the head when he said that some Tories simply did not want a settlement. He might have gone further and said that Eden was one of them and that he was actively determined to have his war. This was apparent to us planners from the start, and throughout. International conferences were called, Menzies went to Cairo, matters were discussed at the United Nations: all that was, for Eden, a front. Behind the scenes military plan after military plan was made, and tinkered with, in collaboration with the French. Up and down the country the argument raged. Families came to blows. When the *Observer* came out for the Gaitskell line, its circulation immediately fell. But the "reliable" Tory press fanned the flames. This was to be Britain's finest martial hour; in a word, the good old days had returned. The Tory Party Conference in September was cock-a-hoop.

At the Labour Conference at Blackpool from 1st to 5th October, Gaitskell spoke strongly on an emergency resolution on Suez. He thanked some newspapers for their support—the *Mirror*, the *Guardian*, the *Herald*, the *News Chronicle*, *Reynolds' News* "and some others"—but accused the rest of destroying national unity by insisting on the use of force. He recalled that the 1955 Labour Party Conference had come out overwhelmingly in favour of a defensive alliance with Israel. (A rather different type of alliance was being cooked up at that moment.) He could not pretend that even now the danger was entirely over. "I agree with our friends from Paole Zion (the affiliated Union of British Jews) that we must not forget the rights of Israel and Israeli shipping." He hammered home the United Nations point and received loud applause.

He received even more when, taking a little time off from his Suez preoccupations, he spoke for the NEC on their document "Towards Equality." This had received most violent abuse in the Tory press. Allowing himself some heavy irony:

"We know how the wealthy gained their wealth: through skill, courage, patience, energy, loyalty, and family affection." Labour's belief in social justice and equality was in no way based on envy or on levelling down. They wanted higher productivity, a democratic educational system, and fairer taxation. Everyone from Thomas More to Marx and the Webbs had passionately hated social inequality. "This is really the heart of our Socialist faith. For the past 30 years this is what I have cared about more than anything else in our programme." He was repeating some of his 1955 speech, but they loved it. We also, he said, want gaiety and colour. Finally, an appeal for unity of purpose between the Trade Union Movement and the Parliamentary Labour Party, and a rousing reference to the future Labour Government. Gaitskell was now right in his stride as regards Conference speech-making, and that stride never faltered to the end. The usual characters headed the Constituency Parties' poll: Barbara Castle, Tony Greenwood, Harold Wilson, Tom Driberg. But as a result of Suez, Gaitskell was now much closer to Bevan, who was elected Treasurer. However, another difficult character was looming up: Frank Cousins, who had recently come up fast from relative obscurity to be General Secretary of the Transport and General Workers' Union, and who had resigned from the NEC in February 1956.

By the time Parliament reassembled on 24th October, the deed of Anglo-French collusion with Israel had been done at the Sèvres meeting the day before. Eden's nerves were now stretched to breaking point, and he was less than ever inclined to tell any important part of the truth to Gaitskell. In reply to a question by him, Lloyd said that the recent Egyptian proposals for a solution were being studied. What he meant was that they looked so reasonable that they were a grave embarrassment to the Government, teed up as it at last was for Eden's war. Also on 23rd October the students made their first anti-Soviet demonstrations in Budapest. Lloyd made a statement on 29th October, mentioning that HMG and her allies had brought the whole Hungarian situation

before the Security Council. Gaitskell expressed his admiration of the Hungarians', and also the Poles', spirit of independence, a matter which moved him deeply. Nobody mentioned Suez. That, I repeat, was 29th October 1956, the day
on which Israel attacked.

At a quarter past four on the afternoon of the following
day, Eden handed Gaitskell, whom he had summoned for
the purpose, a copy of the statement which he intended to
make in 15 minutes' time about the Anglo-French ultimatum,
which in effect ordered the Egyptians to retreat 10 miles from
the Canal and the Israelis to retreat—but in this case a long
way forwards—to within 10 miles of the east bank. The ultimatum sounds ridiculous today, and it did then. Even those
few of us in the Foreign Office who had planned the operation were flabbergasted; and the three officials who had been
completely in on all the planning had since early October
been reduced to two, since the most junior member, myself,
had not been entrusted with the secrets of the collusion with
Israel. As for the large number of other senior officials who
should in the ordinary way have been consulted on the
world-wide implications of such an action, they were very
cross indeed. But none screwed themselves up to resign. Gaitskell, of course, was in a white-hot fury, though he kept his
cool. An action like this by Eden came, by now, as no great
surprise to him. All the same, the effrontery of the man in
launching a sort of declaration of war, for clearly it amounted
to that, without the slightest warning to, let alone consultation with, the leader of roughly half the nation, was not to
be forgiven.

Eden made his statement as planned just after Gaitskell
had had his first sight of it. For the moment Gaitskell, wisely,
played it long. Why was there no reference to the Tripartite
Declaration; and under what authority could the British and
French forces intervene, as threatened? Eden replied, to protect the lives of our citizens and in defence of vital national
and international rights. He was to look silly on all those
excuses. Soothingly, Eden said that the Security Council was

considering the matter and that he was in close touch with
the US Government. A true statement, but hardly complete;
for both bodies were to react strongly and immediately
against the Eden line. Denis Healey drew attention to the
possible repercussions in Hungary, where Soviet forces were
now engaged in what might seem to the world a similar
enterprise to that threatened by the British and French. But
at 5.42 p.m. the House, as arranged some time before, went
over to the discussion of Agriculture (Fatstock Payments).

Not for long. At 8 p.m. there was a further, and much
rowdier, debate though even this one had to make way at 10
sharp for the burning question of White Fish Authority
(Levy). Gaitskell said that he understood, but did not approve, Israel's reasons for attacking. Britain and France
should have waited for the Security Council to finish its discussions. The Tories rolled about laughing at that sally. No
one Power, Gaitskell went on, could appoint itself the world's
policeman. The Government had deliberately not consulted
the Commonwealth or the US Government or, come to that,
the Opposition. The Tories were boisterous and carried the
vote by 270 to 218.

From then on, absolutely no holds were barred. On 31st
October, Eden made a confused and woolly statement—he
himself admitted that he was no longer on top of his job—
and was fearfully harried and told to resign by the Opposition. Gaitskell kept up the pressure. He referred to one
extraordinary omission in Eden's statement: on the expiry
of the ultimatum, had the Anglo-French forces been ordered
to occupy the Canal Zone? Eden refused "in any way to give
the House any details of the action which will follow." Gaitskell said that the situation was fantastic and that he must
assume that the forces were on the move (as indeed they
were). This was "an act of disastrous folly whose tragic con-
sequences we shall regret for years." It was "a positive assault
on the three principles which have governed British foreign
policy for at any rate the last 10 years—solidarity with the
Commonwealth, the Anglo-American alliance, and adherence

to the Charter of the UN." In that body even Australia was against us, and we had vetoed a US resolution. The excuse of protection of British lives and property was the flimsiest possible; Gaitskell was right again, and it was only because of Nasser's orders to his people that they were spared. "There is an even worse story going around, to which I hope we shall have some reference from the Government, that the whole business was a matter of collusion between the British and French governments and the Government of Israel." Later he infuriated the Tories by thanking goodness for the US intervention against us. "This reckless decision," as he described it, came just when events in Poland and Hungary "had given the free world the greatest hope and encouragement for 10 years." (He was over-optimistic here.) "Hon. Members may cheer their own Prime Minister and jeer at us, but all this will not stop the wave of hatred of Britain which they have stirred up." This was meant to madden the Tories, and it succeeded. Labour would oppose the Government's policy "by every constitutional means at our disposal." It was a brilliantly provocative speech and resulted in considerable disorder in the House, as Gaitskell had no doubt intended. After that poor old Hinch let go. About the Opposition: "I entertain the most profound feelings of disgust and degradation"; about his own side: "I find myself proud to be living upon this day." Orotund, but it is possible to penetrate the opaque oratory and see what he meant, and many of his colleagues with him. He added that Labour members were constitutionally cowards and unpatriotic. Major Harry Legge-Bourke—who else?—accused Gaitskell of letting down the troops in action. Harold Davies asked the pertinent question: Oh, have we declared war then? This was loudly treated by the Conservative benches as an impertinence. The witty Captain Pilkington, having maintained that Gaitskell had supported the Government on 2nd August, quoted Gilbert and Sullivan in his direction: "The idiot who praises every country but his own." Dr. Horace King, an objective enough man as we know from his excellent performance as Speaker today, chided the Tories for saying "Let us all be British together" when they meant "Let us all be Tories together." Selwyn Lloyd attempted to wind up under constant interruptions from Labour.

The next day, 1st November, was the same only much more so. The new Minister of Defence, Antony Head—Walter Monckton having quit because he could take it no longer—made a brief report on the military situation. Gaitskell asserted that "millions of British people are profoundly shocked and ashamed." Then it was a free-for-all, with poor Mr. Speaker in the middle. Eventually, he had to take the most exceptional step, "pursuant to Standing Order No. 24," of suspending the sitting of the House for half an hour. Tempers cooled off, but not for long. On resumption, Gaitskell repeated the pointed question: are we at war, and if not what protection do our armed forces have if captured? Eden, as usual, declined to say yes or no, but later admitted that there had not been a declaration of war. We, however, would apply the Geneva Convention "and Israel and Egypt were also bound by its provisions." This was a large and unwarrantable assumption; and just as the great "patriot" had abandoned thousands of British subjects living in Egypt to Nasser's mercy, so it now became clear that the great warrior was doing much the same with the British troops. Nye Bevan made a calm intervention, but the House became a disorderly one again.

On 2nd November, Gaitskell asked whether the Government proposed to accept the cease-fire proposed by the US Delegate to the United Nations and approved by the General Assembly by 64 votes to 5. Eden first hummed and hawed, and then said no. In connexion with one of his remarks, Denis Healey, who was as fiery as Gaitskell throughout, turned to the Speaker: "Mr. Speaker, could you please tell me what is the parliamentary expression which comes closest to expressing the meaning of the word 'liar'?" The commotion was appalling. At one point the Labour front bench rose to their feet and booed Eden as he left the Chamber.

The Parliamentary Labour Party, which had not been wholly behind Gaitskell in August, was now united; this included the 17 Jewish members. They insisted on a session on Saturday 3rd November; very hard on the Tory weekenders. Gaitskell later referred to another very serious event in the last 24 hours, reports of Soviet troops and tanks entering Hungary. The debate continued furiously the next day. Eden made a wet statement. Gaitskell was accused of wanting to "sell Britain," He and Healey went hammer and tongs for Eden. Lloyd made a statement on developments in Hungary, and from then on the catastrophic connexion between the two campaigns was fully realised and debated.

On Sunday 4th November, Gaitskell and Bevan addressed a mass rally in Trafalgar Square on the theme "Law not War," There were cries of "Stop Eden's War." The crowd surged down from Trafalgar Square to Downing Street, which not only Eden but the traditional officials of the Foreign Office considered most unseemly, On the same day Gaitskell replied to a broadcast by Eden. The latter had told his friend Sir Alexander Cadogan, formerly head of the Foreign Office and now Chairman of the BBC Governors, that he considered that his own broadcast was "a non-controversial ministerial statement" and that consequently Gaitskell had no right to reply. For Eden had reached the stage where his war was a national crusade; and "l'état, c'est moi." Cadogan was inclined to agree, but Gaitskell insisted—at one point he lost his temper with the BBC over the matter—and so did some less elevated BBC staff members. He went out on both television and sound. Shortly before he had dined at the house of Ian and Anne Fleming, who were dear friends of his. Also present was Bob Boothby, who had a high regard for Gaitskell. Boothby was one of a group of more intelligent Tories who had reached the conclusion that if the Tory party were to remain in power, Eden must go. Gaitskell also wanted him out, of course for different reasons, and they had some discussion of the situation; enough, indeed, for an unjustified rumour of collusion between them to be spread about. But Gaitskell misread the auspices on this occasion, and his highly emotional statement was only partially a success. His theme was that the Prime Minister must resign, and he appealed to those Conservatives who had doubts on Suez to repudiate him. "We undertake to support a new Prime Minister in halting the invasion of Egypt." The present one was utterly discredited in the world. "This matter is above party." It was reckoned that he had a larger audience than the Prime Minister had had. But with our forces in action, this appeal had the main effect of closing the Tory ranks, and Gaitskell was accused of waging a personal vendetta.

The House was as turbulent as ever on 5th November. The Tories were jubilant at the reported surrender of Port Said; the reverse when it proved to have been countermanded by Nasser. After frantic messages to and from the United Nations in New York, Eden finally announced the staggering news that the Anglo-French forces, who were at last making progress down the Canal, were to cease fire at midnight. The Tories' bitterness against Labour and Gaitskell in particular, against the United Nations, against the United States, in fact against every one but Eden, was unlimited. Gaitskell added some fuel to the fire at another "Law not War" demonstration the next day in the Albert Hall attended by a capacity audience. He said that the cease-fire was a triumph for democracy. He also praised the Hungarian resistance to the Soviet invasion which, he said, showed clearly the true character of Soviet Communism. He was heckled by both left and right, but tremendously applauded at the end. Several hundred "Law not War" demonstrations took place in early November. On 9th November, Gaitskell headed a delegation of protest on Hungary to the Soviet Ambassador. His Excellency said baldly that the uprising was Fascist; Gaitskell replied, equally baldly, that his statement was unacceptable.

The Suez aftermath rumbled on. A significant interlude was a visit by Gaitskell to Winchester, where the headmaster had invited him some time before to speak on the duties of the Opposition. He received a further message from Desmond

Lee shortly before his visit, begging him to keep off Suez and generally to be non-controversial because feelings in the school were running so high. The press were excluded. Gaitskell complied and at the end asked if there were any questions. Yes, replied a master who was in the audience; would he please explain why he had behaved as a traitor to his country? Gaitskell had been needled frequently by better men than this one, and he explained patiently the reasons for Labour's consistent line. By the end the majority of the audience were on his side. So, no doubt, were the other guest speakers in this series, fellow-Wykehamists Sir Roger Makins and Sir William Hayter, who as Ambassadors in Washington and Moscow respectively had fully realised the ghastly folly of Eden's policy.

Gaitskell and his colleagues kept up the pressure both in and outside the House, and incurred great odium in many quarters as a result. At Carlisle on 25th November he accused the Tories of "appalling arrogance" in assuming that only they were right and the whole of the rest of the world was wrong. We must now withdraw the forces unconditionally from Egypt. Only after that could the Canal be cleared, Anglo-American understanding rebuilt, the pipelines repaired, and free negotiations with Egypt resumed. "We have become, in the Middle East, a grave liability to the West." We should leave it to the US and the UN to take the lead. On Hungary, while his indignation was no less than before, he pointed out that we could not have used force to help the Hungarian people "without the virtual certainty that we would have been starting a third world war."

In a big speech in the House on 6th December, Gaitskell put the collusion issue fair and square. He first had some fun at the expense of the Foreign Secretary, who he said had done an involuntary strip-tease—"herself or himself, whichever sex he likes to adopt for this purpose"—thanks to Bevan's very successful participation. "Scarcely a fig leaf is left to the Foreign Secretary." But he was in deadly earnest most of the time. It was well known that France and Israel had collaborated throughout the summer. Equally, Britain and France had been thinking of using force ever since early August. British and French Ministers had met on 16th and 23rd October. "Was it or was it not true that before 29th October, and possibly on 16th and 23rd October, discussions took place with France about Anglo-French intervention when Israel attacked Egypt? That was a question to which there had been no answer." He castigated the Government on the usual lines, not least for going into a war with half their own nation opposed to it. They must return to proper co-operation with the Commonwealth, our other allies, and the United Nations. He was repeatedly and loudly applauded by his supporters. But he got no change out of Eden and Lloyd on the collusion issue: only evasions, amounting two or three times to downright lies.

Anthony Nutting, the very young and up-and-coming Minister of State at the Foreign Office who had been Eden's protégé and had yet honourably resigned because of Eden's folly, had also resigned his seat at solid Tory Melton Mowbray together with his five-figure majority. Gaitskell sent the Labour candidate a letter in December in which he again referred to the Government's secret collusion activities over Suez and called on the electors to repudiate them. Needless to say, they did not. On 15th December he returned to the charge in a speech at Derby. "What is the good of claiming you stopped a war when you connived at the starting of it?" The growing power of the right-wing Tories, as over Suez, was ominous, he said. He named the British Ministers involved in the "secret" meetings as Eden and Lloyd, and the French as Mollet and Pineau. He was right. On 20th December, Gaitskell again pressed for answers on the meeting of the two Prime Ministers on 16th October and the question of collusion. This time Eden did not even hedge; he told a straight lie: "There was not foreknowledge that Israel would attack Egypt."

On 30th December, Gaitskell arrived in New York for a lecture tour of over three weeks. At the airport he told reporters that he hoped the Anglo-US rift would soon be mended and that he welcomed the US Government's move to take the lead economically in the Middle East. Three days later at the University of California, he repeated that the US and the UN must try to settle the Israeli-Egypt conflict and in general bring peace to the area. The Labour Party had approved of the US's policy over Suez. He had a few provocative, for his audience, remarks to make on other international questions. He favoured a withdrawal of foreign troops from Germany and from the "Russian satellites"; also the admission of Communist China to the United Nations. At Berkeley on 4th January 1957 he repeated these themes, again commended the Eisenhower doctrine for the Middle East, and defended Britain against charges of neo-colonialism. After speaking at the Occidental College in Los Angeles, he went off to Harvard to deliver the Godkin lectures. On 9th January he told the press there that he was sorry Eden's health had not recovered as a result of his trip to Jamaica, that he was right to resign, but that as the whole Cabinet had backed his foreign policy, a general election was now required. He declined to go into details: "We have this convention that we do not attack the other Party when we are out of the country." Old Earl Attlee, lecturing at Moline, Illinois, at the same time, made similar comments. A few days later Gaitskell, speaking at the Economic Club of New York, encouraged the US and the UN to be firm with Nasser over the clearance of the Canal and other such matters. Macmillan had formed his government on 10th January, and Gaitskell cut short his tour to return on the 19th. At London Airport he said that he had found the Americans bewildered over Suez, but no longer anti-British. "There is no ill-feeling," but they would be watching the new government's performance. He paid a generous tribute to Eden in the House, skating over the last few months when he said he had been unwell. Our graceless and stupid Tory could not refrain from asking whose fault had that been?

Gaitskell's Godkin lectures at Harvard were published

here in 1957 under the title *The Challenge of Co-existence,* and they provide a crisp résumé of his thoughts on the international situation in January of that year. He thanked his wife, Philip Noel-Baker, Kenneth Younger, and Denis Healey for their help in preparing them; and described the atmosphere thus: "Suez and Hungary had exploded, but the smoke had not cleared away." He modestly began the first one, on Co-existence and the UN, by saying that politicians were superficial people who knew less and less about more and more. Lenin had introduced the "co-existence" slogan, which had been used by the latter-day Stalin and much more by Bulganin and Khruschev. "To us the challenge of co-existence is not merely how to avoid a third world war, but also how to bring to those people who do not now enjoy them the benefits of liberty and true self-government." After speaking of the struggle with Communism in the uncommitted areas, he referred to Suez. Article 51 of the UN Charter defined the only circumstances in which a nation may use force. Even Israel's preventive war of 29th October was contrary to it. NATO specifically accepted the purposes of the UN Charter as its own aims. "My countrymen have taken opposite views over Hungary and Suez." Had it not been for the use of the veto by Britain and France, he believed that the UN could have stopped the Israel-Egypt war; and he warmly welcomed the formation of the UN force. He praised the US's anti-colonialism; but added that they, together with Britain and France as the other signatories of the Tripartite Declaration, should have allowed Israel to purchase arms and shown beyond doubt that they would have gone to her aid if attacked. The Security Council would have to be strengthened by the addition of Communist China (he never seemed to consider whether she would accept an invitation if offered), India, Japan "and Germany when reunification has taken place, if not before." His second lecture, on Co-existence in Europe, reads today as a mixture of the realistic and the unpractical. NATO had led to a considerable strengthening of all sorts of ties between the US and Europe, and also Britain and

Europe; but the alliance was militarily, and indeed politically, very weak. After the passing of the MacMahon Act in 1946, which strictly limited the US Government's freedom to share nuclear information with her allies, the Labour Government had decided Britain could not be entirely dependent on the US and so must make her own H-bomb, though it caused a heavy strain on her resources. The Intercontinental Ballistic Missile would soon appear, but he was confident that the US would keep her bases in Europe nevertheless. The heroism of the Hungarians and Poles had "shown that the rule of the Communist puppet government is only kept in being by the tanks and artillery of the Soviet army": not a completely correct judgment, but no doubt welcome to American ears. We should aim at a withdrawal of the Red Army from all the "satellites" in return for a withdrawal of US forces from West Germany, though not from the rest of Western Europe. (This of course the Soviet Government would, and will, never accept.) If the West German Government would renounce all claims to their pre--1945 territories and recognise the Oder-Neisse frontier, they might well get reunification and the freedom of the satellites to boot. Here he was very wide of the mark. The eventual aim, he went on, must be comprehensive disarmament, but NATO and the Warsaw Pact should remain for the time being. He did not favour a neutralised, reunited Germany; the USSR might come to dominate her and, in "sinister" fashion, bribe her with a piece of Poland, as in the past. (Rather far-fetched.) "We owe it to the peoples of the satellite countries at least to examine what can be done to win freedom for them by diplomatic means." (Music in Foster Dulles' ears.) Britain was in favour of joining "the proposed free trade area though not the so-called 'common market,'" chiefly because of her Commonwealth ties, and because "we also feel that we have a special relationship with the US." At this stage Gaitskell did not understand the Soviet Government's, and their allies', views on Germany East and West too well. He became more realistic as the years passed. The reference to the "special relationship" seems regrettable to me, not because Gaitskell was not absolutely sincere about this, but because this vague phrase is too often used by some British politicians to induce a false sense of comfort and security, and into the bargain assumes something which by no means appeals to all Americans. But the question calls for another book.

In his final lecture on The Uncommitted Areas, Gaitskell pointed out that with 600 million people they had one-quarter of the world's total population. Britain and France had, rightly, given independence to a similar number of people, though there were groups in Europe who opposed this policy. British bases in hostile countries were an anachronism, and the US principle of unobtrusive bases leased without political strings was preferable. We should sympathise with the Bandoeng type neutrals, especially India. Summing up his lectures, he said that nearly all these themes converged on the Middle East. Here the successes of the UN must be followed up, with the help of the US in particular. He would favour the UN's actually administering the Gaza Strip and a corridor from there to the Gulf of Akaba, as well as patrolling Israel's other frontiers. He hoped that in time open collaboration between the US, the British, and the French could be restored; he underestimated Macmillan's quickness of operation on this point. "I would ask that we do not allow any alleged disagreement about 'colonialism' to divide us." Summing up: "For my part I look on the Suez episode as a temporary affair, an aberration." I personally do not think he was right on this, to the extent that there was much in the past record of Eden and his cronies that made it, or something like it, predictable. He ended: "Surely what has happened in Europe gives us, the people of the democracies, the greatest hope and encouragement that we have had for these past 10 years. This surely should encourage our two nations not to part company, but rather to pursue our common struggle with all the greater faith and courage." While his analysis may not have been correct in every detail, here he at any rate spoke for England; and he decidedly

pleased his audience. Indeed the US Government and people
had never turned anti-British as a whole. They had just been
completely opposed to the machinations of Eden and his
government.

What, then, did the balance sheet show for Gaitskell after
his first year and a bit as Leader? On the face of it he had
won a famous victory. He had stood up for what he, a great
many people in Britain, and more still elsewhere considered
Britain's honour. He had laid down with clarity and force
the lines which Britain's foreign policy must follow in the
1950s. He had been instrumental in terminating the Suez
"aberration," and also the political life of the man chiefly
responsible for it, Eden. The Labour Party liked his leadership, and Bevan was back in the fold, as Shadow Foreign
Secretary. But in some important ways the victory was a
Pyrrhic one. The majority of the British people thought
Nasser deserved condign punishment for his seizure of the
Canal. They placed much of the blame for the delay and
eventual fiasco on Gaitskell. Many, particularly in the Conservative Party but also beyond, regarded him as a turncoat
since his speech of 2nd August, and an actual traitor for
continuing his vociferous opposition when the military operation was under way. These feelings persisted, astonishingly,
for years and affected the result of the next election in distant 1959. Cecil King, in his charming memoirs called *Strictly
Personal* but which might better have been entitled Strictly
Poisonous, even produced the extraordinary fantasy that
"Hugh Gaitskell was convinced the Government was bluffing
and that it was his duty to help them bluff." But to return
from his world to that of facts, inside the House the continuing opposition to Gaitskell was so open and so bitter
that he once said desperately that he wondered whether he
could properly fulfil his duties as Leader of HM Opposition
since personal relations were so bad. Moreover, if he had got
rid of Eden, he now had to deal with a far wilier politician
in his place, and moreover one who, unlike Eden, knew how

to get on well with the Americans. He made a final assault on him over Suez a few months later.

In sum, I see the story as a typical Gaitskell operation: logical and wholly sincere from the start, for the 2nd August speech contained all the fundamentals of his policy whatever the Tory wishful thinkers chose to imagine and impute; persistently pugnacious; taking difficulties and opposition head on; smashing them, to the natural accompaniment of much bitterness in the short run; and finally, as in nearly all his operations, proving himself and his policy right in the long run.

EIGHT

The Start of Modernisation

GAITSKELL HAD NEVER found it possible to get on any sort of sound footing with Macmillan. In an exchange in the House about this time, the animosity between them showed through. To a question about doctors' pay, Macmillan replied: "No. Only the Rt. Hon. Gentleman would make so foolish a supposition." This raised a laugh amongst his colleagues, and Gaitskell was furious: "The Prime Minister is, as usual, rude and arrogant." He considered him, with justification, just as dyed-in-the-wool a Tory as Eden and just as deeply involved in the Suez aggression, though with a beady eye on the main chance throughout. He did not relish the idea of coping with him in the House. Macmillan for his part, just like Eden, doubted whether anyone could be a full man unless he had served in the trenches. Moreover, Suez had taken up too much of Gaitskell's time; he wanted to get ahead with Labour Movement matters. He was now chairman of a study group from the National Executive Committee and elsewhere on "Public Enterprise—Labour's Review of Nationalised Industries," which was a subject close to his heart.

He remained, however, most active on all aspects of international affairs. He told the Oxford University Labour Club in February 1957 that he accepted that Britain should get nearer to Europe, but only for the right reasons, which would not include anti-Americanism, and with due safeguards. This lukewarm attitude remained till the end. At the same time he entered Europe personally in a big way on the Socialist International front: at Copenhagen in December

1956; The Hague and then Berlin in March 1957, where he spoke up for a neutral zone in Central Europe; Italy in April; Vienna in July, where he was elected third vice-chairman alongside Ollenhauer and Mollet.

On 23rd March in Shropshire he had resumed the attack on the home front. The responsibility for the grave situation in industry, with strikes and threatened strikes, lay with the Government. There were widespread suspicions that they had been encouraging the employers to be tough; the Tory philosophy was that of a selfish free-for-all, and the Prime Minister was prone to indulging in "swashbuckling" language. This would naturally put up the backs of the workers and the Trade Unions and was the reverse of the Socialist policy of fair shares and co-operation on a basis of social justice. At this time a series of by-elections went against the Conservatives; and there was high optimism about Labour's return to power, for instance at the Scottish Trades Union Congress, which Gaitskell addressed in April.

The repercussions of Suez were not yet dead, and Gaitskell decided on a vote of censure, which he moved on 15th May: "That this House expresses its concern at the outcome of the Government's Suez Canal policy, and deplores the damage to British prestige and economic interests resulting therefrom." He made a deliberately provocative speech of over an hour, and it managed to revive some of the hectic atmosphere of the Suez debates, with loud applause from the Labour benches and violent interjections opposite. Gaitskell went over familiar ground in a colourful way and once more explained how the Labour attitude had been honourable, necessary and consistent throughout. Nasser had recently reopened the Canal, and the Prime Minister was right to swallow his pride and tell British shipping it could go through. It was most regrettable that the United Nations had not established the rights of Israeli shipping. The Government's policy in thinking that their aggression could succeed had been not merely immoral but, on the facts, totally unrealistic and "nothing short of lunacy." Then, snuffing the air of per-

sonal battle as ever, Gaitskell came to his main point. All
that disaster was not just Eden's fault; it was the Cabinet's
as a whole. The present Prime Minister's role remained
somewhat obscure; and yet, as a former Foreign Secretary,
Minister of Defence, and at the time Chancellor, he could
well have given sound advice. Had he told the Cabinet that
the Americans would welcome the escapade? Gaitskell put his
finger on something here; for Macmillan had visited Washington in September and reported to Eden that all was sweet-
ness and light in that quarter. Had Macmillan, asked
Gaitskell, only realised at the last moment that the pound
would be under intolerable pressure? Again, a good question; the answer being that Macmillan had only put this
consideration to Eden at a very late stage, though he was
certainly intelligent enough to have known it long before.
"Was it true that in the early stages he was the most flamboyant and romantic supporter of the whole plan?" The
plain answer is, yes. But, of course, Gaitskell did not receive
it on the day. All the old Tory hackles were up, and the
Government survived the censure vote with ease.

A subject much on Gaitskell's mind at this time was the
proliferation of nuclear tests, with all their threatened
dangers, though our scientific information was that these
were probably exaggerated. Under pressure from Labour,
Eden had said in December 1956 that he would seek an
agreement on the matter, but he did not get around to it in
time. After Macmillan's wise and successful fence-mending
meeting with President Eisenhower in Bermuda in March
1957, Gaitskell repeated that the Labour Party would support
the manufacture of the British H-bomb, though with some
regret, but he was highly doubtful about the necessity for all
these tests. When the Russians proposed in June that H-bomb
tests should be suspended, under proper controls, for two or
three years, Gaitskell was all for agreeing. If we had our
doubts of Soviet sincerity, "surely the right course is to test
the Russians, not the bombs." Another theme that he still

mentioned with emotion from time to time was the disgraceful Soviet oppression of Hungary. While empty gestures on the Western side would be no help, "we can make sure that the rest of the world shows its loathing and contempt for what the Soviet leaders have done," and make greater freedom for the East European nations an object of our diplomacy. In a BBC television programme he denied that Bevan and he any longer had wide differences on foreign policy. "We did once, but not now. In the last year or so we have reached agreement." In August he had a great reception in Yugoslavia by President Tito and the Yugoslav press. In reply to a question about Labour's prospects in the next election, he said: "We hope and believe that we shall win," though he would not be over-optimistic.

As guest of honour at a lunch of the American Chamber of Commerce in London on 17th September, Gaitskell gave an earnest disquisition on the West's economic problems. He advocated closer Anglo-American co-operation in economic affairs, lamented the fall over the last year of the sterling area's gold and dollar reserves, and said that some solution must be found soon to West Germany's surplus. All this has a familiar ring today. He thought there was no case for devaluing the pound: Government and Opposition alike were pledged to defend it. A week later he wrote to Macmillan, requesting an emergency recall of Parliament to discuss the financial and economic situation, as soon as possible after the return of the Chancellor, now Peter Thorneycroft, from his discussions in the US and Canada in about a fortnight's time. Macmillan refused and the House reassembled on 29th October, as scheduled. Speaking at Brighton on 29th September, on the eve of the Labour Party Conference there, Gaitskell took the Government severely to task for raising the bank rate to 7 per cent and generally going for deflation. Thorneycroft was reported as saying in Washington that "full employment must be subordinated to sound currency." This, said Gaitskell, "sounds to me very like a declaration of

war by the Government on the Trade Unions." It was asking
for trouble from them at a moment of national crisis, when
increased production was the most important aim of all.

At Brighton, from 30th September to 4th October 1957,
battle was joined on the nationalisation question. Gaitskell
threw himself into it with zest when he replied for the NEC
on their paper: "Industry and Society and Public Ownership." There had been much emotion, some big misunderstandings, and some good knockabout turns in the debate, he
said. "I do not regard, and never have regarded, nationalisation or public ownership as an end in itself. The ultimate
ends are: equality and social justice; co-operation; accounta-
bility to the community; planning for full employment; and
higher productivity through public ownership and control."
The Labour Party Movement agreed with the tactics embodied by Sidney Webb in the phrase "the inevitability of
gradualness." "We are evolutionary and not revolutionary."
He admitted that the paper had some new ideas in it: "but
you know we must not be too frightened of new ideas." Each
case must be judged on its merits, as in the 1945 election
programme. The object, after all, was to obtain power; and
"the millions of electors we have to convince, including
many millions of Labour supporters, will not be satisfied if
you simply say you are nationalising 'because that is Socialism.'" With the renationalisation of steel and road haulage on the programme, it was full already. "Let us be
confident but not complacent about the next General Election. Though the people have turned from the Tories, they
have not yet turned to us. We have to convince a lot more
marginal voters." He ended with an appeal to the Party and
Movement to face in a clear-headed manner the economic
and political facts. This was a forward-looking speech, hard-
headedly logical and practical, with few frills and much
commonsense. It upset a number of people on both the extreme right and left wings. But the paper was overwhelmingly
approved by 5,309,000 votes to 1,276,000. In the defence debate Bevan declared that if the unilateralist resolution was

carried, "You will send a British Foreign Secretary, whoever he may be, naked into the conference chamber" without the covering of the British H-bomb. Bevan had been Shadow Foreign Secretary for some months by now and was proving a most stalwart and valuable colleague to Gaitskell. This was another outstanding example of the success of Gaitskell's methods of confrontation. Wilson was also in the Shadow Cabinet as Shadow Chancellor.

A week later a curious approach was made by the Communist Party of the Soviet Union in the shape of a letter from Khruschev to Gaitskell, conveyed by the Soviet Chargé d'Affaires in London, covering a document which suggested, amongst other things, that representatives of the two Parties should meet to discuss the dangers of war in the Middle East. It transpired that similar documents had been sent to various European Socialist Parties. Gaitskell referred the letter to the NEC, who in due course replied that such a meeting was out of the question. He also informed the Prime Minister and the Foreign Office, and to deflect any possible smear campaign he related the story to a press conference in Manchester, firmly making the point: "We have no contact with, still less collaboration with, Communist parties in any country." Nevertheless, Khruschev tried again in a letter of 30th April 1958, and duly received the same answer. He appears to have changed his mind about the Labour Party since the celebrated George Brown dinner of April 1956, unless there was some ham-handed Machiavellianism aimed at discrediting them and other Socialist Parties by his apparent friendliness. On the Middle East Gaitskell said that the Arab-Israel dispute was still highly dangerous and that a guarantee of frontiers by the great Powers, including the USSR, was required. That was easier said than done.

In mid-December Gaitskell undertook an extended tour of Asia, visiting India, Burma, Malaya, Singapore, Ceylon, and Pakistan. In India he made some statements which provoked Nehru. He defended NATO and said that, while he respected India's non-alignment, he thought that talk of a "third force" usually came from anti-Americanism and was ineffectual anyway. He proposed that the United Nations should recognise Communist China and should assume the trusteeship of Formosa—totally impracticable, alas. On the Soviet proposal for a Summit meeting, he said that careful preparations would be needed. He arrived home on 27th December. Speaking to 2,500 senior grammar school boys and girls early in the New Year, he said how important it was that European countries should not even appear to be trying to run the new Asian countries' affairs for them.

He now moved towards promoting an early Summit meeting. A joint Labour Party and TUC declaration dated 6th March 1958 on disarmament and nuclear war advocated this, together with a unilateral suspension of H-bomb tests—though not of the British manufacture of H-bombs—and an attempt to get general agreement, with the USSR and the US, to suspend them. A mere two years after becoming Leader of Her Majesty's Opposition, he was already bidding fair to be acknowledged as a world figure.

Meanwhile, Gaitskell was uttering solemn warnings against divisions and disputes in the Labour ranks, and well he might. All kinds of things were looming: Clause 4, unilateralism, Frank Cousins, and, less seriously, Michael Foot. "In a great party like ours there will always be room for personal differences of opinions on some policy issues, but we have to make up our minds as a party and present our views to the country." He called for wholehearted support of the declaration, even by many outside the Labour Movement. The Campaign for Nuclear Disarmament had been formally started by Bertrand Russell and Canon Collins in January, and at its public launching in February at the Central Hall in Westminster several overflow meetings were necessary. This was to prove a great thorn in Gaitskell's flesh. On the one hand it represented a continuation of Labour's old and still respected tradition of pacifism. Members of its extreme Committee of 100 were prepared in 1961 to be sent to prison in the cause, having been found guilty of a breach

of the Official Secrets Act, like other members of the Labour
Party in the first World War. At the same time the Campaign
could exploit the argument that Britain's own nuclear arsenal
was an irrelevance when compared with the equipment of the
Super-Powers. I was closely concerned with defence matters
in the Foreign Office at this time, and I am bound to say
that that argument had some substance in itself. It did not,
however, cover the international and strategic situation as a
whole.

Speaking at Birmingham on 29th March at the first of a
series of regional conferences on the Labour "plan for peace,"
Gaitskell advocated a Summit meeting without delay and
said that the Government's response to the Soviet proposal
had been "confused, clumsy, and inadequate." He had by
now turned against any idea of a preparatory Foreign Ministers' meeting as otiose. And in April he thundered against
a recent speech by Mr. Acheson, which accused Labour, in
effect, of being hoodwinked by the Russians. Mr. Acheson,
he said, was "misinformed," and he mentioned that his own
Party leader, Mr. Adlai Stevenson, had recently confirmed
to him by radio-telephone the importance he attributed, as
he had in the Presidential election, to the suspension of tests,
under proper supervision. Labour stood by NATO, "but we
sometimes feel that Mr. Acheson and others like him are a
little too inclined to be frozen in the postures of 1949." A
few days later, on 23rd April, the joint Labour-TUC body
issued another declaration on Disengagement in Europe,
warmly welcoming the Rapacki Plan. This was very sensible
and forward-looking. We are still today, waiting for practical
results. Unfortunately, the declaration also called for German reunification based on free elections, a scheme which has
never had the slightest appeal for the Soviet and GDR governments and I fancy never will. In May, Gaitskell was the
chief fraternal delegate at the biennial congress of the West
German Social-Democratic Party at Stuttgart. He was already
a friend of Willy Brandt, and the friendship grew closer over
the years.

Gaitskell was always preoccupied with education, which he considered almost as basic as economic considerations in forming the Socialist society. He was a member of a NEC study group which produced a paper entitled "Learning to Live—a Policy for Education from Nursery School to University," under the chairmanship of James Griffiths. He spoke out strongly in Nottingham against the 11 plus: "You cannot pigeon-hole human nature at 11." He commended the Corporation for their new comprehensive school and said that flexibility was required to cope with different children's varying paces and directions of development. He was also a member of two NEC economic committees, Harold Wilson being chairman of both.

After giving the Government rough treatment over their handling of the bus strike in May, Gaitskell paraded with his fellow-Oxonian Macmillan on 25th June to receive their honorary Oxford degrees of Doctor of Civil Law. Such a coincidence had never occurred before, and it only occurred now because Macmillan had twice been prevented from attending. Other recipients included Lord Beveridge, Sir Alan Herbert, and, as Doctor of Music, Dmitri Shostakovitch. The Public Orator referred to Macmillan's "unflappability": "Even though the world were to fall to ruin about our ears, one thing is certain: nothing would shake this imperturbable Scot." As for Gaitskell: "His rapid advancement caused no surprise. Leaders have been known who were guided by Party feeling rather than guiding it themselves. Not he. He does not shirk the task of leadership when the free world is at stake."

Nasser was now stirring things up in the Middle East and had entirely recovered from his Suez setback, which in any case had been accepted in most of the Arab world as a victory over two large colonialist Powers and had thus heightened his prestige. In both Lebanon and Jordan the governments were threatened by Nasserite influences. Gaitskell followed a consistent line. He said in a party political broadcast on 28th June that if British or American forces landed in Lebanon, there would be grave repercussions throughout the Middle East. After what had happened at Suez, no one could blame Labour for being anxious. We should support the UN, and "not do anything against the decisions of the Security Council." By 17th July, when US forces had gone to Lebanon and British to Jordan, he described the situation, in a speech in the House, as very grave. The Soviet Government had expressed its displeasure. He doubted whether Article 51 of the UN Charter applied, though he must admit that forestalling action against a surprise attack might not always allow of prior reference to the Security Council. He accepted that the Prime Minister could not give publicly all his information on the position. But, from a severely realistic point of view, was it right to send British troops to Jordan "to preserve a particular régime in power"? The fact was, he said, that the revolutionaries there, in Iraq, and elsewhere were the only movement in the Arab countries which commanded any popular support. We must try and discuss matters with the Soviet Government. If he was right, he added, the danger in the whole situation was "colossal." "We regard this latest move of the Government, however sincerely taken, as fraught with the gravest risks both to our own interests and the peace of the world." His supporters, many of whom had wanted an even more categorical condemnation of the Government, heartily applauded his oratory. But, as it happens, I was myself in a position, as Foreign Office Adviser to the Chief of the Secret Service (then Sir Dick White), to observe that Gaitskell had acted with more heart than head on this occasion. We had ample and reliable intelligence on Nasser's plans for subverting the Lebanese and Jordanian set-ups; unfortunately, much less on the future in Iraq.

On the critical day in mid-July, I was with Dick White when the final confirmatory intelligence of imminent action by Nasser in Jordan came in. We were asked not to act on it because that would endanger an excellent source. We decided without hesitation to take that risk. Having checked with

King Hussein, whose information pointed in exactly the same direction, we then recommended to the Government that they should comply with his request as an ally that the British paratroopers should go in without delay. They did so within 48 hours. The US looked after Lebanon, and the surging up of human monsters festooned with the most modern lethal weapons on the Beirut beaches gave the recumbent lovelies there the thrill of their lives. I think Gaitskell was wrong on various counts here. Our ally Hussein asked us to help protect his country against almost certain aggression, so that Article 51 could be said to apply. We went in only at his request. We acted immediately, and not against any Security Council resolution. No killing was needed. We were successful; and whatever criticisms some of us may have of Hussein's and Jordan's policies since then, we have remained good friends. In all these ways the operation was totally different from Suez, which was still very much on Gaitskell's mind.

He was on sounder ground when he said in September that it would be "criminal folly" to fight, and risk world war, over Quemoy. "I have never been an appeaser or an anti-American," he said, but occasionally we must tell the US Government when they were being silly. In fact, the danger over that almost forgotten little island appeared such that he moved an emergency resolution on the subject later in the month at the Annual Conference. He had meanwhile announced that he had been invited by the Soviet Government to visit the USSR that autumn, but had declined because of pressure of business. The visit was not to be long delayed.

The run-up to the Conference included some unpleasant incidents that gave him food for thought. On 22nd September he went with Bessie Braddock and her husband to a ceremony in Liverpool of naming two ten-storey blocks after the latter, a local alderman. The ceremony lasted about an hour, and there was continuous booing and shouting from the crowd of some 5000. As Gaitskell spoke he was interrupted by cries of "We want Churchill. We want Macmillan. You made us bankrupt in 1951. On your way," and other such agreeable sallies. For much of the time he was inaudible. The police had to take a hand.

The Annual Conference took place at Scarborough from 29th September to 3rd October 1958. Gaitskell was most active, speaking not only on Quemoy but on relations between Labour and the Co-operative Movement, economic policy, and foreign policy. In Quemoy, after referring to Chiang Kai-shek as the "puppet dictator," he took a bang at Macmillan. "I find it slightly nauseating that Mr. Macmillan, one of the leading figures in the Suez adventure, should now be talking about being against force. I find such hypocrisy almost intolerable."

When he rose to wind up on the NEC's paper on economic policy, he was loudly cheered. He particularly thanked Frank Cousins for his kind words and paid a tribute to Harold Wilson's work on the paper. This was largely a technical economic speech, but it was nonetheless well received for that. Production was now falling, whereas under Labour it had risen by 7 per cent every year. He would like to see every family owning a car. "Labour have plans for the future; the Tories only clichés." But having worked through the difficult stuff, he ended with a rousing peroration: "Let us pledge ourselves to the cause of democratic Socialism, the greatest in the world, the hope of humanity." It went across very big: prolonged applause, the singing of "For he's a jolly good fellow," and three cheers. His speech on foreign policy was quite a different matter, for much of it was devoted to hitting the unilateralists hard. He paid warm tribute to Nye Bevan's various speeches on the theme that he would not go naked into the council chambers. Together with Bevan and George Brown, he had seen General Norstad, who was by no means hellbent on nuclear aggression by NATO. "Would unilateral renunciation of H-bombs on our part bring peace in the world?" There were loud cries of "Yes." "There is not a shred of evidence that if we did this, America or Russia

would do anything of the kind—not a shred." To quit
NATO, as some proposed, would be "disastrously dangerous
to the peace of the world." For one thing, West Germany
would become the leading power in West Europe. All should
remember that Ernest Bevin helped to create NATO. As
always, he spoke up for Anglo-American understanding.

Later in October, Gaitskell toured the depressed areas of
Scotland, and afterwards he devoted a good deal of energy
and a good many speeches to telling the Government what
they should do about the unemployment and general economic mess that they had caused. If they tried hard enough,
they could have full employment. As before, he demanded
more investment and encouragement of exports. On 28th
October, on the eve of the new parliamentary session, he
appeared on television and, according to *The Times,* "made
an altogether engaging, sociable, and candid guest at Every-
man's fireside"—perhaps even "too urbane and charming"
for some of his extremists. (There was, in fact, a good deal
of criticism in the Labour Party of his so-called Hampstead
set.) He proposed his remedies for the economy and suggested that three and a half years after the last election it
stood just where it had then. A Labour Government, unlike
the present one, would work closely with the Trade Unions,
though it would not be subservient to them. He conceded
that recently there had been a recovery in the Conservatives'
fortunes and that their publicity had been pretty good. This
would be a spur to Labour in the General Election which
was to be expected before long.

NINE

Another Lost Election

GAITSKELL'S NEW YEAR message to the Labour Party listed the five "chief issues" on which the next General Election would be fought, "almost certainly in 1959." They were unemployment, pensions, education, housing, and foreign policy. The form he adopted was question and answer, designed to show how complacent and inactive Tory policy was and how dynamic a Labour Government would be, particularly in favour of the poorer classes. On the last item, for instance, he asked: "Are we to make a supreme effort to break through the deadlock of the Cold War and try out fresh proposals for peace and disarmament? That is the Labour view. Or are we to remain mute and paralysed, waiting for the next crisis and leaving the initiative always to the Soviet Union?"

It was good sound stuff, but was it inspiring? And what were the real prospects for the next election as 1959 got into its stride? The biggest factor was that Macmillan was completely in charge of a tough Tory government. These were the days of Supermac. It was for him alone to decide the date of the election. He had had various successes: the repairing of relations with the US Government, and the restoration of a good deal of Britain's position in the Middle East, not least owing to the success of the Anglo-American effort in Jordan and Lebanon in 1958. Cyprus, as I saw for myself from my post there, was beginning to settle down. At home he could tell people that they had never had it so good, and they loved it. Of course, there were two important qualifications which he did not mention. The rich were having it better faster than the poor. And in the world economic contest, although our position steadily improved, that of half a dozen other nations was improving much more rapidly. These were the facts of life which Gaitskell painstakingly tried to explain. But most people tend to get bored with too many facts in politics; they have to deal with so many tedious facts in everyday life that they look to the politicians for some glamour, some élan, some panache. Macmillan was better able to provide these than Gaitskell. Broadly speaking, people, of course, liked Gaitskell, but were to some extent puzzled by him. His intelligence and his complete honesty were never for a moment in doubt, but sometimes he seemed too intelligent and even too honest. The public in general found it hard to dig him; the Macmillan *persona*, with its patrician self-confidence, was something much more familiar and, in a way, reassuring. Besides, people said, if I'm all right, Jack, isn't that a sign of a successful government? And must I really be my brother's keeper? Gaitskell slogged on with confidence because on the swing of the by-elections away from the Tories he was justified in so doing. And other precedents looked encouraging. The Conservatives would shortly have been in power for eight years; surely, the British public would have had enough of them? Conversely, in British politics one Party simply was not apt to lose three elections on the trot. But it was not the whole story. Apart from his other gifts, Macmillan had luck and, as he once remarked in his lofty manner, do you know, people really rather like a man who is lucky. Finally, the Labour Movement proceeded on its self-indulgent way, its members quarrelling amongst themselves constantly and publicly, on any of half a dozen issues. The floating voter either could not be bothered to understand this type of individualism, or positively found it repugnant.

If the sheer deployment of energy and thoroughness could have won an election, Gaitskell would have achieved it. On 6th January 1959 a NEC statement set out in more detail the foreign affairs theme of his message. The Western Powers had once again, by their unimaginative response to the Soviet proposals on Europe, postponed the chance of settling the German problem. "There is no reason why Russia should agree to a reunited Germany being free to join NATO." This may seem an obvious point, but it was never hoisted in, before or since, by the Tory negotiators on the question. Hence the endless series of futile discussions over the years. What was needed instead, the paper proposed, and very wisely, was immediate negotiations on the Rapacki Plan.

On 8th January 1959 a portentous event occurred when de Gaulle became President of France. A mere six days later he received his first foreign visitor: Gaitskell, accompanied by Ambassador Sir Gladwyn Jebb. What is more, they discussed for 75 minutes questions such as NATO, nuclear defence, relations with the USSR, and Algeria. Forewarned, felt Gaitskell, is forearmed.

The run-up to the election was now beginning in earnest. Did Macmillan go to the North-East and broadcast on Tyne-Tees television? Gaitskell followed suit. Throughout February and March he stumped the country, often in the company of his friend Nye Bevan. Indeed they stumped further. Macmillan showed enterprise in going to Moscow, white fur hat and all; not so long after, the friends were to follow him there. This was announced in February for a few months later. Gaitskell was already forecasting an October election while most prophets still hesitated. Also in February he ran into a typical reception from an audience of about 900 at the Oxford University Labour Club: there was much hissing and booing when he attacked the Government, and as much again from the Campaign for Nuclear Disarmament members present when he defended Britain's retention of the H-bomb. He ran into less trouble when he addressed about 1000 people at Heidelberg University and welcomed what he called the greater flexibility of the West on East-West European problems. On 19th February, just before the departure of Macmillan and Lloyd for Moscow, he made a constructive and moderately expressed speech in the House. He paid tribute to Macmillan for being the first British Prime Minister to visit the USSR. He agreed that the Government had been right to reject Khruschev's proposal for a free city of West Berlin and the withdrawal of Western forces. He pursued the theme that a balance of security must be maintained in Central Europe and explained why he considered something on the lines of the Rapacki Plan was the most hopeful approach. He ended: "We wish the Prime Minister and the Foreign Secretary 'God Speed' in this important mission."

After their return Gaitskell said that the concrete results of the talks might seem disappointing, but the personal contacts were worthwhile. We should now accept without more ado Khruschev's proposal for a Summit meeting. There was no call for a preliminary meeting of Foreign Ministers: only one of them, Dulles, counted for anything and unfortunately he was gravely ill. He saw no reason why the West should object to Poland and Czechoslovakia taking part.

On the home front Gaitskell made his attitude on nationalisation absolutely clear in a speech at Middlesbrough. Steel and road haulage would be taken back into public ownership. Further: "We reserve the right if, after full enquiry, we find that an industry is falling down on its job, to transfer it to public ownership. We are not proposing to decide the exact plans until we have won the election." At a lunch of the Industrial Co-Partnership Association in London he mentioned that he had heard it argued that a level of 600,000 or 700,000 unemployed would prevent inflation and refused to consider any such policy. Today, alas, we appear to have the unemployed and the inflation as well.

There was a good deal of speculation at this stage about the membership of Gaitskell's government, if it came to pass. How would he combine the right and left wings, the intellectuals and the Trade Unionists, the bright boys and the heavies? The composition of the so-called Shadow Cabinet, or Parliamentary Party Committee to give it its official name, gave some guidance but was not completely reliable because it was based on election by Labour MPs whereas the actual

Cabinet would, of course, be nominated by Gaitskell. The principal members, *in situ,* aged not more than 65 were as follows: Bevan (61), Foreign Affairs; Wilson (43), Treasury; Callaghan (46), Colonies; Gordon Walker (51) and Greenwood (47), Home Office; Robens (48), Labour; Brown (44), Defence; Jay (52), Board of Trade; together with, ex officio, Gaitskell (now 52), Griffiths (already 68), and Herbert Bowden (54), the Chief Whip. Greenwood was fancied by some for Housing and Local Government; Crossman might well handle pensions in view of his declared interest; there could be a separate Minister for Welsh Affairs; and Gerald Gardiner was thought to be in line for the Lord Chancellorship. Amongst likely backbenchers were Barbara Castle, who never liked Gaitskell, and Roy Jenkins, who did. All in all, pretty good prognostications; but the situation was to be radically altered by the lamentable deaths of the two brightest figures, Gaitskell himself and Bevan.

In April there was an impressive gathering of Socialist leaders from all over Europe in Stockholm to celebrate 70 years of Swedish social democracy. The Prime Minister, Tage Erlander, was host, and his guests included the Danish Prime Minister, H. C. Hansen, the Austrian Foreign Minister Bruno Kreisky, the President of the Finnish Parliament Karl August Pagerholm, Gaitskell, the Chairman of the West German Socialist Party Erich Ollenhauer, and Willy Brandt. Gaitskell was a great admirer of Scandinavian social democracy and its numerous successes in government. Brandt came on to London and discussed with the Labour National Executive and members of Parliament the dangers of Khruschev's "ultimatum" of November 1958 on Berlin, which happily turned out not to be an ultimatum after all.

In April and May, Gaitskell was involved in two brushes with the US press. The columnist Art Buchwald, writing in the Paris edition of the *New York Herald Tribune,* quoted him as voicing some provocative opinions about Macmillan at a private dinner party: "I personally don't trust Mr. Macmillan. My own personal opinion is that Mr. Macmillan is an actor, and I think all this publicity is dragging British politics to its lowest level." On disengagement in Central Europe "he felt Mr. Macmillan had taken the Gaitskell plan and used it as an original Macmillan idea. He scorned disengagement until election year. Then he suddenly invented it." Gaitskell denied that he had used any such language and insisted on a statement of apology by Buchwald. Yet I cannot help a sneaking feeling that his opinions tallied with what was quoted, even if it was highly indiscreet of Buchwald to use them. The other incident developed into a considerable rumpus. Gaitskell chose the May Day rally of some 12,000 people in Hyde Park to accuse the *Christian Science Monitor* of interfering in British internal politics because it had indulged in some speculation about the result of our next General Election. He seemed much incensed, even though the offending article had mentioned that many experts regarded Labour's election chances as nearly equal to the Conservatives'. "As a staunch supporter of Anglo-American friendship, who has never joined in the popular pastime of chucking bricks across the Atlantic," he insisted that even the slightest appearance of any American interference would be fatal. For good measure he castigated Macmillan for hypocrisy in his dealings with the US Government. The *Monitor* acknowledged Gaitskell's services to Anglo-American friendship and denied, firmly but moderately, that it had in any way suggested interference. The *New York Herald Tribune* said it was not like Gaitskell to peddle anti-American sentiments, but "Politics is politics the world around." The *New York Daily Mirror* was nasty. "Mr. Gaitskell accuses the US of interfering in British politics and he wants us to mind our own business. Not such a bad idea. Maybe it would have been a good idea in 1917 and 1941. It was this country which subsidised the Labour Government during the Prime Ministry of Clement Attlee. If the US has more respect for Prime Minister Macmillan than for Mr. Gaitskell, it is only natural," and a good deal more in the same strain. The *Washington Post* remarked that there were some misgivings about a

Labour Government, particularly if Mr. Bevan, "who seems to enjoy tweaking this country's nose at every opportunity," became Foreign Secretary. "Mr. Gaitskell should keep his shirt on." I see this as another typical Gaitskell operation. He laid about him because he sincerely thought he should. This aroused strong resentment in the short term, stronger than he expected, and moreover he exposed his flank politically. In the long term it did good by clearing the air.

Also in May, Gaitskell found it possible to accept an invitation dating back nearly a year from Dr. Nkrumah, Prime Minister of Ghana, to visit his country. By a coincidence the Commonwealth Secretary, then called the Earl of Home, was there in the course of an African tour at the same time, but he made far less impact than Gaitskell. Predictably, Gaitskell had his reservations about the political set-up; but he commented that for any newly independent African country he considered that the essentials were racial equality, democracy, and economic development, and that all of these were coming along in Ghana. He hoped that Ghana would play a full part in Commonwealth affairs. Her union—temporary, as it proved—with Guinea was her own affair. In the course of a tour of East Anglia soon after his return, he made the point that "It is no longer any good trying to resist the great wave of African nationalism which is now sweeping the continent." For him, the "great wave" metaphor; for Macmillan in January 1960, "the wind of change."

At this critical stage in the pre-election period the Labour Movement once again inflicted some painful wounds on itself, this time in the sphere of nuclear policy. In early June no less than 80 Labour back-benchers tabled a motion to the effect "that this House, noting the refusal of the French Government to permit nuclear warheads in American custody to be stockpiled in France, is equally opposed to their being stockpiled in this country, and to any transfer to Great Britain from French territory of American nuclear-weapon-carrying aircraft." At a private meeting of the Parliamentary Labour Party, Gaitskell argued strongly that if General Norstad could show that such a transfer was militarily necessary, Britain, as a faithful NATO ally, should and could not refuse. He received stalwart support from the old guard of Morrison and Shinwell, and the motion was not pressed. A few days later the Labour Party officially adopted Gaitskell's line on nuclear disarmament. This was that Britain should volunteer to give up her nuclear weapons provided that all other Powers except the US and the USSR agreed to renounce them. He explained the line to an audience of miners at Walsall on 27th June. It was a challenge to the Government to explain what was their alternative. Lord Hailsham, he said, had been abusive as always: he had said that Britain would thus become a Tibet or a Hungary. But this also amounted to abuse of the Atlantic Alliance and NATO, and an invitation to proliferation. Sensibly, Gaitskell said: "I view the spread of nuclear weapons to the nations of the world as a prospect fraught with the utmost danger." The three nuclear Powers were within sight of some agreement to stop tests. Yet France was about to explode her first atomic bomb. The truth, we now know, is that the new Labour policy was well devised and justified; but, in view of the attitude of France and China, ineffectual.

At the beginning of July the dates for Gaitskell's visit to the USSR were announced: 29th August, for ten days, then Poland. Also in the party were to be Bevan, Denis Healey, who was a strong proponent of disengagement in Central Europe, and all three wives. In the upshot these plans did not entirely come off.

Frank Cousins and his Transport and General Workers' Union were now on the rampage in opposition to the new nuclear policy, though it had been agreed not only by the Labour Party but by the TUC as such. Cousins had, in effect, now taken over the leadership of the Left from Bevan, and for the first time Gaitskell was having real difficulty with one of the big six Unions. At a press conference on 10th July, Gaitskell said that, in spite of the TGWU's declared opposition, the Party was not split. "We have a democratic constitution which involves us from time to time in arguments in public . . . But you may be sure that once the Party has decided, the decision will be loyally accepted by all concerned." Asked if "that goes for Mr. Cousins too?" Gaitskell repeated: "By all concerned." In a strong speech at Workington the next day he showed that his blood was up. "Our Party decisions are not dictated by one man, whether he be the Leader of the Party or the general secretary of the TGWU. They are made collectively, first in our elected executive after discussion, and later submitted to the vote of our annual conference." (He could have added that even that vote need not bind the Party.) In general, he said, the situation called for hard, clear, calm, and honest thinking. The whole phrase epitomises the Gaitskell style. The Conservatives, he repeated, were bankrupt of ideas on how to tackle nuclear proliferation. But the unilateralists must be clear that their policy meant Britain's leaving NATO, which was "escapist, myopic and positively dangerous to the peace of the world." Strongly as he felt against continuing H-bomb tests, "I cannot give an absolute pledge that we should never never undertake them. That might conceivably jeopardise the future security of our country, and that I will not do under any circumstances." Gaitskell pressed the same line a few days later at the Socialist International Congress at Hamburg and was supported by Willy Brandt. On his return, "pretty well satisfied with the reaction there," he said he was not surprised that a recent poll had shown that over 60 per cent of people in Britain were against Britain's giving up the bomb unless the US and USSR did so as well: "It will take time to make people realise what is at stake." Now all this was indeed hard, clear, calm, and honest thinking. The trouble with it was precisely that it was too much trouble for the electors as a whole. The Tory position of staying put, as usual, was much easier to get across and to hoist in.

Parliament rose on 29th July, and there was some speculation that Gaitskell might be Prime Minister when it reassembled. He was asked who he thought had been the

greatest peace-time Prime Minister and replied Walpole. In
this he was, without knowing it at the time, at one with Macmillan, though he gave the different reason that he had
handled a new situation well. He was frank about the tradition of revolt inside the Labour Movement, which did not
exist amongst the Tories. They were going along well precisely because Labour's Welfare State had disrupted the traditional political loyalties. As some of the working class became better off, they turned Tory. In the rural areas however
"cap-touching snobbery" was going, though I must comment here that ten years later in the shires it has still not
gone. Snobbery, said Gaitskell, was still a great force behind
the Tories; that too is true of today. He was confident that
his Shadow Cabinet was fully equipped to exercise power. He
exuded confidence himself. After a tour in Kent a couple
of weeks later, he said: "We shall have a majority." During
the tour, on which his wife went with him as she frequently
did, he did not neglect various electoral-campaign-type gimmicks, such as a visit to an old folks' home, where eleven
inmates were over 90, and a reunion with the leading Socialist citizens of Chatham, where he had first stood for Parliament in 1935 and failed.

Shortly before setting off for Moscow, Gaitskell again defined his nuclear policy. He said that the prevention of proliferation was the most important objective: true, of course,
but personally I find a certain naïveté in the idea that our
own renunciation could ever have achieved this. Britain
would remain firmly in NATO, but without her own
H-bomb stocks. Blue Streak, which was intended to be our
independent missile with nuclear war-head, should be scrapped, at a saving of some £500 m. to the British taxpayer;
the military atomic research installations at Aldermaston and
elsewhere would go too. He agreed that the US Government
would have decisive control of the West's nuclear capability,
but as well as the "nuclear club" there would be a powerful
"non-nuclear club." Things have turned out rather differ-
ently. The day before his departure he met for the first time

the US Secretary of State Mr. Herter in London and had a long talk. He also wrote to President Eisenhower, expressing his regret that he would be away during his visit to London and received a cordial reply.

On 29th August, the Gaitskell party arrived in Moscow in a Soviet jet airliner for their ten days' visit. His wife recalls today what an enjoyable and stimulating trip it was. The other members of the party were Bevan as Shadow Foreign Secretary, on his fifth visit, while it was Gaitskell's first; the Healeys; and David Ennals, who was then secretary of the international department at Transport House. They were the guests of the so-called inter-parliamentary group of the Supreme Soviet. On arrival, Gaitskell said that he wanted to explain to the Soviet leaders Labour's plans for a non-nuclear club and for disengagement in Central Europe, which he did not think they clearly understood as yet. Bevan said that every time he came to the USSR he found it more exciting and that he brought the greetings of the British working-class movement to the people of the Soviet Union. Evidently, all hard feelings over the fracas at the 1956 dinner were forgiven and forgotten. The following day they attended an exhibition of Soviet economic achievements, and farmer Bevan indulged in some badinage with an elderly Ukrainian farmer about their respective cows' milk production. After two days in Leningrad, the party returned to Moscow for a two-hour talk with Foreign Minister Gromyko, which both sides described as very friendly. So was the meeting between Khruschev and the British politicians in the Kremlin on 4th September, when they discussed Berlin, a European neutral zone, the dangers of nuclear proliferation, and the banning of nuclear tests, as well as Anglo-Soviet relations. Khruschev had allowed the press in for the opening five minutes, which were passed in heavy banter about how Gromyko, who was also present, should be drowned because he gave him no peace, and the virtues of vodka and its US rival, bourbon, described by Gromyko in English as "nuclear whiskey." The talks lasted no less than three and a half hours, and an informal atmosphere was maintained. A considerable degree of agreement manifested itself, not least on the desirability of an early Summit conference. In this connexion Gaitskell warmly welcomed Khruschev's forthcoming visit to President Eisenhower. Khruschev did all the talking on the Soviet side, with only brief interventions by Suslov and Gromyko. On Berlin the two sides agreed to differ. Gaitskell and Bevan came away convinced that agreement on a ban on the testing of nuclear weapons was in the offing.

On 6th September, Gaitskell and Bevan did a combined act on Moscow television to an estimated ten million viewers. Apart from giving their views on the great international issues, they remarked on Labour's achievements, such as the National Health Service, and deplored the ignorance shown even in high quarters in the Soviet Union about contemporary Britain and not least, in connexion with "colonialism," the fact that we had given independence to half a billion people since World War II. Gaitskell freely admitted that most British people, for their part, were ignorant about life in the USSR. As a whole, this was both a refreshing and a puzzling performance for its Soviet audience.

Meanwhile, Macmillan had been craftily developing his election strategy. In Gaitskell's absence he appeared on television with President Eisenhower, thus impressing on his audience his standing as a world figure. And in the middle of the night of 7–8th September, Gaitskell told reporters in the Sovietskaya Hotel that he had received a message "in confidence" from the Prime Minister which necessitated his leaving for London the next day and completely missing out the planned visit to Poland, which he regretted very much. I have little doubt that he muttered a few short Anglo-Saxon words about Macmillan under his breath. Later on 8th September he admitted under pressure from reporters that the message was to the effect that 8th October had been fixed as polling day. And the following day, armed with a four-volume English edition of Sholokhov's *And Quiet Flows the*

Don, which Khruschev had sent him in return for a complete collection of Shaw's plays (not, reciprocally, in Russian), he and his party boarded a Soviet aircraft for London.

Gaitskell, with the help of his wife and Bevan, conjured up the atmosphere of his talks with Khruschev in an independent Television interview on 14th September. Khruschev was a genial character who occasionally enjoyed a bit of a row; he should, in his earthy way, get on well with the Americans when he visited them. Allowing for a slight difference between earthiness and the Wykehamical stance, I wonder whether this does not go for Gaitskell too and account for his own good relations with Khruschev as well as the Americans? On foreign affairs, said Gaitskell, Khruschev was very shrewd. He had clearly gained confidence in the last three years, and he was undoubtedly popular in his country. Dora Gaitskell added that Mrs. Khruschev was very much a person in her own right and incidentally spoke good English.

The run-up to the General Election on 8th October 1959 had been long; the actual campaign was short. Macmillan's strategy and tactics were admirable. The half-truth that "you've never had it so good" had been pressed home by a large propaganda machine for months on end. Macmillan himself was at the height of his powers, in both domestic and international politics. Gaitskell was highly respected; but the programme he had to offer was not all that tempting, especially to numerous floating voters who suspected that Socialist fair shares for all might imply a rather thinner slice off the bacon for themselves. Some of the Socialist intellectual leaders' thinking seemed a bit abstruse: there was no such difficulty over the Conservative leaders, who in any case only included a couple of intellectuals and whose line appeared broadly to be: it's a free-for-all, and may the best man win. And they were united, at any rate in public; while Labour were not.

By all objective standards the result was a disaster for Labour. Up to a few weeks before the election, Gaitskell had been confident of victory, though not indulging in hubris. Then the public opinion polls began to edge the other way. John Harris, who had at the age of 29 been his propaganda adviser for some months, has told me how, right up to polling day, Gaitskell thought Labour would win. Yet as soon as the first results began to come in on 8th October, not least that of the perennial barometer seat Billericay, Harris had to tell him that it had not come off. Indeed it had not, and Gaitskell conceded victory to the Conservatives at an early stage. Their percentage of the total vote was static; but the number of votes cast for them had increased by some 450,000 to a record, for them, of 13¾ million, only slightly below Labour's 1951 all time high. Above all, the seats won had gone up by 21 from 344 to 365. Labour's vote had diminished by nearly 200,000, and their number of seats from 277 to 258. It was their worst performance since 1935, and the number of seats won had now gone down for the fourth election in succession. Of these, they had lost three, a rare and lamentable record. Given luck, the Tories could now prolong their rule from eight to thirteen years. And they did.

These were the facts and the prospects for Gaitskell and his Party in October 1959. The question was whether they would be shattered and splintered by them, or inspired by adversity to a new and successful strategy. The answer, in the short term, was neither. But they were to climb back, laboriously, all the same.

TEN

Fighting Back

THE DAY AFTER the election Gaitskell met the press at Transport House and appeared on television. Both friend and foe agreed that he performed with dignity. He described Labour's defeat as "neither a landslide nor a disaster, but a setback." He believed that the policies put to the nation were right: here was the familiar logic and stubbornness at work. The margin, he said, had been "a very narrow one indeed." On this point the Tories could afford to smile since they had a clear majority in the House of 100. What Gaitskell meant was that the gap in votes cast was narrow. This too was somewhat irrelevant and also inaccurate since the gap had increased by some 650,000. He went on that he had hoped to gain some 40 or 50 seats, which would have given Labour a slender majority. The swing against Labour had come chiefly in the South and Midlands: it could be recouped the next time. Here he was right, but what a long time it was to be. Then a typically fighting statement: "We have attacked, and on this occasion we have been repulsed. We shall attack again and again until we win." This style was to be repeated in two of his greatest Conference speeches. Gaitskell paid a tribute to the organisation of the election campaign by Transport House, headed by Morgan Phillips, and in the constituencies, which he thought much better than in 1955. On this sad day he raised a smile when asked whether a remark which Herbert Morrison was said to have made represented the truth: that he was out of touch with ordinary people. "This is rather like the question: 'Have you left off beating your wife?' If I say 'yes' I am rather silly. If I say 'no' I am pompous and arrogant."

The Gaitskell personality was under a good deal of scrutiny from various angles at this time. A report was published in parts of the press that, during the campaign in which he had attacked tax-free capital gains on the stock market, he had spent £6,000 on shares in an investment trust called "Investing in Success" Equities Ltd. He flatly denied this and explained that he had applied for the shares some weeks before but withdrawn his application. He had always said that people had the right to invest their money in the most profitable way, but they should pay tax on any capital gains. All this was a little puzzling for the vast majority of Labour supporters, who would never have £6,000 to invest anyway, nor indeed ever possess a stock or a share. When addressing the Parliamentary Press Gallery Luncheon Club on 11th November, he remarked that he had frequently been described as dry, schoolmasterish, "toffee-nosed." During the election campaign he had admitted that actually he enjoyed life; so he became overnight a rake. "But now," referring to a recent caricature, "we have hit a very happy medium. I am the 'Mona Lisa' with the mysterious smile. Nobody knows what goes on behind it." He also remarked, provocatively, that for a politician the television could serve as a useful corrective to the press on occasions. The *New Statesman,* which for all its traditional leftism is perhaps more inclined towards destructive rather than constructive criticism, commented peevishly that "the leadership appeared to be manipulated by a small and much disliked group of anti-Socialist zealots who do not only oppose, but even scorn, most of the traditional causes which inspire the rank and file."

The Annual Conference had been postponed because of the election—no doubt Macmillan also had this little piece of disruption in mind when he fixed the date—and gathered at Blackpool on 28th and 29th November. Not surprisingly, it was a bit of a shambles. However, Gaitskell seized the opportunity to make a speech that went to the heart of several matters, fairly and squarely putting the cat amongst the pigeons, of whom there were many as self-confident as those heavy birds which fly in your face in London parks. If, as so often, Gaitskell's tactics seemed unnecessarily rough to many members of the Movement, the long-term strategy was good; now was the time to seize the bull by the horns, for the Party were certain to have all too long a period in opposition during which they could, and must, sort themselves out. Better some constructive disagreement and disunity now than later when another election was impending. On the burning and self-destructive question of Clause 4, for instance, Gaitskell remarked to Griffiths one day that it was imperative to renovate it. Faithful old Griffiths was shocked: Gaitskell, he said, must surely know that Clause 4 was "an article of faith" to his generation. Gaitskell replied sternly: "Maybe, but you know that we do not intend, any of us, to implement Clause 4 fully, and I regard it as my duty to say so to the party and the country." A less thorough Leader would have drawn the opposite conclusion from the same premise, as did many of the rank and file: that in that case there was no reason to cause further disruption and disunity by arguing out in public what was in practice a foregone conclusion.

Barbara Castle, the Chairman, opened proceedings on a low note. "Despite a good programme, better organisation than we ever had, and brilliant leadership by Hugh Gaitskell, we lost." As she was far from seeing eye to eye with him on a good many topics, this was a loyal tribute indeed. Gaitskell opened the debate on the General Election and spoke with both cogency and passion. It is not difficult to criticise the way in which he made some of his points, but it is impossible to question his courage. He started with a little joke. One lady had told him that Labour had lost because twenty-five years earlier they had rejected the Douglas social credit theory, owing to the sinister influence of—himself. One principal reason for the defeat was the most expensive and professional Tory propaganda campaign costing "hundreds of thousands if not millions" [sic]; against this Labour's puny £20,000 was helpless. (The official Labour estimates, pub-

lished later, were that the Conservative Party had spent
£468,000, while industry had contributed another £1,435,000
to their cause.) The Labour programme had been criticised,
amongst other things, for lacking idealism; yet it aimed at
helping old people in hardship, opening the doors of educational opportunity, hastening freedom for colonial peoples,
fighting racial injustice. He could see nothing in that particular criticism. "I believe our programme was excellent
. . . It disproved the idea that we must always adopt an
extremist line." He then commented on the grisly record of
three successive elections lost and four losses in the numbers
of seats—"almost unprecedented in British political history."
The basic cause was a great change in the economic and
social scene; everywhere the labour force was moving away
from heavy physical work towards distribution and staff jobs:
three or four years later he would also have used the word
"technology." Secondly, there was the absence of serious unemployment or even the fear of it. "We take great pride in
the part we played in bringing this about," but few bothered now to be grateful for the Welfare State. Living conditions would continue to improve, even under the Tories. The
affluent society had brought a notable increase in home
comforts and pleasures—holidays, cars, the telly, the fridge,
the glossy magazines. "I fancy that our failure was largely
a failure to win support from the women. We must pay special attention to this." Now, for the future, "It is our job
to get back into power as quickly as possible." There were
some suggested methods that "we can toss out of the window
straight away." One was a pact with the Liberals, who had
increased their vote by nearly a million, but uselessly as their
tally of seats remained at six. Another was to change the
Party's name, presumably to "Socialist" or "Social Democratic": he was wise enough to see that, if this might please
some middle-class voters, it would fatally alienate the Trade
Unions and all those still proud of sporting the "cloth cap."
Thirdly, there was the suggestion that the Labour Party
should break with the Unions. Well, no doubt unofficial

strikes had damaged the Party, and of course the Unions' reputation too; but—optimistically—they would put their house in order. This passage, which does not on the face of it appear all that provocative, came as a thunderclap. For throughout the weeks since the lost election Gaitskell had done two things: kept silent on major issues himself and encouraged ratiocination by his Labour colleagues. It was his personal friends like Jay and Gordon Walker who had put forward precisely these ideas in the magazine *Forward* and run into stiff opposition of themselves personally, and the "Hampstead set" as a whole, from the Left. Gaitskell had slapped them down.

He went on to say that Labour must make a special effort now to attract younger people; and to counteract the Tories' "monstrous falsehood" that they, and not the Tories, were a class party. To appeal to the young, they must put more emphasis on colonial freedom, individual freedom from ham-handed bureaucracy and bumbledom, sport and the arts, and less on heavy political doctrine. The base must be broadened, and "we have to show that we are a modern-minded, mid-20th century party, looking to the future. Obviously, the appearance of disunity must be avoided." (Unfortunately, it was more than an appearance; and this one was a long time coming.)

All this was good, general doctrine. Now Gaitskell became more specific. Nationalisation had lost Labour votes because, first, pernicious Tory propaganda had blamed increased costs in the nationalised industry on the fact of nationalisation itself, and secondly "Thousands, and perhaps millions, of voters were induced to think that we intended to nationalise any and every private firm, out of a doctrinaire belief in public ownership." This was, of course, all rubbish and brought him to the crux. "I agree with neither of the two extreme points of view—stop where we are, or nationalise the lot." Now he ventured on a definition of the base principles of British democratic Socialism. First came what his mentor G. D. H. Cole had called "a broad human movement on behalf of the bottom dog" (for my taste an inept metaphor), not only at home but abroad. Secondly, social justice and an equitable distribution of wealth and income: not "equal," he specified, because that would call for a revolution. Thirdly, a classless society without snobbery and privilege. Fourthly, fundamental equality of all races and peoples, and an end to arrogant white supremacy. Fifthly, an essential element of personal idealism (the contrary, though he did not specify, of Tory self-arrogated "gentleman's honour" and "integrity"). Sixthly, public interest ahead of private interest. And finally, freedom and democratic self-government for all. Now general nationalisation and the other Party shibboleths—he did not use the word—were merely means to these ends. Bevan had put it well: Labour needed to control "the commanding heights of the economy."

Now, into top gear. The Party Constitution was today forty years old. It made no mention at all of colonial freedom, race relations, disarmament, full employment, or planning. For the reasons already given "Clause 4 cannot possibly be regarded as adequate and it lays us open to continual misrepresentation. I do not conceive it as my duty today to be nice and noncontroversial. I am sure that the Webbs and Arthur Henderson would have been horrified to know that their words were treated as sacrosanct forty years later in utterly changed conditions." This was the head-on approach with a vengeance; but who, even amongst the most stick-in-the-mud Trade Unionists, could fail to recognise, when they had recovered from the onslaught, that it represented forward-looking commonsense? Gaitskell then quoted one of the Grand Old Men of Socialism, R. H. Tawney, then a lively 79 years old: "We should treat sanctified formulae with judicious irreverence, and start by deciding precisely what is the end in view." (What a shame that more of us have not regulated our lives on these lines!) Finally, the National Executive Committee must get cracking straight away on the re-thinking. "Our defeat, comrades, must be a supreme challenge to keep up the spirit of attack, the spirit of attack again and again and again, until we win." This echoed some

previous oratorical flourishes and foreshadowed the next
year's peroration that was to ring round the world. The
speech received prolonged applause; but some of the sentiments aroused bitter opposition, not least from Frank
Cousins, who wanted Gaitskell out. There was some angry
discussions. As usual, the left-wingers Barbara Castle, Harold
Wilson, and Anthony Greenwood headed the Constituency
Parties' poll. But both in its positive ideas, and in a negative
way, it put the seal on Gaitskell's pact with Bevan; for the
hard fact, which they both knew, was that if Bevan had
wished, he could almost certainly have overthrown Gaitskell
on this occasion. He refrained, and now became both Treasurer and Deputy Leader of the Party.

In a BBC programme on 3rd December, Gaitskell took a
bit of a pounding and was closely questioned on most of the
leading issues by Socialists from France, West Germany, and
Sweden and by the foreign editor of the *New York Herald
Tribune*. Was his personal position endangered by Bevan?
He replied rather acidly that he did not think so. Nor did he
think they differed fundamentally on nationalisation, though
they might on the extent and timing. "I would certainly not
say that there was any basic split in the Party," with emphasis on the word "basic." He could not agree that the
Labour Party should become more independent of the
Unions, who in any case would not try to dictate to the
Party, although many organs of the press were making mis-
chief over this. The interview certainly showed how widespread were doubts about the unity and morale of the Labour Movement, and undeniably with good reason.

A grim battle over the future of the Party was now engaged behind the scenes as well as in public; and the first
stage alone, mainly concerned with Clause 4, continued for
over three months. In Gaitskell's first newspaper interview
since the electoral defeat, he told the *Observer* on 19th December that he thought the Opposition had cranked up in
lively fashion during the first session of the new Parliament.
Richard Marsh and Anthony Wedgwood Benn had distinguished themselves in debate. Harking back to Blackpool, he

admitted that his speech had been calculated to provoke strong dissent in some quarters; and he then developed again, in detail, his own position on nationalisation and Clause 4. As for his definition of the principles of Socialism, he remarked snidely: "I have never heard that the classless society was a Tory principle"; and Tory policy in East and Central Africa had shown equal cynicism about racial equality. Finally, "so long as we persist with the job of modernisation, I am confident we shall win the next election."

As if all these Party political activities were not enough, Gaitskell set off on 30th December for a visit of over three weeks to the United States and the West Indies. No sooner was his back turned than *Tribune* jumped on it. His proposals on Clause 4 should be rejected, and once that had been done he should resign. A stupid remark by Frank Cousins was quoted as if it were a pearl of wisdom: "You can have public ownership without Socialism; but you cannot have Socialism without public ownership." In fact, of course, Gaitskell entirely agreed and was trying to get the question of degree and timing into these thick skulls. But he proceeded serenely on his tour. In Pennsylvania he tried to dispel some widely held ideas about the Labour Party, such as that they were mostly pacifists, or commie fellow-travellers, or international revolutionaries. While he relaxed to some extent in Jamaica and Trinidad, Michael Foot—attractive and impotent as ever—informed eight million viewers on *Panorama* that he personally intended to oust Gaitskell. By a coincidence the passage in Anthony Eden's memoirs where he described Gaitskell's succession to Attlee as "a national misfortune" was published the same day. At this point Nye Bevan fell ill, and Gaitskell cut short his tour to return to England. Troubles were indeed coming not as single spies, but in battalions. At the same time Macmillan was adding to his stature by making his "wind of change" speech in the Union of South Africa. On Gaitskell's return, his first tactical move was to indicate that he, for his part, was not interested in remaining as Leader if he did not get his way over Clause

4. Even his stalwart supporters on the right of the Unions, who were already a little hurt that he had not consulted them before his Blackpool speech, began to have their doubts at his intransigence. Gaitskell riposted, in the National Executive Committee and in public speeches, by dinning it in that it was not he who was intransigent, but the grass-roots— and intellectual fringe—fundamentalists. For instance, he went over all the ground again in a long speech at Nottingham on 13th February 1960, to which *Tribune* responded, without a tittle of justification, that he had changed his tune and was now speaking with the tongue of men and of angels, or rather of Bevan and Barbara. In spite of critical declarations by Wilson, Greenwood, and Crossman, he stuck to his guns in another firm statement at a dinner of former students of Ruskin College on 22nd February and threw in supporting speeches at Cambridge, Oxford, and Leeds Universities in the following days for good measure.

The climax of the discussions on Clause 4 in the National Executive Committee was approaching, if slowly. On 16th March the Committee approved a long statement which not only textually reproduced Clause 4, "the first full declaration of Party Objects, adopted in 1918," but added another which "amplifies and clarifies Party Objects in the light of post-war developments and the historic achievements of the first majority Labour Government." This consisted of a most comprehensive list of principles and objectives, from (a) to (b), which were largely drafted by Gaitskell and were wholly satisfactory from his point of view. Then, the tiny sting in the tail. After ruminating for three months longer: "At its meeting on 13th July 1960 the National Executive Committee passed the following: The NEC resolves not to proceed with any amendment or addition to Clause 4 of the Constitution, but declares that the statement which is adopted on 16th March is a valuable expression of the aims of the Labour Party in the second half of the 20th century and commends it to the Conference accordingly." Everyone had won; there could be backpatting all round. We shall see that the Conference gave little trouble. Gaitskell sailed onwards and could now devote most of his energies to other matters.

As always, foreign affairs played a prominent part in his life. He contributed largely to a declaration by the NEC in February on the Arab-Israel dispute and followed this up by going with Sam Watson and others to the Socialist International Council meeting in Haifa in April. On 27th March at Largs he spoke strongly to the annual conference of the Scottish Labour Party in favour of accepting the concessions, and also conditions, made by the Soviet delegation in the talks on nuclear tests. "Today we are at a turning-point in world affairs. The great Powers have a new chance, which may perhaps be a last one. The road to peace is open." After this, the general disarmament conference could get going; and thirdly, the Summit. He also slammed apartheid in the Union of South Africa. The style, this time, was emotional. And the dour Scots lapped it up. Throughout April, May, and June, the NEC, in consultation with the TUC, flogged out the crucial paper on Foreign Policy and Defence, and Gaitskell was deeply involved. This was to lead to high drama at the Annual Conference. Meanwhile, he was given no peace in the public arena, where he was constantly and sharply attacked by his own side.

In March, Gaitskell had removed Crossman from his position as Shadow Pensions Minister because he had spoken publicly in favour of unilateral nuclear disarmament by Britain. He was then attacked by that persistent gnat, Michael Foot, in *Tribune* and also by J. P. W. Mallalieu in the *New Statesman* for lack of leadership in not (it was all tremendously negative) reprimanding Douglas Jay and Woodrow Wyatt for their criticisms, from the right wing, of the National Executive's new constitutional statement. Basically, of course, these were renewed attacks on Gaitskell's group of upper-middle-class, well-off, Hampstead-type intellectuals to which group Michael Foot belonged technically but by no means in spirit. Then A. J. P. Taylor alleged vaguely that Gaitskell had forbidden a member of the Shadow Cabinet to take part in the Aldermaston march; he would not say whom or in which year, and Gaitskell, then briefly in the US, seemed puzzled but not too disturbed by the whole affair. The march itself was a great demonstration, and a breakthrough for the unilateralists came when the Co-operative Party Conference came out in their favour. One Robert Willis, then vice-chairman of the TUC, said that Gaitskell had insulted the sincere marchers because he had declared that he would rather consult a Gallup poll than their goodselves for a sensible opinion on nukes. While in Washington, he had spoken, together with two other distinguished Opposition leaders in the shape of Adlai Stevenson and Lester Pearson, to American newspaper editors on the role of the Opposition everywhere. "What we need," he declared virilely, "is party politicians"; in other words, an Opposition's duty was to oppose, all along the line. He certainly satisfied that need, through and through.

While Gaitskell was away on Socialist International business in Israel at the end of April, the Government announced the abandonment of Blue Streak. Gaitskell had recommended this for some time. Critics seized on recent speeches by Harold Wilson, Shadow Chancellor, and George Brown, Defence, to pretend that Gaitskell's line on nuclear policy had been scuppered. The truth was different. The line which the Labour spokesmen would take on the matter had been agreed at a Shadow Cabinet, with Gaitskell in the chair, before his departure. He was met at London Airport on his return by Harold Wilson. He declared roundly: "It is complete nonsense to say that there is any crisis in the Labour Party." Both Brown and Wilson had made "extremely fine speeches." The Labour Party was not going pacifist, unilateralist, or anti-NATO. They would have to think through the complicated issues raised by the new situation, that was all. Asked about his alleged Aldermaston march veto, he replied snappishly—and who shall blame him—"Mr. Greenwood has cleared all that up. It is quite ridiculous." Gaitskell's position as Leader was decidedly rocky at this time, and it seemed clear that he would have to lean heavily on Nye Bevan, whose health was now, in May, improving. He was confident enough, a few days later, to jest that he understood that Labour had a majority inside the Conservative club at South Leeds.

On the eve of the Summit talks, for which Gaitskell had pressed for so long, he made a long speech in the House which was a combination of statesmanship and, it must be said, lack of realism. His object, he said, in this debate—provided out of Opposition time—was to encourage the Government in their efforts at this critical meeting. He dealt at some length with the recent shooting down of the U2. While espionage of all kinds was a fact of life, it seemed stupid of the US Government to have taken just this risk at just this moment. However, Khruschev appeared to be keeping cool. (Not for long, as it transpired.) He hoped to see the Summit result in a ban on nuclear tests and a boost to the 10-Power disarmament commission, which at present was "in full disarray." The two most populous nations in the world, China and India, must be brought in on these talks. Also Britain and France must be brought together to devise a scheme for preventing nuclear proliferation; after all, China would produce nuclear weapons soon. A zone of controlled disarmament in Central Europe was much to be desired. In general, the leisurely diplomatic procedure of the nineteenth century was no longer adequate. The Foreign Secretary should say to his colleagues: "Hurry, hurry, that is what the peoples of the world demand." In the upshot Khruschev hurried all too much, and in the wrong direction. As soon as the Summit had assembled in Paris on 16th May, he taxed President Eisenhower with the U2 affair; the President, contrary to custom in these matters and contrary to what Khruschev expected, came clean and admitted responsibility. Khruschev blew his top, and the abortive Summit was finished three days later. Gaitskell commented that the collapse of the Summit was a great shock and a bitter disappointment. Khrushchev had behaved in an intemperate and offensive manner, but had at least indicated that he would continue negotiations on banning nuclear tests and on general disarmament. We must press on with these, and also with strengthening NATO. This theme he emphasized in a series of speeches in the next fortnight, in the Commons, on television, and elsewhere. All NATO Powers should have responsible Cabinet Ministers as their representatives on the NATO Council, rather than feeble Ambassadors. He seized the opportunity of taking a poke at his unilateralist adversaries in the Party: it would be both unwise and dishonest to give up the British bomb and yet rely on the US to protect us. In fact, "ban the bomb" and you would get a Communist Europe. "I personally, do not want to live in a Communist state." In the House on 30th May he lectured Macmillan and Lloyd on the inadequacy of their efforts at the Summit and after, and said that, since the fiasco, there was all the more scope for British initiative in bringing the US and the USSR together. He was warmly applauded by his followers.

This was a period of intensive struggle inside the Labour Movement. As Gaitskell put it to the Durham Labour Women's annual gala in June, "It would not be a bad idea if we rationed the number of speeches made attacking our own personalities in the ratio of one to ten in attacking the Tory policies." But it was just a phase, he said. On 24th June the Hampstead Labour Party, Gaitskell's own home party, put an end to a call by one of its members for Gaitskell's resignation. The resolution was defeated by an overwhelming majority. It was condemned to "lie on the table." More important, however, was the fact that all this time Cousins and his unilateralists were baying for Gaitskell's blood. Konni Zilliacus expressed it succinctly in a pamphlet called *Anatomy of a Sacred Cow* published by the Campaign for Nuclear Disarmament in July. "His sincere and strongly held economic and political convictions put him so far to the Right as to make him almost indistinguishable from a Liberal in home affairs and from a Tory in foreign policy. That is his personal tragedy and the Party's misfortune." At a press conference at the House, Zilliacus said that but for Mr. Gaitskell the Labour Party would be following a unilateralist line, and he predicted a large majority in favour of unilateralism at the Party Conference. He was not far wrong there. Gaitskell was not much perturbed. He well knew that support from Zilliacus for any given policy was akin to the kiss of death. More seriously, death struck Nye Bevan on 6th July, and Gaitskell was deprived of a man who had become a wise and vigorous helper. George Brown, who had made his mark as long ago as 1939 at the Annual Conference, and since 1945 in the House as an energetic leader of the Trade Union group, succeeded him as Deputy Leader in due course.

July 1960 was in several ways a crucial month for the Movement and for Gaitskell. After months of discussions between the NEC, the TUC, and the PLP, a massive joint statement on Foreign Policy and Defence was issued by the NEC and the General Council of the TUC, for eventual discussion at the Annual Conference. This started by saying that two fiascos—the break-up of the Summit and the cancellation of Blue Streak—had left the Sandys-Macmillan policies in disarray, and new thinking was necessary. In fact, however, the proposals contained little that was new. It was admitted that for practical purposes Britain could not really remain for much longer an "independent nuclear power"; but Gaitskell's influence ensured that emphasis was placed on our duties as a loyal member of NATO. He made these points in a speech at Bristol and was rewarded with an attack in *Pravda*, which said that, having convinced himself a year earlier of the Russian people's peaceful intentions, he had now returned to the stale propaganda of the Cold War. The joint document was to lead to a most lively discussion at Scarborough in October. So was a report by the General Secretary on Labour in the Sixties, which the NEC received also in July and commended to Conference. In the PLP, meanwhile, Gaitskell received an overwhelming vote of confidence.

On 28th July he made a heavy attack on Macmillan's appointment of Home as Foreign Secretary, on grounds both of his personal inadequacy and of the necessity that that particular Minister should perform in the Commons. He used satire, ridicule, and straight crushing argument. Everyone knew, he said, that the House of Commons held sole responsibility for foreign affairs. He quoted at length from Anthony Eden's memoirs, *Full Circle,* his reasons for not appointing the Marquess of Salisbury Foreign Secretary, well qualified though he was. He rounded on Macmillan: he, at that stage, had warmly supported Eden and, of course, was appointed Foreign Secretary himself. Now as Prime Minister he had changed his tune and appointed an earl. Home, said Gaitskell, could not honestly be called "the best available Foreign Secretary"; Rab Butler was far better qualified. Even Sandys or Macleod could fill the bill better. "Have we got a caretaker Foreign Secretary? Is that all it is about?" Home had been in favour of appeasement before the war, and this would scarcely help us to improve relations with the USSR, as we hoped to do. Or was it the case that the Prime Minister would in practice do the job? He recalled Bevan's immortal phrase: "Why bother with the monkey when the organ-grinder is here?" and mentioned the apposite metaphors of the ventriloquist and his dummy, the puppeteer and his creatures. Actually, it seemed that there would be treble control, with Lord Privy Seal Heath understudying the other two. This was a thoroughly bad arrangement in every way. If puppets there must be, "I would prefer to have the puppet show in the House of Commons." Needless to say the Labour motion was defeated by a large margin.

The Conference motion had been fixed for 3rd–7th October, and September was spent in feuding and sparring within the Labour Movement. In spite of Cousins, the TUC narrowly approved the official policy statement on defence. When asked for his view on this vote, Gaitskell offered "no comment." He declared that the crisis in the Movement would be over by the end of the Conference: he was excessively optimistic here. Speaking at Battersea on 25th September, he went so far as to say that if the policy statement were not approved, the Party might well go neutralist and pacifist. There were some cries of "nonsense" and also some applause in favour of Britain's quitting NATO. This was a comprehensive speech, in which he once more put great emphasis on the United Nations and our duty to support it. The speech's mixed reception can only have confirmed his conviction that the NEC were in for a rough time on defence questions at Conference. In a television discussion on "Britain—ally or neutral?" filmed in London a fortnight before but shown in the US on the same day, Gaitskell criticised the US Government both for relying too much on nuclear weapons and for isolating China. (He erred, not for the first or last time, in assuming that China would jump at the opportunity of joining the UN if offered it.) His companions on the programme were a curiously assorted group: Mrs. Eleanor Roosevelt, Bertrand Russell, and Lord Boothby. Not surprisingly, the President's widow and the Earl were sharply at odds on how to cope with Communism. In a laudatory "personal view" of Gaitskell published on 1st October, Lord Pakenham wrote that he had been surprised during the 1959 election campaign to discover "what a ferocious partisan my mild-mannered friend of thirty years had become." He had taken the defeat with much dignity, but since then he had had a hard time and much buffeting about. "Hugh Gaitskell has never failed to make a first-class speech on a first-class occasion, with the possible exception of his Blackpool effort last year."

However that might be, Gaitskell was going to make no mistake in 1960. One of his friends has referred to his "love-hate relationship" with the Annual Conferences, and it is not a bad description. Gaitskell himself accused the press more than once of over-dramatising some of his political activities. But the truth is that he loved the drama of the Conferences, as he did in a different style that of the House, and threw himself into it body and soul. By October 1960 he was absolutely fed up with the unilateralists and what he considered their perverse, disruptive stupidity. He was never one to suffer fools gladly, except innocent fools. So he went for them hammer and tongs. Did he win? As we shall see, no and yes.

There was electric tension in the air as the hundreds of delegates converged on Scarborough. Never have the complexities of the constitution of the Labour Movement on the one hand, and of Gaitskell's character on the other, been more sharply manifested. True, the NEC had approved the defence policy statement; but equally it was clear that a defeat for the NEC at Conference was on the cards. George Brown, always Gaitskell's faithful lieutenant, had suggested certain compromise proposals in a recent article. Other members of Gaitskell's circle begged and pressed him to bend just a little, to accept some honourable compromise. Wedgwood Benn resigned theatrically from the NEC at their first meeting in Scarborough: Gaitskell was very cross and expressed the view that Wedgie had never grown out of being an undergraduate. And through it all he remained absolutely adamant.

Proceedings opened quietly enough on 3rd October. Gaitskell paid a fine tribute to Nye Bevan, all the finer for its frankness. "It is well known that for a period after 1951 relations between Aneurin Bevan and myself were badly strained. I am very glad that for the last four years of his life we were able to work in an intimate relationship together. I particularly enjoyed the visit we paid to Russia last year. Nye was in tremendous form throughout the whole of those 10 days. He never disguised his views on some aspects of the Soviet régime." That afternoon at the traditional Fabian Society tea party, Gaitskell said that he did not consider the Liberals a serious danger provided that Labour settled its internal difficulties, which he hoped would happen in the next day or two. "A great deal of the arguments on principles have been tremendously confused." He thought Liberals could be Liberals for only one reason—the snobbery which prevented them from joining Labour. The following day the usual left-wingers were duly elected at the top of the Constituency Parties' poll, in the shape of Barbara Castle, Tony Greenwood, and Harold Wilson. The NEC's report on Labour in the Sixties, on which Wilson wound up, was approved with acclamation.

On 5th October the Joint Statement on Foreign Policy and Defence of the NEC and the TUC was moved by Sam Watson, and a wide debate followed. A great deal of heat was generated. Cousins put forward a rival, unilateralist resolution. Gaitskell wound up, at length. He began in a deceptively cool manner. He was, he said, going to try to lower the temperature a little. He listed all the points on which delegates were agreed: the United Nations, disarmament, disengagement in Central Europe, China, the banning of nuclear tests, the necessity for changes in NATO, the prevention of nuclear proliferation, the stopping of British production of nuclear weapons. But "we disagree about what is called unilateral nuclear disarmament." His own opinion, he said reasonably, was that this was not a matter of principle and "morality," as the CND claimed, but of a careful balance of the various factors, economic, military, technical, and so on. As long as the USSR had nuclear weapons, the West must have them too. The unilateralists in effect relied on the US to protect us; but if we withdrew from NATO, we should lose our influence on them as an ally, and moreover they might well withdraw too. West Germany's influence would replace ours. Khruschev would not start an aggressive war, but short of that the Communists' policy was constantly expansionist. He also believed that NATO was our best hope of improving East-West relations. Labour opposed the arming of West Germany with nuclear weapons, as indeed did the Social Democratic Party also. But it was unrealistic to say that she should not be armed at all. The Amalgamated Engineering Union had put in a resolution which amounted to pro-neutralism, "and I must ask Conference to reject it." Similarly, the Transport and General Workers' Union's resolution, pressed by Frank Cousins and backed by sixty other resolutions demanding withdrawal from NATO, must be rejected. At this point Gaitskell shifted into top gear and really got cracking. "There is one other possibility of which I have read much—that the issue here is not really defence at all but the leadership of this Party." Then, categorically: "The place to decide the leadership is not here but in the

Parliamentary Party." Giving Cousins fair warning: "Frank Cousins has said that this is not the end of the problem. I agree with him." Everyone knew that the vast majority of the PLP supported the policy document and opposed unilateralism. Here he gave rein to real anger. "So what do you expect them to do? To go back on the pledges they gave to the people who elected them from their constituencies?" Were they to support unilateralism "like well-behaved sheep"? They would not do so, for the reason that they were men of conscience and honour. "People of the so-called Right and so-called Centre have every justification for having a conscience, as well as people of the so-called Left. Do you think that we can become overnight the pacifists, unilateralists, and fellow-travellers that other people are? How wrong can you be? As wrong as you are about the attitude of the British people." Most of the votes, of course, were predetermined; and he thought this a bad system, which should be looked at in a calmer moment. Finally, the magnificent peroration, echoing to some extent his 1959 speech, but with greater force and passion. "I say this to you: we may lose the vote today and the result may deal this Party a grave blow. It may not be possible to prevent it, but I think there are many of us who will not accept that this blow need be mortal, who will not believe that such an end is inevitable. There are some of us, Mr. Chairman, who will fight and fight and fight again to save the Party we love. We will fight and fight and fight again to bring back sanity and honesty and dignity, so that our Party with its great past may retain its glory and its greatness. It is in that spirit that I ask delegates who are still free to decide how they vote, to support what I believe to be a realistic policy on defence, which yet could so easily have united this great Party of ours, and to reject what I regarded as the suicidal path of unilateral disarmament which will leave our country defenceless and alone."

All, as it seemed at the time, in vain. The juggernauts rolled on. The AEU's resolution was carried on a card vote by 3,303,000 to 2,896,000; the TGWU's by a flimsy 3,282,000 to 3,239,000. Finally, the Joint Statement was rejected by

3,042,000 to 3,339,000. Obstinately, Gaitskell declared in a radio interview the same evening that he thought the Executive had done "extremely well" to get as many votes as they did, which probably included some two-thirds of the Constituency Party votes. He declined to say whether he would stand for the leadership in three weeks' time. Stephen Swingler, the Labour MP for Newcastle-under-Lyme, then declared that sixty MPs already opposed Gaitskell, that a candidate supporting the Conference's decisions would be put up, and that he thought that Gaitskell "had declared himself as being unfit to do the job." In a television broadcast Gaitskell was asked whether his reference to fellow-travellers might be regarded as a "smear," but he stuck to his guns. He was supported by William Carron, President of the AEU, who said that of the fifty-two members of the Union's policy-making body, twelve were identified members of the Communist Party and another six to eight were fellow-travellers. Cousins added a typically unhelpful bit: he would like to see a Labour Government telling NATO to give up the H-bombs.

Gaitskell's third contribution at the Conference was his winding-up speech on 6th October in the general debate on Labour's Aims. Here once more he was opposed by Cousins, but in this case the NEC's paper was passed by a large majority on a show of hands. Gaitskell deliberately played this one cool. He patiently explained, for the umpteenth time, that after Blackpool he had been misrepresented as being opposed to all public ownership. As for the compromise on Clause 4, the NEC had let it pass because so many Labour adherents were deeply attached to the 1918 Constitution. He used the same tactics as he had used over unilateralism: "It was never an issue of principle, but of presentation." He got away with it this time. He repeated his belief in "the inevitability of gradualness."

So how did Gaitskell emerge from the 1960 Conference? On the face of it, battered and bruised, and with an uncertain future. He had aroused much resentment; in some cases it seemed deliberately. He had been signally defeated on defence questions. He had, in effect, told Conference to take a running jump at itself. In the lion's den he had taunted the lion with impotence and stupidity. Of course, he had calculated, correctly, that the lumbering Trade Union creature was in fact no lion, but a drayhorse. He had smacked down the powerful Cousins and indicated that many of his supporters were fellow-travellers or worse. He had made it absolutely clear that on major policy the Conference's votes and decisions were in no way final, and that he and his friends would fight them, to the end. He had emphasised the importance of the PLP, who had chosen him as Leader, as the representatives of the Labour Movement who, unlike the Trade Union delegates, were freely elected by the public at large. As to his own future, he kept the Party on tenterhooks, though his friends had little doubt, from discussions behind the scenes, that the fighting back would include a new bid for the Leadership on his part. In sum, he had deployed his usual methods. Tactically, he had gone head on into collision with the opposition. In the short term, he had lost. But strategically, and in the longer term, the impact of his battering-ram was such that his opponents in due course came to a delayed-action shuddering halt, while he pressed on with all the force of his lucid and cogent analysis of the problems on hand and with constructively elaborated proposals for their treatment. As the Marquess of Montrose once wrote:

> He either fears his fate too much
> Or his deserts are small
> That puts it not unto the touch
> To win or lose it all.

There was most definitely no sign of a loss of nerve by Gaitskell at this critical point in his career. From his personal point of view he was not seriously disheartened, though from the Party's, more so.

The bickering continued and was happily exploited by the right-wing press. Barbara Castle and Tom Driberg, both members of the Executive, said that Gaitskell must go if he persisted in his determination to reverse Conference's decisions. Greenwood threw his cap into the ring, and Driberg said he would vote for him as Leader. On the other hand, George Brown, the Shadow Defence Minister, said categorically that the Conference's decision must be reversed. Harold Wilson now declared that he would stand for the Leadership. Years later he was to say that this was a most unhappy time: "I didn't like doing it, and it was a pretty hateful experience and a hateful time." He did so not, of course, as a unilateralist but because he was asked by a wide variety of Labour members to go forward as a compromise candidate who might avoid a further serious split in the Movement. Desmond Donnelly, the National Union of Agricultural Workers, and various other bodies came out in support of Gaitskell; some local Labour parties came out against. Donnelly accused Wilson of neutralism. Gaitskell obdurately followed his own line. Addressing a special meeting of constituency workers in South Wales on 23rd October, he went carefully and persuasively over the whole argument of his Scarborough speech. "I believe in all sincerity and with passionate conviction that it would be utterly wrong for us to agree to unilateral nuclear disarmament by the West." It would also be a "practicable impossibility" for Conference to direct the policy of the PLP. He announced that he had decided to accept nomination for reelection as Leader: this was no great surprise to his audience. He said that he expected the PLP to stick to its guns and, in consequence, the next Conference to reverse the Scarborough decision.

Gaitskell romped home on 3rd November with 166 votes to Wilson's 81 and 7 abstentions. Thus his margin was a mere 2 votes less than in 1955. His supporters cheered the result lustily; and when William Warbey asked Gaitskell to show his magnanimity by accepting the unilateralist decision of the Conference they rolled about laughing. The first round voting for the Deputy Leadership, vacant since Bevan's death, was inconclusive: George Brown easily led Fred Lee and James Callaghan, but lacked a clear majority over both together. At the second round, however, Brown was safely home. Gaitskell and his closest associates immediately set in motion a campaign throughout the country to disrupt the unilateralists. A group of energetic younger members of the Party, calling itself "the Campaign for Democratic Socialism," led by Bill Rodgers, Denis Howell, and Dick Taverne, with great support from Roy Jenkins and Anthony Crosland, did much to help Gaitskell restore sanity to the Party over the months. This was something novel. The Left had always felt free to organise and lay about them; now the moderates were replying in kind. Gaitskell welcomed their efforts, but, as Leader of the Party as a whole, he thought it right to stand back a bit and let them carry on with the good work. Both he and the Campaign for Democratic Socialism group ran into stormy opposition at times. Employing his favourite method of taking the bull by the horns, Gaitskell said at Manchester on 5th November that he supported the proposal to station the US Polaris depot ship in Holy Loch, which had outraged the CND supporters probably more than any other single development. He did so, he said explicitly, because he regarded Polaris as more effective, less dangerous to the population, less likely to lead to war, and thus more likely to preserve peace, than any other weapon. About a third of his audience of some 500 booed and indulged in general rowdiness. At Liverpool the next day the audience was greater and more violent still; they howled him down. There were frequent cries of "resign" and "go to the back benches." However, Gaitskell, though red in the face with the effort, battled on and got across the point that persistence in unilateralism would lead to Labour being "massacred" at the next election. He was rewarded with the singing of "For He's a Jolly Good Fellow" by his supporters. In the more peaceful atmosphere of a private meeting with members of the Trade Union group of the PLP on 7th November, a resolution was carried deploring the antics of the previous weekend and calling on everyone to refrain from personal abuse. The view was expressed that Trotskyites and Marxists had been behind the demonstrations.

Gaitskell was determined that both in the House and in

the country Labour should continue to attack vigourously the Government's policies at home and abroad, but it was only natural that the Government could afford to laugh off criticisms from a Party which seemed to be looking in about four different directions at once. In a series of speeches in November and December he covered a very broad spectrum: unemployment in the car industry, the desirability of peers being able to renounce their peerages, the mishandling of the Central African Federation, excessive independent television profits, and in general the Government's lack of planning which favoured the "get-rich-quick boys." He devoted a speech on 11th December in Yorkshire to foreign affairs. Britain should now be doing four things: pressing strongly for a new Western attitude to China, seeking a controlled disarmament zone in Central Europe, keeping the cold war out of Africa, and trying to clear up the confusion in NATO. These were not new themes, but they were to the point. The Tory Government was "sluggish, inert, and dumb. The Foreign Secretary, being in the Lords, is seldom seen or heard." Gaitskell had severely criticised the Earl of Home's appointment in July, and as a member of the Diplomatic Service at the time I warmly agreed with him. This was one of the early signs of Macmillan's mishandling of public feelings where personal appointments were concerned, and the whole Home story from then on was to cost the Tory Party dear. Gaitskell then said that Heath, the Foreign Office spokesman in the Commons, "offers us nothing but platitudes. The Prime Minister is unusually evasive." But Britain could and should use her influence to mitigate the Cold War. Nineteen-sixty-one held promise: "What we hear of Mr. Kennedy suggests that he will not be content to regard the Cold War as something we must accept indefinitely," and in Moscow Khruschev's theory of peaceful competitive co-existence had been accepted. Meanwhile, however, nearer home, the National Union of Railwaymen stiffened their attitude, and their executive agreed unanimously to "uphold and reaffirm" the unilateralist Conference decisions. And the Coventry Borough Labour Party also unanimously announced that they did not want a visit by Gaitskell which had been planned. He caused trouble wherever he went; it would give rise to "a mischievance" in the city. These were hard words. Coventry's two Labour MPs, Maurice Edelman and Richard Crossman, had as it happened both voted in favour of Wilson as Leader. Inside the Labour machine, nevertheless, an offshoot of the Policy Committee began work in December on Signposts for the Sixties, with Wilson in the chair and Gaitskell a member; and he also served as a member of the Finance and Economic Policy Sub-committee under Mikardo's chairmanship. Through all this difficult period there was no denying that the Movement was seriously at odds within itself, or that this gave the Tories and their press— that is, the great majority of the national press—golden opportunities for destructive criticism which they seized with gratification. But what they were unable to grasp was that the Labour Movement, with all its disparate elements and controversies, kept moving towards its main goals, under its elected Leader. Tories, of course, had never up to this point had one of those.

That was not Gaitskell's happiest Christmastide. He had had a hard year, and more of the same was to come. But his confidence in the future, based solidly on the great vote of confidence which the PLP had given him, never wavered seriously. His New Year message to the Movement was understandably sombre in parts. "Nineteen-sixty was a year of difficulty, disappointment, and disillusion. International relations deteriorated sharply; so did the economic situation at home; 'You have never had it so good' became a bad joke; Tory poster promises have gone with the wind." The Labour Movement must clear up its internal differences in a "courteous manner." In foreign policy the Government produced "only a deafening silence" when new initiatives were required. At home, "You just don't get expansion, price stability, and full employment from Tory free-for-all economic policies. So there is a great job to be done both in criticising the weaknesses of the Government and in putting forward our own constructive proposals." Considering the state of the

Labour Movement, and his own position, at that time, it was a fortifying message.

However, the tide was not to turn for several months yet. Gaitskell stumped the country, preaching the multilateralist doctrine. At Croydon in early January 1961 he was greeted by some neo-Luddite pickets with placards saying "Long live Clause 4." At Derby on 14th January the rowdies cut loose, not in large numbers but so persistently that the police were called in. One demonstrator weighing some 14 stone insisted on being carried out. Nevertheless, Gaitskell got across a sharp attack on the Chancellor, Selwyn Lloyd, and the ineptitude of the Government's economic policy. He also called for a full investigation into the origins of the disturbances. In a press interview Gaitskell, described as looking relaxed and well despite the "political drubbing" of the past year, said that while affluence and "You've never had it so good" were all very well, many people in Britain were still far from affluent and "you cannot get away from the fact that our production record is the worst in Europe." There were other black spots: too few council houses; not enough public money spent on education—the Russians for instance spent three times as much per head; and all the time class differences and snobbery were encouraged by the public schools.

On 17th January 1961, Gaitskell left on an important mission to the United States: he was not only to appear on television but he expected to meet the President-Elect, John F. Kennedy, of whom British Labour had very high hopes. He was given a charming send-off by a unilateralist group calling itself Appeal for Unity, whose representative requested the US Embassy to forward to the future President a letter stating: "We feel that you should know that Mr. Gaitskell no longer represents the official view of this Party on defence and foreign policy." This effort daunted neither Gaitskell nor Kennedy: "Gaitskell's reaction was "It's too silly for comment." In fact, Kennedy saw him straight away, at a private lunch given by Averell Harriman on 18th January, at which only two other guests were present. They struck up an excellent relationship from the start. Gaitskell did not attend the presidential inauguration on 20th January, but went to the inaugural ball that night. On 21st January he gave an impressive performance in an hour-long television interview on the National Broadcasting Corporation's network, in which he covered the whole sphere of world affairs. He did not pull his punches. He urged that China was "a force you must reckon with" and that the West should try to get nearer to the USSR on the basis of the Rapacki Plan. He remarked that in Britain there was only "a very small minority" of pacifists and others who favoured our leaving NATO. He returned to England on 23rd January and gave his most favourable impressions of President Kennedy and his administration. Kennedy, with whom he had had two hours' talk, was highly intelligent, very much on the ball, open-minded, but not cynical; "a man of great competence." He had chosen a strong team of youngish, practical-minded realists. Gaitskell hoped for early discussions between the US, British, and West German governments on economic matters. He was sure that the Kennedy administration would be more realistic about absurd charges of colonialism made against the British and would work steadily towards better relations with the USSR. He had made it clear to Kennedy that not only was Britain as a whole not going neutralist, but the Labour Party was not either. The Kennedy-Gaitskell collaboration was to prove fruitful in many directions. So, in fact, was that between Kennedy and the avuncular Harold Macmillan. One of Gaitskell's great achievements was to lead Labour to a new view of the US as not being forever the bastion, or bogeyman, of capitalist reaction. He strongly supported throughout the Atlantic Alliance and community. He was a "mid-Atlantic man." He got closer than any other Labour leader to Democratic and liberal-minded Republican leaders. And, it goes without saying, far closer than Eden and his lot ever did.

Gaitskell brought back with him a heavy cold which, however, did not prevent him from continuing his hard-hitting campaign, until it developed into laryngitis and, very temporarily, silenced him. To the Oxford University Labour

Club he foretold doom: if the Government was not more active in the economic sphere, this country would in the 1970s
have a standard of living definitely lower than that of the
most advanced industrial nations." This prophet must often
have felt during these months that he was not without
honour save in his own country. Women members of the
Labour Party at their annual conference called for the strong-
est possible protest against his attitude on unilateralism.
Michael Foot at a meeting of the PLP condemned him for
nominating Labour peers: Gaitskell pointed out that this
had gone on since 1958, and, of course, he won his point. A
left-winger called John Baird had called him "this stubborn
little man" and a few other things in a recent speech: he now
formally withdrew the epithets. In February a committee of
twelve from the NEC and the TUC, which included Gaitskell, Brown, Healey, Padley, Crossman, and Cousins, voted
by 8 votes to 4 in favour of a new draft, mainly Healey's
work, on defence principles, to be called Policy for Peace.
Crossman saw fit to attack Gaitskell personally for not accepting an alternative draft of his supported by Cousins and
Padley. Brown came down on Crossman like a ton of bricks.
Gaitskell pointed out yet again that it did the Party no good
if the public was constantly reminded that the Leader and
the Party Chairman of the year, Crossman, did not see eye
to eye. On 2nd April it was the turn of the Young Socialists
at their first annual conference to resolve by 210 votes to 114
that the 1960 Conference's decision should be observed and
that Gaitskell must go. Delegates admitted that they would
rather have been taking part in the Aldermaston march ther
in progress. On the same day, however, the Clerical and Ad
ministrative Workers' Union voted clearly in favour of the
Policy for Peace statement. Slowly, slowly the log-jam was
beginning to shift. A whistle-stop tour of eleven LCC constituencies by motorcade a few days later was a success except
that a Conservative loudspeaker van intruded with the reiterated comment: "Here is Mr. Gaitskell and the Labour
Party—but which Labour Party?" In the Bristol by-election

he praised Wedgwood Benn for wishing to give up his peerage and called on the voters, in unusually strong language,
to vote against "stupid snobbery, muddled mysticism, absurd
dishonest nonsense, timid obscurantist complacency," etcetera.
Benn won, but was disqualified from taking his seat. In Gaitskell's May Day message, he described the same issue as "a
smug retreat to Tory folklore" on the part of the Cabinet,
who, he added broadly, believed in "government by gim-
mick." On defence policy he raised his sights: 95 per cent of
the new statement, he said, could be agreed by everybody in
the Movement. And within the same week three major
Unions endorsed it. By mid-May he was able to say that the
end of the controversy on defence was probably in sight. By
early June he was expressing high hopes of unity at the 1961
Conference. The real issue, he said to the National Union of
Vehicle-Builders at Bridlington, was a clear-cut one: did
Britain stay in NATO or did she get out?

Gaitskell often showed his alertness on security matters,
and he took a positive interest in the trial of the spy George
Blake. Macmillan's attitude to espionage and intelligence, as
I had the opportunity to observe at first hand within the
Foreign Office, tended to be one of boredom. However, he
invited Gaitskell to discuss the matter with him. Gaitskell
said in advance that everyone must be convinced that, while
secrecy up to a point might be essential, it was not used to
cloak incompetence. It would be necessary to consider
whether a high-level independent enquiry into security pro-
cedures was now essential. On 11th May the Prime Minister
announced that, after discussions with Gaitskell, just such an
enquiry would be launched.

Gaitskell now appealed to those who had "gone up in the
world" not to cease voting Labour just because they had a
car or a telly. On this theme he was caustic about Tory
propaganda when speaking to Northumberland miners. The
latest effort to the effect that the Tory Party was not "a class
party" was "breathtaking." Half the Cabinet were educated
at Eton; out of 350 MPs "they can muster precisely one trade

unionist." The Chancellor tried to pretend that the £5,000-a-year man was not rich. "Come off it. This hare won't run. The Tories are just as much a class party as they always have been." Someone shouted: "What about Winchester?" To this Gaitskell retorted, primly: "The Labour Party is drawn from all classes. It has never blamed anybody because they were born of better-off parents." In one sense I think he was right, in another wrong. In Britain it is regularly the middle-middle and lower-middle classes who decide the results of elections. The key question, therefore, is not so much one of class, objectively; but rather one, as Gaitskell said on other occasions, of a deeply encrusted snobbery: do these floating voters prefer at any given moment to be governed by the well-established, traditional governors, or do they prefer to give those who are more truly representative of the whole people a chance? And here once more, as regards Gaitskell personally, the difficulty was manifested that, however strong his sincere devotion to Labour principles, he was upper-mid born and bred and a rich man to boot, as well as an intellectual. All this led to doubts, never indeed of his sincerity, but whether he was not bound to be influenced by his heredity and social environment in a direction away from the lives of ordinary people.

On foreign affairs Gaitskell pursued a logical line of support for the United Nations. On the Bay of Pigs he said that President Kennedy had at least forbidden the use of US forces, but he should have stopped the "futile escapade" altogether. After "the horrifying events in Angola," the Portuguese colony in Africa where Dr. Salazar's government had recently taken harsh repressive measures, it was disgusting that the Tory Government should have shown "in at least seven different ways in a few weeks" their support of that government. They should join with the US Government and others in denouncing the massacres and insisting on a UN enquiry. As for our intervention in Kuwait at the ruler's request in response to Kassem's threat from Iraq, this was justified under our agreement with the ruler; but as soon as possible we should get out and ask the UN to replace our forces. Gaitskell was perhaps a bit starry-eyed about the UN's capabilities, but his line was consistent and worth hammering home.

On 12th July a nicely balanced Labour team appeared on television to present the policy document Signposts for the Sixties: on the one hand Gaitskell and Brown, on the other Crossman and Wilson. The broadcast helped to show Gaitskell as Labour's now acknowledged dominating personality and was in effect a build-up for him. What he actually said was perhaps not momentous: chiefly an attack on Tory "I'm all right, Jack" methods and on British complacency in general. What it signified to the Labour faithful, and to many floating voters, was that the Gaitskell line was now predominant and would carry the day at the October Conference and beyond.

In the meantime, he kept up the pressure on the Government. His theme was that after ten years of Tory rule, we were drifting into a major economic crisis, and it was no good for the Government to try to blame other countries or adverse international conditions. He summed it all up in a rousing speech opening a debate on the economic situation in the House on 18th July. His supporters were uppish. They cheered as he rose, and cried "Rub it in." He did. The facts, he said, were unpalatable: over the past ten years we had the worst export and production records of any industrial country and a steadily declining share of world trade. Did the Chancellor really expect wage restraint from the Trade Unions, given that dividends were rising at three times the rate of wages and salaries and that Tory tax changes had all favoured the rich? There were four constructive measures to be taken: industrial planning, such as was succeeding in France; control of imports; the encouragement of professionalism in business and exporting, as it was practised in the US and West Germany; and the abandonment of the "sealed lips" policy, to which the Prime Minister was particularly prone. "Is it not rather surprising that the Prime Minister has made only one speech in the House of Commons since November 1st last, and that on South Africa?" Britain suf-

fered from complacent management and bad labour relations.
He did not want austerity—"There is no need for us to become kill-joys"—but he did want fair shares for all and, in
consequence, a new industrial climate. "Stop-go, stop-go" was
not good enough. Nor was the Prime Minister's smug "You've
never had it so good." Here Macmillan was stung to interject:
"I did not devalue the pound"; to which Gaitskell riposted:
"The Rt. Hon. Gentleman devalued something else. He devalued our moral standards." If we continued on our present
course, we should become a backwater, an historical relic, a
nice people dreaming of the past, "despised, perhaps in an
affectionate way, by other countries." New leadership was
desperately needed. This was Gaitskell in his best House of
Commons style. He was constantly interrupted by cheers
from his own side and received a great ovation at the end. It
was the speech of a confident leader, on the aggressive
against a government that was beginning to look shop-soiled.
His new authority showed itself again at a meeting a few
days later when he brushed off some unilateralist demonstrators as "boring," and his audience tore up their leaflets.

After representing Britain at a meeting of Socialist leaders
in Copenhagen, Gaitskell flew to Canada on behalf of both
the Labour Party and the Socialist International to attend the
founding convention of the New Democratic Party. Here he
spoke up strongly in favour of negotiations with the Communists, as well as of support for the UN and NATO. On
31st July, HMG had announced that the UK had decided to
make formal application, under article 237 of the Treaty of
Rome, to join the European Economic Community; this was
to be one of Gaitskell's chief preoccupations for the short
remaining period of his life.

As the Annual Conference approached, he was able to say
in a couple of speeches that he was "delighted with the general spirit of the Party," that he expected membership to
increase from now on, that the period of internal squabbles
was practically over, and that the Tories were becoming
more discredited with every week that passed.

ELEVEN

Annus Mirabilis

THE LAST YEAR and a bit of Gaitskell's political life, beginning with the Blackpool Conference of 2nd–6th October 1961, brought him success after success. At home the fearful storms over unilateralism and his leadership subsided. The Labour Movement still had its deep internal disagreements, which is an endemic state of affairs, but the Party began to look like a serious contender in the next election in one, two, or three years' time. The Conservative Government, constantly harried by Gaitskell and his revived supporters, lurched down a slippery slope; and Macmillan's powers and judgment showed signs of failing. And as Gaitskell consolidated his position as Leader at home, so he grew steadily in stature in the eyes of the world as a whole.

The Conference went very much according to plan— Gaitskell's plan—and he made two masterly speeches. Winding up on Signposts for the Sixties, he flayed the Tories' record over the past ten years as "disastrous." The workers were now being penalised under the wage freeze. The document described the proper way ahead, and readers would note that it definitely supported public ownership where appropriate. (That was another of Gaitskell's battles won.) He dealt Cousins a zestful blow for suggesting that less attention should be paid to the floating voters and more to the old faithfuls. Was he aware, asked Gaitskell, that in his own TGWU three out of every ten males, and four out of every ten wives, voted Tory? Collapse of stout party. He renewed in colourful terms his constant appeal to the Movement to look to the future. "I am not suggesting a return to a glori-

ous past, power, and empire. I have no patience with nos-
talgic dreams of that kind; the time for all that has gone. Its
final epilogue was written by the Suez fiasco, which the Prime
Minister so readily supported and used then as the stepping-
stone by which he slipped to power." So much for the past.
"Comrades, there is another kind of greatness which I believe
beckons us today. It lies in the quality of the civilisation we
create here in Britain. The most important thing is that it
must involve an acceptance of values appropriate to the
second half of the 20th century." He mentioned amongst
other priorities racial equality, the struggle against poverty
world-wide, and in the UK improved housing and education.
Then a theme very dear to his heart: above all, we must
despise and laugh at snobbery and class distinctions. For all
these objects "Our Party is the only instrument." Signposts
for the Sixties was approved by acclamation: another complete victory for Gaitskell.

Others followed when he wound up on "Policy for
Peace." Having paid a tribute to Hammarskjöld, whom he
had known well personally, on his death, and said that his
ideal of world government must remain the ultimate aim of
everyone who wanted peace, he turned and rent the unilateralists who had discomfited him a year earlier. He insisted
that the TGWU's critical resolution should be rejected; and
so it was, by the huge majority of 4,309,000 to 1,891,000. This,
for a start, was a sensational reversal of the 1960 form and
proved that Gaitskell's stubborn counter-attack against those
who had handled him roughly for a year and more had
struck its target. On two items his recommendations were
not carried: that Conference should express its approval of
the Polaris base, and of West German troops training in
Berlin. But these were incidental. On Berlin, which had
been in a most critical state ever since the Wall went up on
13th August, Gaitskell said that while we must never start a
war, we must be prepared to retaliate if attacked. Above all,
in the tense new situation it was more, not less, important
and urgent to negotiate with the Communists; and the Ra-

packi plan would provide a basis. He heavily criticised the Government's obscurantist policy in Africa, and ended magniloquently: "Last year, Mr. Chairman, our task was to save the Party. This year it is to save the nation." "Policy for Peace" was approved by 4,526,000 votes to 1,756,000. That was for practical purposes the end of unilateralism. Its deathknell had sounded. It was true that, as usual, Tony Greenwood, Barbara Castle, and Harold Wilson topped the poll in the constituencies section. But nobody had the slightest doubt that as a whole the Conference was a triumph for Gaitskell.

Thus fortified, Gaitskell set about belabouring the Government. Under pressure from him, the National Executive Committee decided to launch a pre-election campaign—a good deal pre, as it transpired—and appointed a campaign committe. On 17th October, Gaitskell made in the House the first of a series of powerful onslaughts in the field of foreign policy. Two horrible events had changed the scene: the erection of the shocking Berlin Wall and the resumption of nuclear tests by Khruschev. Yet HMG "maintained a rather unnecessarily coy silence" and seemed unable to formulate a policy together with its Western allies. It was really not good enough for Macmillan to remark to some press representatives on the 18th green at Gleneagles, as he had a fortnight after the Wall was started, that nobody was going to fight over Berlin, that Khruschev was on holiday like himself, and as regards the frightening Berlin situation: "I think it is all got up by the press." I myself had been British Minister in Berlin since June and had reported fully, together with my US and French colleagues, on the appalling dangers and stresses of the situation; so that Macmillan had, of course, not the slightest excuse for his light-hearted attitude, which was in no way shared by Presidents Kennedy and de Gaulle. Gaitskell went on that we must stand firm over Berlin, but also try to get negotiations moving with the Communists. We needed better physical control over access to Berlin (this was certainly true), and he believed that a reasonable bargain could be struck on these lines: West Germany should accept the existing frontiers of East Germany as final; the Rapacki Plan, or something like it, should be negotiated; and "there should be some recognition de facto of East Germany as part of the price we should pay." (From my advanced outpost in West Berlin, I was reaching similar conclusions.) A considerable degree of de facto recognition already existed in practice, and he was not advocating anything which would prevent the eventual reunification of Germany. The United Nations should be associated with any such agreement and possibly supervise the access facilities to Berlin. Some UN agencies might be physically transferred to West Berlin; this would, in time, make the division of the city far more difficult for the Communists to maintain. He was glad that the US and British governments had worked fairly closely together on the Berlin issue. I could confirm that this was a fair assessment.) But the British Government should improve its record where freedom in other parts of the world was concerned, notably in Asia and Africa, and both support the US more strongly in this direction in the UN and refrain from measures to restrict coloured immigration into this country. The Labour side liked, and applauded, this speech very much. For myself, I found that Gaitskell's ideas on Berlin and Germany appealed to me more and more as time passed, though in some ways my own ideas were to go further than his.

Gaitskell went to Rome for the meeting from 21st to 27th October of the World Congress of the Socialist International and took the opportunity to berate Khruschev on his latest little jape, the explosion of a 50-megaton H-bomb. This, he said, had caused not fear but "deep disgust and cold anger." Did it mean a change in Soviet policy, just when disarmament talks were looking more hopeful? He had done "a terrible thing." Though Gaitskell did not say so in public, he realised that Khruschev had lost his temper because the West were staying steady over Berlin; and that the monster explosion, one of twenty-five in a new series of tests, was also part of Khruschev's campaign to test young President Kennedy's nerve and judgment to the utmost. Gaitskell went on to repeat the constructive suggestions about Berlin and Germany that he had made in the House a week before. He was loudly cheered by the delegates. Willy Brandt, then Lord Mayor of West Berlin, made it clear that he could not agree with his proposal for the de facto recognition of the German Democratic Republic. But he cordially invited him to visit the city soon. This was the period of several perilous incidents which, as I knew in my official position but the public in the West was, quite rightly, not allowed to know, led President Kennedy to consider the possible need for nuclear war. He wisely decided against; and Gaitskell on his return from Rome equally shrewdly remarked that such incidents were a "try-out by both sides," that the position was not desperate, and that the best course was to keep calm.

On 7th November the PLP elected its Leader, Deputy Leader, and Chief Whip. The Left Wing still took part in the contest, and they were heavily defeated. Gaitskell got 171 votes against Greenwood's 59, George Brown 169 to Barbara Castle's 56, and Herbert Bowden romped home with an even larger majority over Ben Parkin. This was a supererogatory confirmation of the strength of Gaitskell's position.

Gaitskell made the first of a long series of statements about Britain and the Common Market in the course of an interview for the Columbia Broadcasting System recorded in London. He did not think Britain was at all ready to sink her identity in a European federation, though we were prepared for close association with European governments. He himself was not against this, but Labour reserved its position until it knew the exact terms of entry. He added that Britain should give up some of her more far-flung and out-of-date commitments and concentrate more on NATO. In Cardiff a few days later he said that the Commonwealth should be trusted and consulted more by the Government, on such matters as immigration and conditions of entry into the Common Market. It was not enough merely to inform them ex post facto. At Blackburn on 9th December he said that if entry meant the break-up of the Commonwealth—"and I

think it well might"—we should stay out. The best thing
would be to go in, but with a satisfactory plan for the Commonwealth. Meanwhile, Labour must wait and see. Remem-
bering his rough handling in Lancashire a year earlier, he
remarked that he did not want another internal Party row
over the Common Market. (He was going to get one, however.) Nearly 600 Party and Trade Union delegates this time
welcomed him enthusiastically. He said that Labour now had
a great opportunity of gaining power, but hard work would
be needed to get disgruntled Conservative voters to switch to
Labour.

On 3rd January 1962, Gaitskell arrived in West Berlin on
a four-day visit as the guest of Willy Brandt and the Senate,
or local Government. He told Brandt on arrival that he had
come partly to see with his own eyes the Communist "Wall
of shame" and its effects. He did so the same afternoon and
remarked that you had to try to imagine a similar wall
through the heart of London. There appeared to be complete
desolation on the other side. "What an advertisement for
Communism!" He had lengthy talks not only with Brandt,
but with the Allied commandants and Ministers, including
myself; our commandant was on leave at the time, and I was
in full charge of the post. I found his attitude to Berlin's
problems most refreshing and practical; but his ideas did not
at all appeal to the British commandant, a major-general of
remarkably stick-in-the-mud views, when I informed him of
them on his eventual return. Gaitskell also saw, in my company, President Kennedy's personal representative, General
Lucius D. Clay. This hero of the Berlin airlift had been
superimposed on the US commandant and, to that extent, on
the British and French too; and his fire-eating methods did
not make him universally popular. He had asked me whether
he could meet Gaitskell in my office, and as this was the only
time during his eight months' tour of duty that he set foot
in the British Headquarters, I agreed with gratification. We
had a good hour's talk together, and the differences in
opinions were constructively, and amicably, aired. I think it

fair to say that I got on better with Clay than anyone else in the three Western allies' staffs, including the Americans, and Gaitskell hit it off well with him too. So much so that I suggested a short combined television appearance after our talks, and this was readily agreed. I also had much pleasure in entertaining Gaitskell at my house, and at one meal I told him how George Brown, also a guest during a visit before Christmas, had sprung from his chair on learning that one of my sons was at Winchester, knelt in supplication to him, and pronounced: "The school of my masters." Gaitskell commented, rather testily I thought: "Oh dear! George at it again, I suppose!" I was able to assure him that Brown had not in fact been "at it."

On 4th January, Gaitskell made a reassuring statement to British correspondents. There seemed to be fears abroad that West Germany was so disillusioned with her allies that she would try direct bilateral negotiations with the USSR; and also that the Allies would desert West Berlin. In fact, there was not a shred of evidence for any of these fears. In Britain there was also an impression that the inhabitants of West Berlin were quitting in a flood, but this he now knew was an exaggeration. He thought the West had dithered for too long over seeking a realistic solution of the German and Berlin problems. He had had valuable talks with Brandt and Clay, and "there is no disagreement between us on any major issue." This was slightly misleading, for he went on to say that East Germany should be recognised de facto and included in a newly devised international control system for the access routes; neither Brandt nor Clay would have gone along with that though it seemed sensible to me. As for the Wall, it struck him as being like the surround of a prison; and after a brief visit to East Berlin on 5th January, he said that it looked even worse from that side. At another press conference he said that if he were a West German or West Berliner, he would feel that some recognition of East Germany would be a price worth paying in return for properly, internationally supervised access routes, particularly as the

East Germans had always had—and sometimes exercised—
the power to interfere with them in practice. He would not
propose anything more than de facto recognition. He strongly
supported President Kennedy's similar recent proposals on
these matters. On his return to London on 6th January he
repeated his views on a solution, but admitted that the idea
of recognising East Germany was repugnant to the West
Berliners. He thought that possibly the United Nations' Economic and Social Council, the International Labour Organisation, and some other UN agencies might set up in West
Berlin and have a calming effect; but he did not suggest that
UN troops should be stationed there. A few days later at my
suggestion, the Foreign Secretary, the Earl of Home, came on
to Berlin from Bonn, where he was visiting with the Prime
Minister. He curtailed his visit to the minimum that polite-
ness demanded, well under 24 hours. It was not productive;
he and his Foreign Office senior officials had nothing like the
rapport with Brandt that Gaitskell (and I myself) had. Macmillan had decided that he could not even spare those few
hours to visit "the front-line city." At this time Clay had
gone to Washington for consultation, and unquestionably
his attitude to his colleagues on his return a few days later
had radically changed. I asked if I could see him both to report on Home's visit and to hear anything he might care to
tell me about his talks with his government. I was referred
to a junior official. From then on, Clay was positively brusque
with the British commandant, though in fact they had never
hit it off together anyway. Why? The mystery was never
solved. Had he reported to President Kennedy his discussions
with Gaitskell and myself, and been told to keep a more
open mind and eat less fire? If so, did he resent our involvement and our views, which were closer to his President's
than his own? He was suddenly removed, at a moment's notice, in May. So was I, in June.

For the next month Gaitskell grappled authoritatively
with problems on the home front. On 26th January he attended the annual dinner of the Bosworth divisional Labour

Party at alluringly named Coalville. Woodrow Wyatt, the local Labour member, opened proceedings by declaring that he had always been one of Gaitskell's staunchest supporters and that any ideas he put forward were designed to help him to become Prime Minister. Gaitskell thought otherwise and said so bluntly. Wyatt's persistent advocacy of a Labour-Liberal combination for the next election was no longer funny, he said; it was "irresponsible action" and could undermine Labour's hopes of victory. He had not intended to mention the idea: "I thought everyone realised it was a red herring which had become a dead duck." But that very day Wyatt had popped up once more with the idea in the *New Statesman*. He proceeded to explain in detail why it was "an absolute non-starter," and how Labour must now forge ahead and win its own victory. Master Wyatt left the headmaster's study nursing his sore behind. The next day at Nottingham the workers received their lecture: though the Government was responsible for shockingly bad labour relations through their "appallingly clumsy" handling of affairs, the workers must not fall into the trap of alienating public opinion by unofficial strikes and the like. The 2½ per cent annual expansion aim set by the Chancellor, Selwyn Lloyd, was "a miserable target": Labour would hope to achieve 4 per cent, since after all the French were achieving 5. Speaking at Cambridge on 4th February he called the recent government White Paper on incomes policy half-baked, unrealistic, confused, and unconstructive. In particular, the Government had never seriously tried to encourage our exports, a basic matter.

The next day, 5th February, Gaitskell seized with both hands an opportunity for which he had long lain in wait, when he moved a vote of censure on Foreign Secretary Home, specifically for the attack he had made on the United Nations in his speech at Berwick-on-Tweed on 28th December 1961. Gaitskell had considered Home deplorable enough as Commonwealth Secretary, with his lordly manner towards underdeveloped countries and their people, coupled with the assumption that gentlemanly, old-style English amateurism must surely win all hearts. He had been outraged when this denizen of the Upper House, who could not answer to the Commons, was given the yet more significant post. So now he did not mince his words. It was rare, he said, for the Opposition to put down a motion of censure on a single speech by a single Minister. But this speech had also been endorsed by the Prime Minister and the Government. Home had gone as far in attacking the UN as he dared without actually pulling Britain out. This line was damaging to Britain's reputation in the world and to the interests of the Western democracies. Home had seen fit to state that 82 of the 104 members were in arrears on their subscriptions: in fact only six were behind with their regular payments. He had indulged in humbug and hypocrisy when he claimed that the Security Council vote on Goa had approved the use of force by India, which it did not. In any case, a more honest attitude would have been to say: "Well, we have all done it. We must admit it. Russia, Britain, France, the United States, and now India. Let us make a fresh start." Secondly, Home called the UN resolution on colonialism of December 1960, reaffirmed in November 1961, "reckless and careless of peace." The fact was that "there were 97 votes for the resolution, none against, and five abstentions. Who was careless of peace? The whole of the Commonwealth, apart from Britain, 12 Western European countries, and the US, who had all voted in favour? The five who abstained were: France, Britain, Spain, Portugal, and South Africa." Here the Labour benches burst into ironical laughter. Home had attacked the new nations for adopting a double standard and generally siding with the Russians and against us. The facts? The Assembly had ridden off the Soviet troika proposals, heavily defeated the Soviet line on the Congo, asked the USSR not to explode the 50-megaton bomb, condemned the Communist line on Tibet and Hungary, and refused to condemn the US over the Bay of Pigs. What they did attack was the tiny group of dictatorships with whom the Foreign Secretary chose to align Britain. "To regard the UN as simply representing the status quo—and the Foreign Secretary goes far towards this—is to be false to its past and dangerous to its future." It was only natural that former colonies wanted freedom from colonialism everywhere. Also, Home's speech was calculated to upset the US. Perhaps it had been made mainly to impress the Tory Party? They had always been suspicious of the UN, as Suez had shown in an extreme form. And they had always resented the passing of the colonial empire. In fact, however, Britain's proud record of giving freedom to her colonies should lead her to repudiate the policies of Portugal and South Africa. It was intolerable that the Foreign Secretary should associate Britain with this reactionary minority. Our ideals all pointed in the opposite direction. Home's speech "should never have been made, and it should now be emphatically repudiated." This comprehensive condemnation received the ovation it deserved from the Labour benches.

Gaitskell kept up the pressure on the home front and outside the House. Opening the Labour Party's conference on local government at Harrogate on 10th February, he slated the Government as a group of "tired, stubborn men who know that all their cherished nostrums have failed, but have neither the courage nor the energy to change their course." Their recent White Paper on prices and incomes was "so utterly negative and unrealistic that it was a waste of time and effort ever to have written it at all." On housing, Labour had seven main objectives: get rid of the slums, provide a decent home for everybody, house workers nearer their work, clear up the appalling traffic congestion in the cities, redevelop the cities in a planned manner, preserve the countryside, and ensure that rising rents and land values should accrue to the nation and not to individuals. An ambitious programme indeed, of which regrettably little has been achieved as yet.

On 16th February, Gaitskell left for a ten-day visit to the US, forestalling Macmillan who was to go in April. The following day he chose a lunch given by the New York Liberal

Party—hardly a major event—to speak in favour of negotia-tions with the Communists, and against the Portuguese and similar dictatorships. He warned that if the EEC were to be-come a tightly knit political unit, inspired by its own nationalism and with a high external tariff, the relations of the West as a whole with the new nations would suffer. He also saw U Thant, then Acting Secretary-General of the UN, and discussed the Congo and other affairs for 45 minutes. At a press conference he said that a Summit conference might give impetus to the 18-nation disarmament conference due to begin in Geneva in March. On 18th February, Gaitskell lunched with President Kennedy at the White House: their friendly relationship prospered and they had long and fruit-ful talks. The President had announced that the US would probably have to resume nuclear testing some time after the middle of March. Gaitskell begged him to postpone the tests if at all possible so as to let the disarmament conference get into its stride; and, if they were essential, to explain the mili-tary reasons clearly and, of course, to keep them clean, as the last Soviet series had been. The discussions, in which Dean Rusk also took part, ranged over Berlin, Germany, and the Common Market. A couple of days later Gaitskell attended a meeting of an American and British group of parliamen-tarians in the agreeable surroundings of Bermuda. On his return to London he explained US policy in detail. Military evidence on the significance of the recent Soviet tests was still being evaluated. If Kennedy concluded that they had upset the balance of deterrence, for instance in the anti-missile missile sphere, he would order further US tests; but he would never do so for reasons of mere retaliation or prestige. "Pres-ident Kennedy is a very, very reluctant tester. He would much prefer even now a cast-iron agreement with the Russians." But he had been shaken by Khruschev's extreme truculence over both tests and Berlin when they met in Vienna in June 1961. The US Government thought little of Khruschev's proposal for an 18-nation Summit conference, but were ready to consider a smaller one at the right moment.

The tail-end of CND was still giving an occasional twitch, and Gaitskell devoted some time to telling it to stop. He deprecated "just squatting in Trafalgar Square" and emphasised that Labour must seriously close their ranks with a view to winning the next General Election, which they now had a great chance of doing. In a message to a by-election candidate he outlined a Labour Government programme of seven points. "A radical reform of the tax system to help those who get their money the hard way and catch those who get it the easy way. Firm action to deal with the land price scandal. Erective steps to curb the prodigious growth of monopolies. A government drive to increase investment, research, and efficiency in industry. A genuine national superannuation plan giving half-pay on retirement. Firm support for the UN and its efforts for world peace. Acceptance of the Monckton Commission report on Central Africa." Also in March he set up a commission of enquiry into the role of commercial advertising in present-day society, a subject he considered of high importance, with Lord Reith in the chair and Nicholas Kaldor and Francis Williams amongst its members. They reported in due course to the Labour Party, with suggestions for remedying some of the worst abuses; but little action was taken. A series of by-elections at this period was going favourably for Labour, and Gaitskell pressed two points in this connexion: that there was nothing incompatible between owning a motor-car and voting Labour, as he put it, and that voting Liberal was a sheer waste of time. He laid into Selwyn Lloyd's last Budget in April as being "sour and dull" and fiddling about with tax rearrangements when the basic need was to encourage increased production and exports.

On 14th April, Gaitskell addressed a special meeting of the Fulham Labour Party and put forward his maturing ideas about Britain's entry into the Common Market, which from now on until the end of his life was to be the foreign affairs topic that occupied most of his attention. Present was the member for Fulham, Michael Stewart, known at that time as one of the many Labour MPs who were opposed to entry. First, Gaitskell insisted that the people of Britain should be kept properly informed on the progress of the negotiations and on what were the real issues. Here he had a strong point. As both a member of the British public and a member of the Foreign Office, I can testify that the whole question was handled by Edward Heath in a manner that combined blundering superciliousness towards the Six, a sort of basic frivolity, and ineptitude in reporting progress, or the reverse, to ordinary people. Foreign Secretary Home himself had only a shadowy idea of what it was all about anyway. Gaitskell put four questions which he said were vital. Will the Government insist that Commonwealth countries will enjoy the same tariff preferences as former French colonies? Was it intended to agree to discriminate against manufactured imports from the Commonwealth and in favour of those from Europe; and if so, what would happen to manufacturers in India, Ceylon, Pakistan, and Hong Kong whose trade was mainly with Britain? Should we have to abolish our agricultural subsidies, with all the grave effects on our agriculture and on imports from the Commonwealth? And, very fundamental, were the powers of the House of Commons to be transferred "in any respect" to an elected European Parliament, or was Britain to retain a right of veto in a council of governments? What, too, about the interests of our EFTA allies? On no account must the Government just accept any terms and present them as a *fait accompli* to the British public. On 8th May, Gaitskell went so far as to devote the whole of his Party political broadcast to the question, being the first British Party leader to do so. His theme was, again, that the terms of entry must be good; not to go in would be a pity, but not a catastrophe. "History would not forgive us" if we went in on bad terms implying the end of the Commonwealth. He had already said privately that, according to the advice of the best economists, the economic arguments were very evenly balanced, about fifty-fifty; he now repeated this in public. There would probably be a small advantage in the

long run, but some sharp disadvantages in the short. Politically, the danger was that without Britain an "inward-
looking, rather reactionary, conservative, and nationalistic"
state might come into being. It would be important to see
whether the Commonwealth Prime Ministers at their meeting in September were satisfied with the safeguards. "There
is no need for us to be suppliants in this matter, and Ministers too often talked as if the whole matter was settled.
Labour's attitude would continue to be decided strictly on
the merits of the case at each stage. This was a carefully
thought through, low-key performance, convincing in its sincerity, but to some viewers rather puzzling. It contained
nearly all the arguments which Gaitskell was to develop in
his last great speeches on the topic, but it lacked the fire.

The CND was now displaying all the frenetic energy of
a hen whose head has just been severed. At the May Day
rally in Glasgow on 6th May it came to a show-down.
Gaitskell indulged in some judicious losing of his temper and
in some very fierce language indeed. Amongst a crowd of
some 5,000, about 300 CND supporters, including a number
of Communists, proved so unruly that the police had to be
called to hustle them away. "Let them go to the Kremlin
and wave their placards there," shouted Gaitskell. "Let them
ask Mr. Khrushchev to ban his bomb. When it comes to the
elections, these people are not worth a tinker's cuss." (An
echo of a provocative speech by Bevan.) "They are peanuts."
There was uproar for ten minutes, with cries of "Traitor"
and chants of "Gaitskell Tory." A young woman held her
baby up and shrieked: "I want my child to live." Gaitskell
snapped back: "So do I, and I have two daughters." He
replied in kind to a barrage of abuse and said witheringly
that CND "formed a group which could do nothing for the
peace of the world." Also they were bidding fair to wreck
Labour's electoral chances, which after a series of successful
by-elections now looked most promising. Gaitskell deservedly
received a standing ovation from the great majority of those
present. What angered him was not only the boorishness of

the demonstrators, but their arrant refusal to consider any logic or reasoning. A few days later at Leeds University some hundreds of students mobbed him and shouted: "In with Socialism, out with Gaitskell, out with the bomb." Gaitskell patiently lectured them on the necessity for maintaining NATO, with Britain playing her part. In the press these rowdy incidents were deprecated, and Gaitskell's balanced attitude to the campaign, as to other more fundamental issues, was generally approved. One sanctimonious interrupter at a meeting at Gloucester said: "I happen to be one of those 'peanuts,' and as a Christian who believes that the threat of nuclear weapons is anti-Christian, I feel very hurt." This was well calculated to irritate Gaitskell, not least because he did not claim to be a Christian himself and saw no monopoly of goodness in the Christian faith. He replied that he did not mind honest heckling, but at Glasgow there had been a deliberate attempt to stop him from speaking at all. He then repeated his charges. "What I said was 'these people, when it comes to the ballot box, don't count'; nor do they. After that I said they were peanuts. Maybe the word was a little fresh, but then the atmosphere was rather unusual. If the cap does not fit, you need not worry. I can only say that I think that my language was more than restrained." A half-hearted demonstration even dogged him at the May dairy festival of the National Dairy Council, to which he had been invited instead of the customary Cabinet Minister. "All milk is radioactive," declared one banner. Gaitskell, undeterred, proposed a toast to the dairy cow in a mellifluous ode, and the toast was drunk by the company in milk. He vigorously tackled the Young Socialists at their conference at bracing Skegness on 31st May. His main theme was, once more, that internal discord in the Movement must be ended: "We have a tremendous chance now, perhaps the greatest we have had in the decade since we lost office. Our job is not to be monks, but missionaries." They should forget about any Lib-Lab pact; Liberal policy was "amorphous, obscure, and opportunist." Questioned about the proscribing of *Keep Left*, the unofficial paper run by a group of Young Socialists, Gaitskell said that such proscriptions were a good old Labour custom and that as it was associated with other proscribed bodies which constantly attacked the Labour programme—it was clear he meant Communist or Communist-controlled bodies —action was necessary. He explained that there was a list of some forty proscribed organisations: they had "very nice, specious names" such as Artists for Peace, Teachers for Peace, the British-Soviet Friendship Society, and the World Peace Council. It was because of the association of Bertrand Russell and Canon Collins with the last one that their expulsion from the Party was now being considered by the National Executive. He received some boos, but more cheers; a contrast indeed to the previous year's "Gaitskell must go" atmosphere. Later he gave a good account of himself on the dance floor, jiving until two in the morning.

Gaitskell preached his Common Market doctrine to a wider audience when he attended a meeting of the Socialist International Council in Oslo from 1st–5th June. He warmly welcomed the support given by the Socialist Parties of the EEC countries to the idea of Britain, Norway, and Denmark joining. He hoped that they could help to secure favourable conditions and, as always, stressed the Commonwealth aspect. He looked forward to EEC being "an association of neighbours very conscious of their wider obligations to the world in general, anxious to see freer trade everywhere, progressive, radical, and fundamentally international in outlook." As regards Berlin he regretted that Chancellor Adenauer was so hostile to President Kennedy's forward-looking proposals. On his return to London he observed that the reactions of the Prime Ministers of Australia and New Zealand, Menzies and Marshall, to our Common Market negotiations in their joint statement were sharp and showed how dissatisfied they were. Labour would make up their minds in due course, he said again. He made these points once more in a long speech in the House next day. He strongly criticised Lord Privy Seal Heath for his conduct of

the negotiations and his gross exaggeration of the economic
advantages of our entering. He admitted that some critics
exaggerated the political dangers of going in, and he ruled
out the practical possibility of the Commonwealth as a sort
of alternative Common Market. It was true that the rate of
economic growth of the Six had been much greater than
Britain's, but not necessarily because of the Market. "It
would not do to speak, as the Lord Privy Seal did, as though
if we went in, we were prosperous and if we did not go in,
we were not." He was cheered for this sally, as he was again
when he repeated that we must at all costs safeguard the
Commonwealth's interests. New Zealand could be ruined if
we accepted the "pretty frightening" EEC proposals in the
agricultural sphere as a whole. On the political side, as votes
were allocated to countries at present, the one-third of the
votes necessary for a veto meant in practice those of one
large country—France, Italy, or Germany—plus those of one
small; if Britain went in, we should insist that the one-third
stipulation should be cut out and the other should remain
independent, or we should be at the mercy of the other three
large countries. The EEC Commission at present seemed to
him too independent, and it should be put under a strengthened Council of Ministers. He was decidedly against all swift
moves towards a European federal state. At a further conference of the Socialist International in Brussels from 15th
to 18th July, however, Gaitskell, who was accompanied by
Shadow Foreign Secretary Harold Wilson, ran into criticism
from the Belgian Foreign Minister M. Spaak, who commented that Britain seemed to be presenting conditions for
the entry of the Common Market into the Commonwealth,
and to expect the Six to beg them on their knees to join.
He was very much in favor of Britain's membership, but
some of Gaitskell's points were "rather dangerous." The
unification of Europe was "the most essential feature of the
Treaty of Rome" and must not be blocked. The political
will to join did not appear very strong in Britain. Gaitskell
was rather hurt and surprised and said so on his return to

London. It looked, he thought, as if our official negotiators had not put our conditions firmly enough; but he was in the dark on this. "For Britain next month to become merely a province of Europe is to me out of the question." His personal relations with M. Spaak were extremely cordial, but Spaak was a "passionate European federalist" and he was not.

On 20th July, Macmillan had taken the panicky measure of sacking seven members of his Cabinet, including some of the most senior. It looked indeed as if there were some tired men in the Government, as Gaitskell had said. He exploited these developments, which were in one sense a great success for him and his relentless hammering of Macmillan and his men, to the utmost. Speaking at the Durham Miners' Gala on 21st July, Gaitskell taunted Macmillan that he had only escaped being sacked himself "by the skin of his teeth." The "sanguinary events" constituted an unprecedented purge. Never before had a third of the Cabinet, and a dozen other Ministers, been "dismissed with ignominy." The Prime Minister had, desperately and discreditably, tried to shuffle off his own responsibility on to his friends. "The British people will neither forget nor forgive such conduct." The Tories themselves were bitter and angry over the affair; nevertheless, in the censure debate which he had called for 26th July, they would "dutifully record their votes for a man they no longer trust or admire." Their votes would be of no importance. But the British people's verdict would be—guilty. When he duly moved: "That this House declares that Her Majesty's Government no longer enjoys the confidence of the country" (Opposition cheers) "and accordingly calls upon the Prime Minister to advise Her Majesty to dissolve Parliament so that a General Election can be held" (more cheers), Gaitskell let himself go and enjoyed every moment. He had for a long time wanted to shake Macmillan's supercilious calm; now he had him on the hop, and he was going to keep him hopping. The recent sensational events, he said, were a complete confession of failure. He offered the Tories an apt quotation from Kipling's "The Song of the Dead":

If blood be the price of admiralty
Lord God, we ha' paid in full.

These were the actions of a desperate man in the desperate
situation of the decline of Conservative fortunes in by-election after by-election, due in its turn to the Government's
shocking economic and social record. The Home Secretary,
for instance, did not really want the slums cleared. They
had cut back expenditure on education. Their incomes policy
was in ruins and had hampered production. Had there been
disputes in the Cabinet behind the appearance of unity?
The Prime Minister had congratulated the late Chancellor,
Selwyn Lloyd, on the morning of 20th July and sacked him
at six o'clock the same afternoon. The Prime Minister's letter
to him did not suggest that there would be any alteration of
policy, "but we are accustomed to the Prime Minister saying
one thing and doing another." It would be a change to have
a budget for expansion instead of for dealing with a crisis.
Was it all a belated realisation by Macmillan that his colleagues were tired? He should carry the dismissal process
further. "How many of the old comrades who voted him into
power in 1957 now remain? Six out of nineteen. Not since
Stalin liquidated the old Bolsheviks has there been such a
successful process of elimination. Prime Ministers who lived
in history set more store by their policy objectives than by
the time they remained in office. That is true of Peel,
Gladstone, Churchill, and Attlee. It was true of Lord Avon,
however mistaken one might think his policy. It is not true
of the present Prime Minister. His government will be remembered not for the leadership it gave the country, but as
a conspiracy to retain power. Men and measures have been
equally sacrificed for that purpose. Let him do this last service to the British people and give them the freedom to
choose a new government." This was one of Gaitskell's most
constantly and loudly applauded speeches. It struck numerous
tender spots amongst the Tories; it also angered a good
many. The ranks were closed; and for more than two long

years, with an increasing lack of success, the Government soldiered on.

On 31st August, Gaitskell and his wife arrived in Warsaw for a five-day visit as the guests of the Polish Institute of International Affairs, thus making up for the visit which he had had to cancel three years earlier because of the sudden announcement of the General Election. After a tour of southern Poland he had a two-and-a-half-hour meeting with Adam Rapacki, and they discussed his plan, which Gaitskell had supported from the start and which had now got as far as the agenda of the Geneva disarmament conference. They also talked about Berlin and the Common Market. Gaitskell lunched with an old friend, Vice-President Professor Oskar Lange, a leading economist, and lectured on "Security Problems in Central Europe" to the Institute. At their request no Western correspondents were admitted. The next day he had no less than three and a half hours with Gomulka and Prime Minister Cyrankiewicz. This talk he described as "perfectly friendly" in spite of numerous differences of opinion. At any rate, they agreed that the Rapacki Plan and the very similar Labour Party plan deserved most serious consideration. "This is one of the most positive aspects of my visit." He found the Poles much concerned over the future of their exports to Britain if we joined the Common Market. On his return to London he stressed that Poland had "very considerable fear" about possible future aggression by the Germans; and in view of the Poles' experiences in the last war, who could blame them? He had, however, tried to reassure them.

From here on, two subjects occupied most of Gaitskell's time and attention, until the end. They were interconnected. One was the campaign for a General Election; and in the press, in Westminster, and in the world Gaitskell was widely canvassed as the next Prime Minister, and with widespread approbation. The other was the Common Market. An unusual gathering in London in early September brought together Commonwealth Labour Party leaders. At the end

Gaitskell was asked whether the three days' talks had altered his attitude. He replied that they had not. Labour recognised, as before, that there were important political considerations in favour of entry. But if the conditions offered as a whole were not satisfactory, "then undoubtedly we should ask for a General Election." He repeated this in an ITV programme on 13th September and shifted a little further against entry. "As things are, we are giving everything away. We are completely disrupting our previous trading system. We are being asked to discriminate against our friends in the Commonwealth in favour of Europe. What do you give us in exchange? Nothing but promises." He was particularly worried about New Zealand and India. Lord Boothby made some shrewd comments on the same programme. Asked whether Macmillan was likely to crack under the strain of opposition, he replied certainly not; he would do all he could to get Britain into Europe—"I think he is dead right"—but would President de Gaulle and Chancellor Adenauer let us in? Gaitskell went further than before in a speech at Rochdale next day: the last week's meeting had left him in no doubt of the Commonwealth's reservations about British entry at this stage. He expressed emotionally his feelings about the Commonwealth as a whole: "You cannot be in a conference of this size without being moved by the friendliness, the warmth, and affection of these people from so many different parts of the world towards us. This association of equal nations, where you give people who have been subject races their rights and equality with you, is not something to be ignored." This declaration was well timed as it came on the eve of the Commonwealth Prime Ministers' meeting. On 19th September he issued a statement through Labour Party headquarters about the communiqué covering that meeting. "The communiqué confirms that the Commonwealth Prime Ministers believe that if Britain enters the Common Market on the terms so far negotiated, much damage would be done to their countries and to the Commonwealth as a whole. It follows that we must either obtain better terms or stay out." The next day Macmillan broadcast a report on the Prime Ministers' Conference, and the Labour Party within minutes demanded Gaitskell's right to reply on the grounds that this had been a party political broadcast. He did so next day, 21st September, in a nationwide television and radio broadcast. He was more categorical than ever before. Not a single Commonwealth Prime Minister "of an important state" was satisfied with the existing terms, he said. The Six' vague promises must be turned into precise agreements. He repeated his assessment of the balance of economic and political arguments for entry. Politically, it meant the end of Britain as an independent nation. "We become no more than Texas or California in the United States of Europe. It means the end of a thousand years of history." Finally, a General Election must be held before entry: "It is utterly wrong that a decision of this tremendous historical importance, which determines our whole destiny as a nation, should be taken before the people themselves can pronounce on it. I have no doubt what the British people will think. I do not think they will want to break the links with Australia, New Zealand, and Canada. They are British countries with our institutions and language." The Commonwealth was a tremendous force for peace because it embraced so many races and continents. "I do not think the British people, given the choice to decide as they should be, will in a moment of folly throw away a tremendous heritage of history." This was a strongly emotional speech and, in my humble opinion, less than vintage Gaitskell. But I will reserve my comments for the super-tearjerker that was to come at Brighton.

Some of Gaitskell's close friends in the Unions and elsewhere were by now trying to persuade him to pipe down a bit. A slightly ominous sign was that he received backing from Michael Foot in *Tribune*. Some twenty MPs who supported entry, with Roy Jenkins as their spokesman, had a discussion of ninety minutes with him about his broadcast. He tried to convince them that he was not leading the Party into complete opposition to entry, and the meeting was described as helpful. The *Washington Post* came right out with what many were thinking in Britain and Europe. Its leading article said that the most surprising sounds were emerging from the Leader's lips. The voice was Gaitskell's, but the words were more in the style of Lord Beaverbrook. "The anxiety he expresses about Great Britain's losing her independence in foreign policy just does not sound like the Gaitskell known in this country. These are the accents of a narrow provincialism. This Cassandra is not the Gaitskell whose moderation, internationalism, and intellectualism have won him in the US an unofficial 'constituency' quite as admiring as any he has in England. What is alarming is the prospect of an election on the issue with Hugh Gaitskell in the role of a fearful, foot-dragging, little-England isolationist, facing the challenge of the century with quaking fears and dreadful doubts about the dangers of the new world that the European Common Market is ushering into being." A little turgid, perhaps, but it expressed some widespread qualms.

So now we come to the apotheosis of Gaitskell, at the 61st Annual Conference of the Labour Party held at Brighton from 1st to 5th October 1962. He made only one speech, on the statement by the National Executive Committee entitled "Labour and the Common Market" and dated 29th September. Just one speech—but an overwhelming triumph. He followed his usual line on the subject, but he spoke with a fullness and a passion which he had not displayed before. Characteristically, he began by commending the statement "for its compelling logic." He asked that people should not get "over-heated" and that the level of discussion should be kept high. "It should not be decided because on the one hand we like Italian girls, or on the other we think we have been fleeced in Italian hotels." The issue was crucial, complex, and difficult, and "anybody who thinks otherwise is a fool." To three economic questions he gave the answer "no": are we forced to go into Europe; would we necessarily be the stronger for it; and would the Commonwealth automatically gain as a result? After giving facts and figures, he concluded that we would gain in those markets where we sell one-fifth of our exports, but lose in those where we sell about half. "Silly and dangerous nonsense" was often talked about the Commonwealth's no longer being an important market for us: the facts were otherwise. Food prices in Britain would undoubtedly rise. Certainly, a home market of 220 million people had its attractions, but we sell to the world. The size of the Market would not automatically deal with the question of the relative efficiency of our firms: some of the most efficient concerns came from small countries like Switzerland and Sweden. The idea of "dynamic Europe" was attractive too, but the Common Market was not in itself the cause of European expansion. Several Commonwealth countries were expanding their trade very fast, though it was true that we were failing to keep our share of it. What an indictment of the Tory economic policy, of stop, go, stop, and so on in the late '50s, entry would be! "If I have spoken strongly about these economic arguments, let me say particularly to those who favour our entry, that it is not because I start with a prejudice; it is because I am sick and tired of the nonsense and rubbish that is being written and spoken on the subject." In sum, the economic arguments were "no more than evenly balanced." Gaitskell then turned to the political aspects. Of course the idealism of this European getting-together, which the various social democratic parties particularly supported, was to be admired. The idea of a powerful united Europe was tempting, but it would have to unite on the right lines. "Europe can claim Goethe and Leonardo, Voltaire, and Picasso, but there have been some evil features too—Hitler and Mussolini, and today the attitude of some Europeans to the Congo and to the UN." If "belonging" just meant talking, that would be all right, but would it affect de Gaulle's views on NATO or Adenauer's on Berlin? If it meant majority decisions on political issues, the power of the British veto must be assured. Then there is the idea of Federal Europe. "It means—I repeat it—that if we go into this, we are no more than a state, as it were, in the

United States of Europe, such as Texas and California. It does mean the end of Britain as an independent state. It may be a good thing or a bad thing, but we must recognise that this is so. It means the end of a thousand years of history. And it does mean the end of the Commonwealth." And he personally wanted to "cherish" the modern Commonwealth, which the Labour Government had created. To build a bridge between the two would of course be fine, and here he came back to the five conditions that must be satisfied. On our independent foreign policy "we need to lay down that there is no commitment whatsoever which involves any political institutional change of any kind. The right of veto in this matter is imperative. I do not believe the British people at this stage are prepared to accept a supranational system on the vital issues of foreign policy." But the White Paper issued in August was a great disappointment and met none of the conditions adequately. It was not surprising that the Commonwealth Prime Ministers "in no uncertain terms made it plain to the British Government how totally unsatisfactory the present arrangements were." The Tory press and Mr. Sandys at the Commonwealth Relations Office had tried, but failed, to bulldoze the Commonwealth into accepting them; the result had been bitterness. The alternative to entry would not be disastrous at all: there were EFTA, the Commonwealth, the rest of the world. In any case, neither de Gaulle nor Adenauer was "over-enthusiastic to have us in." Why was the Government in such a hurry? Because they wanted to slip it across the British people before they could have an opportunity of commenting. "We are now being told that the British people are not capable of judging this issue—the Government knows best; the top people are the only people who can understand it. This is the classic argument of every tyranny in history." It was reactionary nonsense, "an odious piece of hypocritical, supercilious, arrogant rubbish," and an appeal to snobbery. It was said that the young favoured entry, and he welcomed their idealism. But if he were a young man in search of a cause, he would look beyond Europe and prefer to work for the Freedom from Hunger Campaign, or War on Want, or the Peace Corps formed by his friend Kennedy. The bad side of Europe was anti-American, anti-Russia, pro-colonial, obstinate over the Congo, Algeria, Berlin. "We do not close the door. Our conditions are not impossible or unreasonable. I profoundly hope that they can be met. But if this should not prove to be possible; if the Six will not give it to us; if the British Government will not even ask for it; then we must stand firm by what we believe, for the sake of Britain, and the Commonwealth, and the world; and we shall not flinch from our duty if that moment comes."

They went mad. They had been riveted for over eighty minutes; they gave him an unparalleled standing ovation of well over eighty seconds. On the platform people like Driberg, Crossman, and Mikardo clapped themselves sore; though faithful personal friends of Gaitskell like George Brown and Sam Watson did not conceal their lack of enthusiasm. Tony Crosland and Roy Jenkins looked glum; Douglas Jay, elated. The Chairman, Harold Wilson, said that he was sure he was speaking for the whole of the Conference in proposing that "this historic speech should be immediately printed and made available to every Party member and to the wider areas outside." This was agreed with acclamation. Supreme irony, when there was some temporarily embarrassed discussion at lunch about who would pay, Frank Cousins himself said that the TGWU would, for up to one million copies. Even Shinwell, a relentless critic of Gaitskell, welcomed this warmly. On reflexion, the leading marketeers, including many Trade Union leaders, were dismayed, and so were many of their younger followers. It was generally agreed that Gaitskell had abandoned his fence-sitting posture, had delivered the most devastating attack yet made by any British politician on the European idea, and had gone considerably beyond the NEC's brief in doing so. George Brown grappled manfully with the difficult task of winding up the debate. His main point was that Gaitskell's prime objective was to destroy the gimmicks and double-talk of HMG. His speech was also circulated to Party members. When interviewed on the BBC on 5th October, Gaitskell persisted that he had not intended to give the impression that Labour were coming out against the Common Market. He did not enjoy disagreeing with some close personal friends, but he was bound to do so as he had some in both the pro- and anti-entry camps. When asked if he was gambling on an early election, he replied: "No, on the contrary." Heath got it right when he said: "I am not aware that Mr. Gaitskell has definitely opposed entry. It seems to have been the manner of his delivery that created that impression."

Why exactly did he do it? That is a complex question indeed. First, because he was honestly annoyed with the way the Tories were negotiating and with their totally inept handling of the important question of keeping the British public properly informed. Secondly, because of his deeply sincere attachment to the Commonwealth and its interests. But he seems to have worked himself into a lather and to have been carried away by the Conference atmosphere. It could not objectively be said that this was a non-committal speech. The conditions he posed, and not least his vehement insistence on the British veto, were not objectively possible and were bound to strike people in Europe as arrogant. The repetition of the references to Texas and California and to "a thousand years of history" were rather shameless and have a reactionary smack about them. And sure enough he was immediately accused in France of "nationalistic demagogy" and deliberately hampering the European idea; and in Bonn of "Machiavellian cynicism" and of selling out to his "dubious" friends of the rabid Left Wing, though Brandt loyally continued to press for Britain's entry. What he succeeded in doing was to make it easier for our opponents in the Six to hamstring the Macmillan Government's efforts since it appeared that about half of Britain was solidly against entry; and by his bulldozing methods Gaitskell broadly appeared to have the bulk of the Labour Movement behind him and thus to have avoided another serious split. In spite of his remark about his friends, he was in fact deeply distressed that some took his speech so hard, especially amongst his faithful Trade Union supporters. What is more, he was genuinely surprised, which was itself surprising as he might have expected it, and he was not an insensitive man. In a small circle he admitted that emotionally he must all along have been more against the Common Market than he realised; another rebuff to desiccated calculation. Finally, it is possible to be too sophisticated in judging such big issues: on the form then and since, is it not conceivable that he was simply right?

However that may be, nothing daunted, he had on the evening of the speech accepted nomination as Vice-Chairman of the NEC for the next year, after Arthur Skeffington and Anthony Greenwood had withdrawn. Barring an act of God, he would therefore be both Chairman and Leader of the PLP in 1963–4, when the General Election was bound to take place. He would be in a more powerful position than any man in the whole history of the Movement. Do I hear the Eumenides in the wings, whispering cruelly to each other of the fatal price of the sin of hubris?

Gaitskell did not leave his Common Market campaign at that. On 11th October the Conservative Party Conference voted for entry. But, said Gaitskell, this was stage-managed: its members would jump into the sea off Llandudno, tear down the Union Jack, or sing the "Internationale" if it kept them in power. They had thrown out of the window the Government's pledged safeguards. They had sold the Commonwealth down the river, and no doubt the EFTA allies too. "We still believe in the Labour Party that Britain has its own part to play in world affairs." Asked by Lord Boothby on television whether he would repudiate the present terms if he became Prime Minister, he replied: "I am not commenting on that one." But Britain must not be "submerged" in Europe. He agreed that the US seemed anxious that we should join, as a prelude to a build-up of the Atlantic union.

But he thought the Americans were wrong, and dangerously so, in thinking that a European state would necessarily be a stabilising influence. On 25th October, with that energy that seemed inexhaustible, he paid a flying visit to Paris and addressed the World Parliament Association. He pointed out that Britain was already heavily involved in Europe, militarily, commercially, and culturally. He hoped that suitable entry terms could be negotiated, but the alternative was not isolation. On the contrary, "the British relationship with countries of the Common Market would be even closer and friendlier than at present" while her special links with the Commonwealth would be maintained. He also pressed at some length for the modernisation and activation of the United Nations. Amongst other things he suggested a permanent international police force, a World Development Agency, a UN Disarmament Agency, the reform of the Security Council by the co-opting of more of the newer nations, and the admission of China. On 7th November he returned to the Common Market theme in what was to be his last major speech in the House. He spoke for a full hour, as usual with exiguous notes. His line was the same as before, and he supported it with numerous telling statistics.

But Gaitskell by no means devoted all his time to Common Market affairs. Speaking at Derby on 20th October, he said the plan put forward a few days earlier by the National Economic Development Council was "the most devastating indictment of ministerial folly ever presented to a government by its own officials." In showing what could be done in future, it indicated what had not been done since Labour's planning set-up was scrapped in 1951. In exports, for instance, the new plan provided for an annual rise of 5.7 per cent, against the 2½ per cent so far achieved under Tory rule. When Labour had put forward just such a plan Macmillan had described it as "a recipe for national bankruptcy." Who could trust the Government's economic judgment now?

This was the time of the Cuba crisis, and Kennedy took the trouble to send his White House CIA aide, an old friend of mine, to show the photographic evidence not only to Macmillan but to Gaitskell too. While Gaitskell agreed that the US Government had ample cause for alarm at the installation of the missiles, he said it would be both illegal and unwise to attack Cuba, and in particular it might lead the USSR to attack similar bases in Turkey. He hoped that U Thant could bring the two sides together, and he criticised the US Government for not consulting HMG, as her NATO ally, at every turn. This was less than fair. First, it was impossible, in the very subtle diplomatic game, where the situation varied significantly from hour to hour, which Kennedy played so well. Secondly, we were in effect consulted since Kennedy treated our excellent Ambassador, David Ormsby Gore, practically as a member of his Cabinet. In another speech soon after, Gaitskell said that the unity of Western Europe was not all that important; what mattered today was relations between East and West and between the richer and poorer countries. He did not believe that the creation of a large new state would help to achieve the greatest aims of all, complete disarmament and some form of world government. Thus Gaitskell's broad idealism never flagged.

With all these major matters on his plate, Gaitskell still found time to intervene forcefully in the question of my premature retirement from the Foreign Office. In early June, I had been informed in a brief letter that the British Ambassador in Bonn and the British commandant in Berlin had complained that I was an unsatisfactory colleague and that consequently I was not only to leave Berlin but to retire forthwith from the Service. I was 49, and I decided that it would be best to accept the verdict, but also to bring into the open the Foreign Office's ham-handed behaviour. The press were soon on to my story, and after the retirement formalities were through in September, some newspapers fairly let the Foreign Office have it. The *Observer* also published very prominently a long article of mine on Berlin. In this I embodied the Gaitskell line, though working quite independently of him and going further on two counts. I thought that the German Democratic Republic should be fully recognised *de jure,* and I gave several good reasons: she existed, actively, and would continue to exist (she is now the eighth most powerful industrial state in the world); and from the diplomatic point of view this was the only approach that might eventually bring about German reunification. I also proposed that West Berlin should become an independent entity, with the usual right to invite friendly forces to be stationed on her soil and with properly guaranteed access routes. All three parts of Germany would then have representatives in the United Nations. This piece caused a considerable stir. On the day of Parliament's reassembly, 25th October, Stephen Swingler put a question about my case, which was answered in writing by Peter Thomas, then Parliamentary Under-Secretary at the Foreign Office. The answer was quite inadequate, and Gaitskell immediately invited me to discuss the matter with him. He, Harold Wilson, and I had a thorough-going hour in his office in the House, and their grave doubts about the justice of my treatment were confirmed after a friendly but detailed probing of all the circumstances by Gaitskell. He then asked Wilson and Anthony Greenwood to deal with the matter, which they did most effectively, their actions culminating in a House of Commons debate on the case in which they made mincemeat of Peter Thomas. This was a period when the Conservative Government, and the top officials in some government departments such as the Foreign Office who came from the same stable, were becoming increasingly careless and arrogant in their treatment of individuals and personalities who were not of their way of thinking. As the Government now consisted largely of Dukes and their connexions, including Macmillan himself, the gap was frequently wide. It was at this time that Rab Butler, who remained a friend of Gaitskell's throughout, asked him in personal conversation whether he had ever known such a bunch of shits as his own colleagues in the Government? And at this time, as Edward Heath recently remarked, people generally were getting awfully bored with the Tories. Gaitskell himself was on to any case of flagrant injustice like a knife. I remember him vividly from that time. Not impressive in looks or dress, but a very shrewd, often quizzical expression, the left eye usually more closed than the right. The manner was gentle and friendly; the intellect behind it, steely and sharp. Anyone hoping to put anything across him would have to get up very early in the morning. Above all, he gave the impression of being a politician who, though he had achieved great success, was interested primarily in human griefs and pleasures, and had, in fact, achieved that success through constant solicitude towards the everyday life of everyday people.

The Vassall Spy case had just broken, and Gaitskell gave it the full attention he always devoted to such security matters. In Manchester on 10th November he said that the resignation of a junior Minister—Galbraith—was not enough. This was the third scandal of the same kind in two years. Yet again, since much of the information was secret, Parliament could not do its job effectively. "How can we be sure that those responsible for negligence, including Ministers, are brought to book?" An enquiry was needed by people completely independent of the Government, and the Opposition should be informed of all that came to light. These admirable suggestions did not have any great effect, and though I myself and others more influential have echoed them since, we still stumble along in this country from one spy case to the next.

However, a sign that Macmillan was prepared, no doubt reluctantly, to recognise Gaitskell's influential standing came when they had a meeting lasting an hour and a half on the subject of the Chinese invasion of India; though here too the concrete results were hardly perceptible. Next Gaitskell hammered the Government on its Central African policy, demanding the dissolution of the Federation and early independence for each of the three territories in accordance with the wishes of their populations. When Heath turned down flat a new proposal by the Polish Government to discuss the

Rapacki Plan, Gaitskell expressed great disappointment. He pointed out that this reversed the conclusion embodied in the Moscow communiqué issued at the end of Macmillan's visit in 1959 and was also contrary to the favourable attitude recently adopted by President Kennedy.

On the economic front, he told the Oxford University Labour Club that the new Chancellor Reginald Maudling's efforts had been "very tardy, very sluggish and very timid." As a result of the "obstinate,, obscurantist attitude" of his predecessor, Selwyn Lloyd, unemployment now stood at 540,-000 and would almost certainly rise above 600,000 before long. These were all "gross errors of judgment on the part of what is really a very tired administration." All this time he kept in touch socially with a very wide circle: at his dinner-parties in Hampstead you could meet anyone ranging from his personal Labour friends to tycoons and intellectuals of numerous shades of opinion and nationalities.

As December 1962, his last active month, arrived, he refused to admit to any tiredness himself; and he pursued his multifarious activities. On 2nd December he made a long speech at a lunch in Paris of the Anglo-American Press Association about the Common Market. He stood absolutely pat on Labour's five conditions and made no concessions, though his tone was less emotional than it had been at the Brighton Conference. He pinpointed the provisional agreements of July and August as being "profoundly unsatisfactory." The offers in respect of the Commonwealth were most vague, and the assembled Prime Ministers had been highly critical of them in September. "Having said all this, I must repeat once more, to avoid misunderstanding, that I would greatly prefer, instead of the failure of the negotiations, that our conditions should be accepted by the Six and that Britain should then be able to join the EEC in the kind of Europe with the qualities and characteristics I have outlined." This was bound to annoy the French, who were in any case in an increasingly arrogant phase themselves. It was a transfer to the field of diplomacy of Gaitskell's favoured technique in domestic politics, that of the head-on collision. As we have seen, on many occasions this had worked in the long run, after much initial resistance. Could it have worked similarly over the Common Market? He was not to be allowed the longer run. On the same visit he had talks with Georges Pompidou, then Prime Minister; Couve de Murville, the Foreign Minister; and Guy Mollet, the Socialist leader. Mollet suggested some kind of treaty of association with the EEC, and Gaitskell agreed that the idea was interesting and worth discussing. Mollet also said that French Socialists had always tried to understand the Labour Party's attitudes, but as regards the Common Market they just were not on the same wavelength. Nor, he might have added, had they been over Suez. "European" circles as a whole in France were dismayed by the speech, which suggested to some that even if Britain joined, she would not think and act as a good European. Gaitskell also sent President Kennedy a carefully elaborated description of Labour's case. Kennedy asked for a reasoned reply to be drafted, but alas time was too short.

Gaitskell's interest, and achievements, in international relations had grown steadily over the years, though as early as 1956 he had made a great impact over Suez. His strong feeling for the Commonwealth was, of course, shared by many Labour supporters. So was his consistent support for the United Nations, even if he expressed his attitude of "the UN right or wrong" more forcefully than most. His most original achievements lay in three apparently diverse directions. First was his profound, and often expressed, attachment to the US alliance, though he never kow-towed to that country. Many in the Party, including Bevan, were less than lukewarm on that score. Secondly, his courageous and consistent stand in favour of the Rapacki Plan and the de facto recognition of the GDR put his thinking way ahead of most Labour supporters, and all Tories, in that sphere. It was also way ahead of almost all Americans' ideas, with the exception of President Kennedy and his circle. Finally, there was Gaitskell's leadership over the question of British entry into the

Common Market; whether in the right direction or no is debatable, but leadership it certainly was. Being throughout not only a man of the Left, but also a highly sophisticated politician, he could both have worth-while dealings with the Communists in the Soviet Union and elsewhere, which is always difficult for the Tories, and keep a clear judgment on the possibilities of rapprochement. No one could be more wholly opposed to the tenets and many of the methods of Communism, as we have seen time and again. But he was always prepared to talk with Khruschev or Rapacki and to put forward his objective suggestions as a result of these discussions. I think he showed over-optimism, and hence lack of realism, regarding the conditions on which the USSR would agree to help a détente in Central Europe and the Middle East; but I have no doubt that further direct contact with the Soviet Government would have remedied this. All in all, it came about that although Gaitskell had never had responsibility for the conduct of our foreign relations, he was most highly respected not only in the Socialist international movement world-wide, but far beyond it by leaders of every colour and kind.

In mid-December, Gaitskell made some plans for fighting the good fight abroad and at home in January. In the first week he and his wife would visit Moscow as the guests of the Soviet inter-parliamentary group. He would have talks with Khruschev on world affairs generally, and specifically on disarmament, disengagement in Central Europe, and the future status of West Berlin. (Would he have come around to my views on that, I wonder?) On his return he would undertake a fact-finding tour of the areas worst hit by unemployment in Scotland, North-East England, and Lancashire. He would round it off with an embattled speech on Labour's plans for tackling that problem, which he foresaw would be one of the Government's tenderest spots in 1963.

It was not to be.

TWELVE

The Last Enemy

ON 15TH DECEMBER 1962, Gaitskell came down with influenza and had to cancel his engagements for the coming week. He entered the Manor House hospital in Hampstead and expected to stay there for a few days. He would then have a medical check before his visit to the Soviet Union. John Harris, who had been Gaitskell's personal publicity adviser over the 1959 election and was now the Party's director of publicity, announced that "There is nothing seriously wrong with him, but he wants to get quite fit before his visit to Russia." After all, plenty of people get 'flu in England in December. Thinking back, one or two of his friends have told me that he had in the preceding months shown something less than his customary social verve and a slight tendency to get irritable as a boring party wore on. An MP who entered the House in November still has a strong impression that he was a tired man. As we have seen, he had not spared himself for a moment, over a long period. On 23rd December he was allowed to go home from hospital to spend Christmas with his family.

It was a sad one. On Christmas and Boxing days it became clear that the virus infection from which he had been suffering, influenza plus a mild attack of pleurisy, had come back. John Harris stated: "Although this will clear up within a week or ten days, his doctors have advised him that it would be most unwise to contemplate a journey to Russia, with its much colder climate, at present." The Soviet Ambassador made the trip to Hampstead, and Gaitskell explained matters to him and sent messages of regret to his hosts, the Soviet interperliamentary group, and to Khruschev. He told the press: "I am exceedingly disappointed as I have been much looking forward to my visit and to my talks with Mr. Khruschev. I hope to go a little later on."

But if the flesh was weakening, the spirit was still more than willing. Gaitskell's New Year message to the Labour Party was as pugnacious as ever. As 1962 came to an end, it ran, the Macmillan Government's policies were collapsing everywhere. Half a million people had Christmas on the dole, the highest number for about a quarter of a century. The Tories, oh yes, produced expansion—every one year in four, conveniently for successive General Elections. On defence they showed sheer misjudgment and incompetence; "time and again we warned them that Skybolt (another missile project) would come to nothing." On the Common Market they had shamelessly ignored their pledges. In Central Africa they had at last been forced to abandon "the long foolishness of imposed Federation." Labour were now ready for responsibility. More and more people were turning to them. "We have to earn and confirm that confidence by remaining united; by being honest with ourselves and with others; by applying in our traditional fashion Socialist ideals with practical commonsense; above all, as always, by the simple, devoted hardwork which has made our movement what it is." A powerful swansong. But the pleurisy lingered on, and the tour of areas of heavy unemployment planned for mid-January had to be cancelled too. George Brown and Douglas Jay would go instead.

By 4th January 1963 things were not so good, and Gaitskell returned to hospital, this time to the Middlesex. His room had previously been occupied by Churchill. To the pleurisy had now been added pericarditis, the inflammation of the smooth membrane surrounding the heart. The medical bulletin stated: "The condition, although serious, is not giving rise to immediate anxiety." A further bulletin was promised for the following day, and this reported him "a little better." His wife was hopeful. "I shall be spending a good deal of time with him. He likes to have me with him. When he wants me to, I read to him." The improvement continued slightly during the next few nights and days, though he suffered a good deal of pain. Four distinguished doctors looked after him. The Queen and Macmillan, amongst many others, sent his wife wishes for his recovery. The slight improvement continued until 14th January. It was reported that "exhaustive tests have not so far revealed any other underlying disease." Yet the fever lingered obstinately on. Of course, no one who knew him could contemplate the possibility that this exceptionally vigorous and commanding man was about to die.

Matters took a decided turn for the worse on 15th January; it was the beginning of the end. A bulletin recorded a "deterioration" in his condition. The inflammation had extended, a secondary infection had developed, and this was not responding to intensive treatment. "His condition is now giving rise to some anxiety." The next day things were worse again, with serious renal and abdominal complications. The outlook was described by spokesmen as very grave, critical, but not hopeless. His brother and his daughters visited him; his wife stayed in the hospital day and night. He received blood plasma transfusions. George Brown cut short his northern tour, flew to London by RAF aircraft, and went straight to see him on landing in the early hours. By this time we all, still incredulously, feared the worst. On 17th January it was decided to use an artificial kidney; members of a team of eight doctors were on constant vigil. "He has held his own during the day." Innumerable messages arrived, from the great like Adlai Stevenson, Nkrumah, Adenauer, Mollet, the Soviet Ambassador Soldatov, and from masses of ordinary people.

He died at 9:12 p.m. on Friday 18th January. His wife was with him. A brief bulletin said: "Mr. Gaitskell's heart condition deteriorated suddenly and he died peacefully."

John Harris said that the doctors told him he had put up
"a tremendous fight for life" and shown "quite extraordinary
courage. He showed a degree of fortitude and courage which
the doctors have rarely witnessed." He was a fighter to the
last.

Condolences and tributes began to pour in immediately
from all over the world, amongst the first being those from
the Queen and Duke of Edinburgh, Macmillan, Attlee,
Churchill, President and Mrs. Kennedy, Dean Rusk, the
Canadian Prime Minister Diefenbaker, the Norwegian Prime
Minister Gerhardsen, the chairman of the West German
Social Democratic Party Ollenhauer. Over the weekend the
list swelled to enormous proportions: Khruschev, Nehru,
President Ayub Khan, Robert Menzies, President Julius
Nyerere, Sir Roy Welensky, the Prime Minister of Nigeria
Alhaji Sir Abubakar Tafawa Balewa, Sir Alexander Busta-
mante of Jamaica, General Eisenhower, President Luebke,
Willy Brandt, Walter Ulbricht, U Thant, President Tito,
Gomulka, President Nkrumah, and scores of other personalities far too numerous to mention. And once again, what
Gaitskell would have appreciated at least as much, the messages came from hundreds of thousands of ordinary people
all over the world. Up and down Britain flags were flown
at half-mast, a privilege normally reserved for Heads of
State or royalty. Harold Wilson cut short a lecture tour in
the US and cancelled a meeting with President Kennedy to
fly back immediately.

Macmillan paid him a handsome tribue on television the
day after his death. "Why did he outclass his rivals? Primarily, of course, because of his clear brain and intellectual
power. But he had something more: that indefinable thing,
character. He had real humanity, not paraded, but genuine;
a warm heart with a real affection not just for mankind in
general but for individuals. He was courteous and sympathetic even to bores. He had no hatred, except a deep and
genuine hatred for injustice of any sort." Macmillan spoke

again when Parliament reassembled on 22nd January, and on his initiative the House paid an unprecedented tribute to Gaitskell: the Government moved the adjournment after questions, that is a mere one-and-a-half-hours' sitting, as was customary only in the case of deceased Prime Ministers or former Prime Ministers, and had last been done in 1881 in honour of a Leader of the Opposition—Disraeli, himself a former Prime Minister. On this occasion Macmillan commended Gaitskell's parliamentary skill: very lucid exposition was combined with "rhetorical and emotional appeal of a very high order." As a debater he was formidable. "I feel sure that he would have taken his place in the ranks of some of our greatest figures, and he was clearly destined to play an ever-increasing role in world affairs." He was also an attractive companion who "commanded deep devotion from his more intimate friends and colleagues." George Brown, pale and emotional, recalled how well they worked together in spite of their temperamental differences. He had been largely responsible for a new approach, a new method, on the part of the Labour Party. His superb clarity "incidentally made arguing with him a nightmare." He was sometimes impatient with others and failed to recognise that their limitations were genuine. "I can think now of one major national controversy where he was utterly surprised and deeply distressed by the reactions of friends." Brown too described him as the gayest and warmest of companions. Jo Grimond and Sir Thomas Moore, deputising for Sir Winston Churchill as Father of the House, paid him due honour. Finally Miss Alice Bacon spoke on behalf of Leeds and particularly the people of South Leeds. She said that Gaitskell often went and stayed in a small house on a housing estate there and had always been an excellent constituency member in spite of all his other preoccupations. "Last weekend the curtains were drawn in the small houses in the streets of South Leeds, not just for a Member of Parliament but for a very dear friend whom they knew and loved." Then the

House, subdued with grief, adjourned for the day. Members filed out in melancholy fashion; and the Gaitskell family, in deep mourning, left their places in the gallery.

It was now revealed that Gaitskell had probably died of a rare and little understood disease called disseminated lupus erythematosis, and eventually this was confirmed. This disease attacks all the basic tissues of the body—skin, membranes, heart valves, kidney glands, and smaller blood vessels; its origins are mysterious, and it is virtually incurable. It might well have struck anyway in two or three years' time. Gaitskell's funeral service on 23rd January was a private ceremony at Hampstead Parish Church. Numerous close friends from the Labour Movement attended, and there were flowers from many foreign Socialist parties, amongst other bodies. Cremation followed at the Golders Green crematorium. More than 300 people attended a memorial service in Leeds. On 31st January, at Westminster Abbey, the congregation numbered more than 2,000. Apart from a representative of the Queen, Macmillan and his Ministers, the Shadow Cabinet, and so on, there were very many visitors from abroad, including the Prime Minister of Denmark, J. O. Krag, and Willy Brandt from Berlin. Above all, and as always, there were the people honouring their man.

For that was Hugh Gaitskell. He had made a good many enemies in the political sphere; very few, including those same political enemies, in the personal. Frank Cousins and Harold Macmillan, from their somewhat different angles, both testified to this effect, at the end. He had established himself as a most successful Leader of the Opposition, having surmounted a lost election, ridden fearful schisms in his own Party, and never ceased to wear down the Tories. He had left Labour poised and prepared for victory whenever the General Election should come. He was regarded by more than half the people as the probable next Prime Minister, and no doubt a highly able one. The same view was held by many politicians, and others, across the world.

I see Gaitskell confronting the last enemy, Death, with his

usual verve and nerve. Tactically, he is defeated. In the
longer run Death takes his place amongst those who have
been, in a good cause, overcome. Hugh Gaitskell had fully
qualified as a citizen of the world. He could speak in the
sense of the wise Latin saying, but more positively: I am a
man, and I reckon that the whole human condition is of
concern to me. He was, in truth, a man for all seasons.

THIRTEEN

The Loss

How often do my Tory friends remark to me: ah, a shocking loss, Gaitskell's death. If only we had him now, the whole country would be much better off. After which they proceed to various pejorative remarks about Harold Wilson as Prime Minister. This is pure hypocrisy, of course. Many Tories hated Gaitskell during his life because he was such a skilful and effective politician. Very few top Tory politicians approached his intellectual calibre, and this caused much jealousy. Moreover, apart from Butler, they were Hogg, a bit of a buffoon; Ian Macleod and Edward Boyle, suspect to many of their colleagues as being too far left; and Enoch Powell, guilty of *la trahison des clercs*. Furthermore, a large proportion of the Tory rank and file, colonels and other types of backwoodsmen, muttered under their breath that he was a traitor to his class, the anointed ruling class who must always be Tory. Also it is a superficial judgment; for very few people indeed, whether Tories or not, have tried to work out what his probable impact since 1963 would have been.

The press did not wait for Gaitskell to die before indulging in speculation about the future of the Labour Movement. "Gaitskell has no challenger" proclaimed one paper on 7th January 1963, and: "When Hugh Gaitskell falls ill and is taken off to hospital, there is nation-wide concern. Almost with surprise people realise suddenly that, on the Opposition benches, there is no other alternative Prime Minister in sight." Moreover, he was now a statesman of world stature, and universally recognised as such, who had discussed world matters with President Kennedy and would shortly do so with Khruschev. "With the Common Market decision imminent and a General Election looming, Britain needs this imaginative, experienced, and dignified public figure." In fact, on 14th January President de Gaulle firmly stated his objections to Britain's entry, which may have brought a wan smile to Gaitskell on his deathbed; and by the end of the month de Gaulle had clarified his position with a decisive "non."

The point was freely made that if Labour had once again come to be considered as an alternative government, instead of as the Party of permanent opposition, Gaitskell could take much of the credit. Having successfully converted a majority of his own Party to his views, he now stood a good chance of also convincing a majority of the electorate. The country, as well as the Labour Party, needed his leadership. *The Times* on 19th January, while heading the top third of a two-column spread "Death of Mr. Gaitskell," made no bones about heading the remaining two-thirds "Electoral Disadvantages for Labour Party." The theme was that the Labour Party was now "almost rudderless at a crucial time. While politicians in all parties mourn Mr. Gaitskell's death, simply because they are politicians they must make calculations, however untimely or ghoulish the duty must seem, and Gaitskell had left no heir." George Brown had defeated Harold Wilson by 30 votes the previous November for the Deputy Leadership, but that was in no way decisive for the Leadership stakes. Neither seemed overwhelmingly acceptable for that, but to be fair nor had Gaitskell in 1955. So it seemed likely that the Conservatives might well exploit Labour's disarray by calling an early General Election. One commentator referred to the "heroic dimensions of the gap that Gaitskell has left"; and there was much speculation that, while Labour under Gaitskell would almost certainly have won the next General Election, all was now in the balance. Both George Brown and Harold Wilson deprecated discussing the leadership at a moment when Gaitskell had only just gone. It was "an agonising issue." After a decent interval Wilson defeated Brown and Callaghan in early February, and Brown on the second ballot on 14th February.

If Gaitskell had been spared, his first priority would have been to recover his strength, his second to use it in harrying the Macmillan Government on all the numerous issues on which they became increasingly vulnerable, and his third to have further talks with Khruschev. He would have issued a statement from his place of recuperation saying that de Gaulle's rejection of British entry on 29th January was not only to be welcomed on the merits of the conditions HMG had so far negotiated, but served Macmillan right on another score too: his obtuse diplomacy in trying to bribe de Gaulle with Kennedy's offer of Polaris, which Macmillan, acting as Kennedy's messenger-boy, had conveyed to the proud President hotfoot on his return from Nassau. In February he would have flayed the Government on the unemployment figures of 878,356, an increase of nearly 64,000 in a month; and he would have exploited the various gratifying Labour by-election results in March. He would, no doubt, have smelt a rat when John Profumo, Secretary of State for War, made his untrue personal statement in the House, which he was to correct in early June when he resigned. Gaitskell would not have kicked Profumo when he was down, as that was not his wont; he always preferred attacking those who were riding higher than they deserved, and he would have treated the affair as a symptom of the decrepitude of Macmillan and the decadence of his administration. So indeed it was. In April he would have hammered Reginald Maudling's Budget on the usual, and justified, grounds that it was designed to make the rich richer and in no way to improve Britain's economic standing in the world. On a matter of financial fact, it was announced at this time that in his will Gaitskell had left some £80,000, a sum which surprised a good many people (including his friend Rab Butler, as he told me). No doubt he was, like Keynes, a shrewd practical investor as well as a good theoretical economist. Duty paid was some £30,000 and the property was left to his wife, with a bequest to his stepson.

In early May, Labour gained over 540 seats in the borough elections in England and Wales, and Gaitskell would have demanded again that the tired and discredited men should go. In June Macmillan said on television that if all went well with his health, he hoped to lead the Tories at the next election. He would have got short shrift from Gaitskell. At the end of June President Kennedy paid a brief visit to Macmillan. He would certainly have found time for a talk with Gaitskell. In early July Heath announced that Kim Philby, who had disappeared from Beirut several weeks earlier, had in fact been the third man concerned with Maclean and Burgess in 1951, contrary to what Macmillan had previously announced. At the end of the same month, Philby turned up publicly in the USSR, and a great many people wanted to know why he had been allowed to get away. No satisfactory answer has been given to this day. We have seen that Gaitskell took these security cases with the utmost seriousness, and he would have turned the heat on over this one. He would have taken some credit for the passage of the Peerage Bill into law, accompanied by Wedgwood Benn's immediate disclaimer of his peerage and entry into the House of Commons; and for the partial nuclear test ban treaty signed in August by the US, USSR, and Britain.

On 30th September the Labour Annual Conference assembled at Scarborough, sadder than usual. Tony Greenwood was elected to the chair that Gaitskell would have occupied in the ordinary way. Suitable respect was paid to him both there and in the official report on the proceedings. A full-page photograph was followed by an account of his outstanding career; this included the comments that "his determination to modernise the Party led to misunderstandings" and "his handling of the complex Common Market issues earned him yet more respect and affection." All perhaps a trifle jejune, as were the tributes at his prep and public schools. At the Dragon, where he had first leaned towards Socialism, there was a small and totally unmemorable ceremony. At Winchester a senior master whom I questioned could not say whether there was any memorial to him or not, though I insisted that an admirer had tracked down a tiny one somewhere. After all, said my friend, we can't have memorials to every Wykehamist politician, can we? Now, if he had been a Field-Marshal (he was thinking of Wavell) or a Bishop, it would be a different matter. Bishops, I replied, are ten a penny; Gaitskell was something special. Eventually, with perseverance, I found it. A small plaque, some six inches across, in an undistinguished room in the house where he had boarded. It relied heavily on the pale all-purpose word "integrity" and appeared to be made of tin; I was assured it was actually pewter. New College also ran to a small plaque. Altogether more appropriate was the elevation of Dora Gaitskell to the peerage that same year. Not only had she brought Hugh much aid and comfort throughout; she had always been an articulate fighter for Socialism herself.

Conference for their part decided to set up a Hugh Gaitskell Memorial Fund under James Griffiths' direction. The appeal for funds "to establish an educational foundation for giving grants to students from the Commonwealth at British universities and colleges, and to assist British students who go to Commonwealth countries to complete their training," in accordance with Gaitskell's firm belief in "the need to forge closer links between the peoples of all races," was launched in January 1964. It was sponsored by representatives of all the political parties, the churches, the TUC, the academic world, and many others. Joint honorary treasurers were Lord Monckton, chairman of the Midland Bank, and David Robarts of the National Provincial Bank. Amongst the signatories were the Archbishops of Canterbury and Westminster; the Chief Rabbi; Rab Butler, then Foreign Secretary; Lord Robens of the National Coal Board; John Betjemen; Kenneth Clark; Maurice Bowra; William Hayter; Noel Annan; Desmond Lee; John Sparrow; and the Labour

and Liberal leaders. The appeal was also to be sent to overseas universities, and already a number of prominent Americans had offered to help. It must be recorded that it has not
really flourished. Some £20,000 were raised, and the first
Commonwealth student recently arrived and is at work in
this country now.

Gaitskell would have enjoyed and exploited to the full
the Tories' antics in October 1963. In a sense these developments were another success for Gaitskell, posthumous this
time, for they represented the cracking of the Tories under
the strain that he had relentlessly imposed on them. Macmillan's health was not up to it, after all; and, dramatically,
on the day before the Conservative Party Conference began
on 9th October, he had to go into hospital for an operation.
His acknowledged deputy, Butler, went to Blackpool (Why
do all those Tories go to Blackpool, I wonder?) to conduct
affairs. On 10th October the operation was successfully performed, but Macmillan sent a message to say that he would
not be able to lead the Party at the next election and that
he hoped that the customary process of consultation within
the Party about the future leadership would not be carried
out. He could say that again. The most undignified scramble
imaginable took place. Poor Butler was swept aside in the
rush; he resents it to this day. Within hours the ambitious
Viscount Hailsham announced that he would disclaim his
peerage, in exchange for the leadership, he hoped. But the
winner when all the infighting had finished was, almost
incredibly for the 1960s, the 14th Earl who had not even
troubled to disclaim as yet, though he did so shortly after
and was found a safe seat. Now Gaitskell would not have
been surprised at the goings-on in Blackpool, which he would
have slated as typical Tory behaviour. But he would have
given Douglas-Home no quarter. He had for years regarded
him as an anachronism in the high offices he held. He would
have ridiculed him mercilessly as Prime Minister. Those
little jokes of Home's about doing the country's economic
sums with matchsticks would not have amused Gaitskell one

bit: he would have condemned them for what they were, supercilious and snobbish amateurism and frivolity on matters of vital importance to the people as a whole. My guess is that he would have had Douglas-Home in tears before long and would not have let him alone until he had forced him into an early election, say in June 1964. And the Labour majority would in all probability have been larger than the skimpy five which they achieved in October.

None of these speculations are intended to belittle what was achieved, and continues to be achieved, under the leadership of Harold Wilson. Gaitskell himself had the highest opinion of both his and George Brown's abilities. Indeed a close friend of Gaitskell's, who is now a Minister of State in Wilson's administration told me he thought things could well have been difficult under Gaitskell, in two ways. First there was the economic shambles to be cleared up, though it would have been marginally less catastrophic if Douglas-Home and Maudling had had rather less time to do their deadly work. But secondly there was the Gaitskell *modus operandi,* which would certainly have led to some troubles and conflicts in the Labour Movement. For a start they would have arisen over the four aspects of policy mentioned in the first chapter. Gaitskell would have refused to play safe. On the devaluation question he would probably have gone ahead and devalued without much delay. He would have been quite prepared to push through legislation on unofficial strikes, if necessary at the cost of a head-on collision with the Unions. He had, after all, been involved in such collisions before. This man had infinite patience with anyone who had a real grievance against the system. At the same time he did not suffer fools gladly, and he would have been quick to say frankly when he thought certain wild-cat strikers were smugly putting their own petty interests above those of the Labour Movement and the nation. Latterday Luddites were not for him. Nor the Enoch Powells of the Labour Movement, such as the London dockers who took time off their work to visit the House and applaud Powell's racialist ideas. He would probably have agreed, privately, that the political spectrum broadly looks like this, reading from right to left: most women, though there are outstanding exceptions; right-wing Tories; most Trades Unionists; other Tories (such as Butler and Boyle); and the Parliamentary Labour Party. Quintin Hogg put it broadly, if perhaps over-confidently, the other day when he said: "The facts of life are Tory." Gaitskell would not have been amused by the attitude expressed by Victor Feather when acting General Secretary of the TUC: "Laws don't make motor cars or build ships. Laws don't make anything except work for lawyers." Similarly, I was assured by Douglas Houghton that if Barbara Castle's original tough bill on industrial rela-tions had become law, the Unions would simply have broken the law. Gaitskell would not have stood for this. He might have been forced to acknowledge that in Britain "full em-ployment" was too often a euphemism for slowness of work spread out over an unnecessary number of people and often with unnecessary and expensive "overtime" at the end. In another sphere, he would have been fairly ruthless both about his own selection of Cabinet colleagues for the appropriate jobs and about dismissing them if they were not up to it.

Gaitskell would have kept the question of entry into the Common Market under review, but would probably have vetoed any positive steps by Britain so long as de Gaulle was in power. And in the search for world peace and East-West détente, he would have been constantly active. Sick at heart at Kennedy's assassination in November 1963, he would have discussed the issues just as frankly with President Johnson; and he and Khruschev would have achieved a meeting of minds on such matters as the recognition of the German Democratic Republic, the Rapacki-Gaitskell plan for Central Europe, and many others besides. As he always tried to judge problems, whether international or not, on their merits rather than starting out with prejudices, he had no more inhibitions in talking to Khruschev than to Kennedy. In domestic matters he would have given high priority to dealing with the socially divisive character of the British educational system. It goes without saying that, if almost all of these policies would have caused flare-ups in the Labour Movement, they would without exception have run into the stiffest and most resentful opposition on the part of the Conservatives.

Would his government have achieved more, and "done better" than the present one? That is more a subject for the novelist than for the serious political commentator, and it would be carrying speculation altogether too far to give a judgment on it. For one thing the present Government's achievements are in many ways underrated, even if the more honest critics admit that the alternative looks uninspiring. When the tally is drawn up for the next election, it will show that the achievements in all spheres connected with the social services, the humanities, the restructuring of industry, the rationalisation of our defence deployment, and many other basic elements of our life, are very considerable. In the spheres of foreign affairs and our economic standing in the world, the Government have been less successful, though the latter is now improving fast; and Gaitskell's presence might have had an appreciable effect here.

What is certain is that Gaitskell had, by character and courage, firmly established himself as *primus inter pares,* and obviously any team is the weaker for losing its best man. Wilson, Brown, Callaghan, Jenkins all agree on this. He might not have succeeded in reversing our gentle, and on the whole painless, decline in economic and diplomatic influence. No democratic government can do all that on its own; success depends in the end on the will of the citizens. But Gaitskell, without doubt, would have fought and fought and fought again for what he considered just and right for the British people, and for the peoples of the whole world as well.

Bibliography

Attlee, C. R., pc, om, ch. *As it Happened.* Heinemann, 1954.
A Prime Minister Remembers. Heinemann, 1961.

Avon, Earl of (Anthony Eden). Memoirs, 3 vols. Cassell, 1960–5.

Ball, George W. *The Discipline of Power.* The Bodley Head, 1968.

Bromberger, Merry and Serge. *Secrets of Suez,* translated. Sidgwick and Jackson, 1957.

Butler, David and Freeman, Jennie. *British Political Facts, 1900–60.* Macmillan, 1963.

Citrine, Lord. *Two Careers.* Hutchinson, 1967.

Dalton, Hugh. Memoirs, 3 vols. Frederick Muller, 1953–62.

Griffiths, James. *Pages from Memory.* Dent, 1969.

Hansard passim. 1945–63.

Hayter, Sir William. *The Kremlin and the Embassy.* Hodder and Stoughton, 1966.

Hitler, Adolf. *Mein Kampf.* 1929.

Hughes, Emrys. *Macmillan: Portrait of a Politician.* George Allen and Unwin, 1967.

Hunter, Leslie. *The Road to Brighton Pier.* Arthur Barker, 1959.

King, Cecil. *Strictly Personal.* Weidenfeld and Nicolson, 1969.

Labour Party Research Department. *Twelve Wasted Years.* Transport House, 1963.

Macmillan, Harold. *Tides of Fortune, 1945–55.* Macmillan, 1969.

McDermott, Geoffrey. *Berlin: Success of a Mission?* André Deutsch, 1963. *The Eden Legacy.* Leslie Frewin, 1969.

McKenzie, R. T. *British Political Parties.* Heinemann, 1963.

Magee, Bryan. *The New Radicalism.* Secker and Warburg, 1962.

Moncrieff, Anthony, ed. *Suez Ten Years After.* BBC, 1967.

Northedge, F. S. *British Foreign Policy, 1945–61.* Allen and Unwin, 1962.

Nutting, Anthony. *No End of a Lesson.* Constable, 1967.

Page, Bruce; Leitch, David; Knightley, Philip. *Philby.* André Deutsch, 1968.

Pakenham, Frank, Earl of Longford. *Five Lives.* Hutchinson, 1964.

Pelling, Henry. *Modern Britain, 1885–1955*. Nelson, 1960.

Pritt, D. N. *The Labour Government, 1945–51*. Lawrence and Wishart, 1963.

Reports of the Annual Conferences of the Labour Party, 1945–63. Transport House.

Rodgers, W. T., ed. *Hugh Gaitskell, 1906–63*. Thames and Hudson, 1964.

Sampson, Anthony. *Anatomy of Britain*. Hodder and Stoughton, 1962.

Shinwell, Emanuel, MP. *The Labour Story*. Macdonald, 1963.

Williams, Neville. *Chronology of the Modern World*. Barrie and Rockliff, 1966.